Foreign Direct Investment

NEW HORIZONS IN INTERNATIONAL BUSINESS

Series Editor: Peter J. Buckley
Centre for International Business,
University of Leeds (CIBUL), UK

The New Horizons in International Business series has established itself as the world's leading forum for the presentation of new ideas in international business research. It offers pre-eminent contributions in the areas of multinational enterprise – including foreign direct investment, business strategy and corporate alliances, global competitive strategies, and entrepreneurship. In short, this series constitutes essential reading for academics, business strategists and policy makers alike.

Titles in the series include:

The Structural Foundations of International Finance
Problems of Growth and Stability
Edited by Pier Carlo Padoan, Paul A. Brenton and Gavin Boyd

The New Competition for Inward Investment
Companies, Institutions and Territorial Development
Edited by Nicholas Phelps and Philip Raines

Multinational Enterprises, Innovative Strategies and Systems of Innovation
Edited by John Cantwell and José Molero

Multinational Firms' Location and the New Economic Geography
Edited by Jean-Louis Mucchielli and Thierry Mayer

Free Trade in the Americas
Economic and Political Issues for Governments and Firms
Edited by Sidney Weintraub, Alan M. Rugman and Gavin Boyd

Economic Integration and Multinational Investment Behaviour
European and East Asian Experiences
Edited by Pierre-Bruno Ruffini

Strategic Business Alliances
An Examination of the Core Dimensions
Keith W. Glaister, Rumy Husan and Peter J. Buckley

Investment Strategies in Emerging Markets
Edited by Saul Estrin and Klaus E. Meyer

Multinationals and Industrial Competitiveness
A New Agenda
John H. Dunning and Rajneesh Narula

Foreign Direct Investment
Six Country Case Studies
Edited by Yingqi Annie Wei and V.N. Balasubramanyam

Japanese Multinationals in Europe
A Comparison of the Automobile and Pharmaceutical Industries
Ken-ichi Ando

International Joint Venture Performance in South East Asia
Craig C. Julian

Foreign Direct Investment

Six Country Case Studies

Edited by

Yingqi Annie Wei
Lecturer in International Business, Department of Economics, Lancaster University, UK

V.N. Balasubramanyam
Professor of Development Economics, Department of Economics, Lancaster University, UK

NEW HORIZONS IN INTERNATIONAL BUSINESS

Edward Elgar
Cheltenham, UK • Northampton, MA, USA

Published by
Edward Elgar Publishing Limited
The Lypiatts
15 Lansdown Road
Cheltenham
Glos GL50 2JA
UK

Edward Elgar Publishing, Inc.
William Pratt House
9 Dewey Court
Northampton
Massachusetts 01060
USA

Reprinted 2014

A catalogue record for this book
is available from the British Library

ISBN 978 1 84376 467 0

Contents

List of Tables

List of Figures

List of Contributors

V.N. Balasubramanyam (Professor of Development Economics, Department of Economics, Lancaster University, UK)
Peter Buckley (Professor of International Business, Leeds University Business School, University of Leeds, UK)
John-ren Chen (Professor of Economics, Department of Economics, University of Innsbruck, Austria)
Roger Clarke (Professor of Microeconomics, Cardiff Business School, Cardiff University, UK)
Nigel Driffield (Professor of International Business, Aston Business School, Aston University, UK)
John H. Dunning (Professor of International Business, University of Reading and Rutgers University)
Richard Eglin (Director, Trade and Finance Division, World Trade Organisation, Geneva)
David Griffiths (Associate, Risk & Research Department, The Financial Services Authority)
Yasheng Huang (Associate Professor of International Management, MIT Sloan School of Management, US)
Sanjaya Lall (Professor of Development Economics, Oxford University, UK)
Vidya Mahambare (Research Fellow, Cardiff Business School, Cardiff University, UK)
Abdul Halim Mohd Noor (Associate Professor, Institut Teknologi MARA, Malaysia)
Robert Read (Senior Lecturer in International Business, Department of Economics, Lancaster University)
Frances Ruane (Professor of Economics, Department of Economics, Trinity College Dublin)
Mohammed Adaya Salisu (Lecturer in Economics, Department of Economics, Lancaster University)
David Sapsford (Professor of Economics, Department of Economics, Liverpool University)
Frederik Sjöholm (Associate Professor, The Stockholm School of Asian Studies, Stockholm School of Economics)

Nicholas Snowden (Senior Lecturer in Economics, Department of Economics, Lancaster University)
Yingqi Annie Wei (Lecturer in International Business, Department of Economics, Lancaster University)

Acknowledgements

This volume contains six case studies on foreign direct investment, along with comments from discussants on each of the six papers, presented at a workshop, held at Grange-over-Sands Hotel in the Lake District on the 13 and 14 September 2002.

We are deeply indebted to Professor John Dunning for chairing and guiding the proceedings of the workshop. We acknowledge with gratitude financial assistance from the British Academy and Lancaster University. We would like to thank all the participants at the workshop and Ms Vicki Shaw for her assistance in preparing the manuscript for publication.

Foreword

John H. Dunning

I greatly appreciate the opportunity of contributing a foreword to this volume. This is partly because I was fortunate enough to have attended the conference, the proceedings of which form the basis for the book; and partly because I regard its subject matter as extremely timely as interest in the interaction between foreign direct investment (FDI) and economic development is gaining a new lease of life. Such interest has, I think, been largely stimulated both by the emergence of new players on the global economic stage – notably China and India – and by the questioning of some of the earlier tenets of economic development by such scholars as Gerald Meier and Joseph Stiglitz in a volume entitled *Frontiers of Development Economics* (2001). If there is one message coming out of this book, it is that development is a multi-faceted, yet contextual, phenomenon; and that, in seeking to understand its objectives, determinants and outcomes, and in advancing the welfare of its participants, a holistic and interdisciplinary approach and perspective are required.

However, in reading the otherwise excellent collection of papers in Meier and Stiglitz, I was disappointed that although the advent, and, to some extent, the implications of (what I shall term) 20/21 globalisation[1] were well rehearsed, very little attention was paid to one of its main facilitating entities, viz. the multinational enterprise (MNE), or indeed to the principal modality by which it conducts its cross-border value-added activities, viz. FDI.

This is why I particularly welcome the initiative of the editors of this volume in commissioning a series of case studies on this subject.

In recently rereading the contributions, I was especially struck by three things. First, the high quality not only of each of the chapters, but also of the constructive and prescient remarks of the commentators; indeed, rarely have I seen such 'value added' by discussants.

Second, the volume embraced a wide range of countries – large and small, more and less developed, resource and manufacturing-based, those catering mainly for export or domestic markets, those pursuing open or more restricted policies towards inbound FDI, and so on. In making comparisons between these contributions the reader is then given a good sense of how *country-specific* characteristics are a key determinant of FDI; of how the *motivation* for MNE activity (market *cf.* resource and efficiency-seeking) varies according to these characteristics; and of how 20/21 globalisation and its concomitant technological advances are affecting the attitudes towards, and the strategies for, structural transformation, of a selection of developing country governments.

Third, I think the readers will also appreciate the description and critical appraisal by the various authors of the ways in which the institutions of developing countries, and the policies of their host governments, have evolved in response to recent economic and political events. Here, the reader is able to make a number of fascinating comparisons between, for example, the reactions of India and China to the opening up of world markets – including financial markets; those of the Mexican and Malaysian governments to their countries' participation in free trade and liberalised capital movements within their regions; the lessons which many small and export-oriented countries can learn from the experiences of Ireland; and the reasons for the successful development of some Sub-Saharan countries, and the failures of others.

What were my own memories of the 2002 conference at Grange-over-Sands in the Lake District? What would I regard as the main insights and conclusions of the current volume? I will confine myself to three observations, which I shall set out under the umbrella of 'three Cs' – which I shall name respectively the *Contextual*, *Counterfactual* and *Conditional*.

As regards the first C, the *Contextual*, I would assert that countries likely to be the most successful in both attracting and benefiting from FDI, know how best to distinguish between its *generic* costs and benefits, and those which are *specific* to their particular economic and social situations. Like firms, countries – or more particularly national governments – need to 'glocalise' – i.e. pursue both global and local strategies which will advance their particular development goals, while recognising that foreign investors are often able to implement a global strategy in deciding where to locate their value-added activities. Such policies embrace the whole gamut of those affecting the determinants and effects of FDI. They range from investment promotion schemes and targeting particular kinds of FDI, to ensuring that the local activities of inbound foreign investors (including the decisions relating to these taken outside the host county) are consistent with the latter's dynamic comparative economic and social advantage. As we have already hinted, such host-country specific characteristics include the size of the country, its geographical position, the history, traditions and ideology of its people, its stage of development, the quality of its institutions and organizations, and the structure and quality of its resources and capabilities.

Such context-specific structural variables as these are well known to international business scholars, but in my experience as a consultant to UNCTAD, so often, in their expectations and assessment of FDI, host country governments do not sufficiently take them into account. In this respect, I would recommend that all policy makers – from both developed and developing countries – should carefully peruse this volume.

My second C stands for the *Counterfactual*. I am encouraged that several contributors to this book asserted that it was not possible to measure the specific or unique consequences of FDI without comparing them, either with the next best alternative, e.g. a licensing agreement or the performance of domestic firms, or the effects of a similar FDI in another country.[2] In this regard, I was especially intrigued with the debate between Yingqi Annie Wei and Yasheng Huang, the outcome of which – to my mind at any rate – seemed to rest not only on the quality of the data and the objectives of FDI, but on the counterfactual situation (including, in this case, the policies of the Chinese government towards promoting indigenous investment).

Once again, I believe it is extremely important that, in assessing the contribution of FDI to a country's economic and social goals, one should seek to compare and contrast that contribution to that which might have been obtained by the next best alternative means; and also the likely impact which different institutions (either actual or possible) and government policies (e.g. towards research and development, intellectual property rights, bilateral investment agreements etc.) might have on both the extent and quality of both kinds of contribution.

My third C is that of *Conditionality*, I think the experience of the last three decades has quite clearly demonstrated that inbound FDI will only help achieve the goals sought by host countries if the economic, social, and human environment offered to the investing firms is conductive towards this end. While again this may seem obvious, several chapters in this book observe that, in the past, FDI has failed to meet the expectations of recipient countries in at least three respects. The first is that the complementary indigenous endowments sought by foreign MNEs, if they are to provide the resources, capabilities, management skills, competitive stimuli and markets desired by recipient countries, are not available – or are not available at the right price. The second is that micro-management policies of the host country governments are not conducive towards the upgrading of and/or structural transformation of indigenous firms. The third reason is that the incentive structures and institutional framework of the recipient countries are unable to guarantee that the unique intangible assets offered by inbound FDI are deployed and disseminated to their fullest and best effect.

In short, by Conditionality we mean that FDI can often (though not always) provide real benefits to the host country, but *only* if its constituent stakeholders, and particularly its governments are prepared to offer the conditions conducive to making this possible. More often, however, than not, in the past, governments have preferred to ensure that inbound FDI does nothing to adversely affect their existing economic and social policies, rather than adjusting these policies so that the net benefits of such investment may be fully exploited.

The history of FDI over the last century provides ample evidence on the importance of the conditionality factor in both attracting inbound FDI, and analysing its contribution to development. During the 1960s, there were few restrictions on inbound FDI. At the same time, there was little acknowledgement of the particular institutional and policy-related imperatives necessary for it to offer the maximum net benefits to the recipient countries. As a result, FDI tended to foster uneven development, while the business practices of MNEs often operated (or were perceived operating) to the detriment of the economic welfare of the recipient countries.

As a result, the conditions of FDI imposed by most (but not all) developing countries' governments changed dramatically in the 1970s. Regulations and control replaced open-door strategies. Yet for many countries pursuing import-substituting development policies and insisting on performance requirements by foreign affiliates, FDI still failed to yield the benefits hoped for. Too many of the wrong conditions replaced an unduly *laissez faire* institutional set-up. Now in the late 20th/early 21st century, as the essays dealing with India, China and Ireland show, the conditions have changed again. These might now be best described as a *controlled liberal policy* towards FDI, plus a recognition, at the same time, that positive extra-market measures may be necessary to facilitate and best guide the kind of FDI most suited to the (contextual) needs of the country in question.

But, perhaps, nowhere is the importance of appropriate conditionality more clearly seen than in the efforts of the erstwhile Communist countries to attract inward FDI. Here there has been abundant research summarised in a recent thesis of a PhD student of mine, (Yakova, 2004), which reveals the importance of upgrading of institutional infrastructure as a critical determinant, both for inbound FDI, and for the structural transformation of Central and Eastern European economies which is needed if they are to raise living standards. The evidence suggests that those countries which, in May 2004, became members of the European Community, have imposed or offered the right incentive structures (or conditions) to FDI; while those offered by the latecomers in the transition process, e.g. Romania, Albania, and some of the ex-Soviet Union satellites, are attracting the least FDI. At the same time, *relative* to the availability and quality of location-bound resources and capabilities, the upgrading of institutions is likely to offer more incentives to foreign investors in the early stages of their structural transition.

Contextuality, the *Counterfactual* and *Conditionality* – the three Cs – then must surely form the basis of assessing the value of FDI to developing countries in the early 21st century. But above all, each needs to be set within an overarching framework of globalisation, rapid technological change – including that of communications, the uncertainty and volatility of financial markets, and the need for more networking and cooperation among firms. These events and characteristics in turn make huge demands on the institutions embedded in firms, national governments, supranational entities and – not least – civil society. It is the reconciliation of the location-bound stakeholders preferences, values, belief system and incentive structures with the economic and social advantages which globalisation and the cross-country integration of valued-added activities brings, which is perhaps the greatest challenge facing developing countries today.

It remains to be seen in what respect and how far both inbound and outbound FDI[3] can help these countries meet this challenge.

Reading and Rutgers Universities
May 2004

NOTES

1. To distinguish it from the globalisation (or as some would prefer the term internationalisation) of the world economy in the 19th and the first half of the 20th century.
2. E.g. comparing the performance of US affiliates in China with those of Chinese indigenous firms (also in China) or those of US subsidiaries in (say) India, Taiwan or Malaysia
3. This volume does not address the determinants and welfare generating effects of outward FDI. Yet, increasingly all of the countries considered in this volume apart from those in Sub-Saharan Africa are becoming quite important outward investors in their own right; and this in turn has important implications for the Cs of economic development.

References

Meier. G. and Stiglitz, E. (2001) *Frontiers of Development Economics: The Future in Perspective*, Oxford: Oxford University Press.

Yakova, N. (2004) *Foreign Direct Investment and Structural Change as Factors in Transition: A Study of Central and Eastern European Countries*, Ph.D. Thesis, Rutgers University.

1. Introduction

Yingqi Annie Wei and V.N. Balasubramanyam

Whilst research on foreign direct investment (FDI) has always been vibrant, recent developments have enlivened an already rich menu. Foremost of these is the dramatic change in attitudes towards FDI on the part of developing countries. In the past limited exposure to FDI was almost a virtue, but now it is a disadvantage. Yesteryear's distrust and suspicion of FDI appears to have yielded place to a newfound faith in its ability to foster growth and development. This change in attitudes, which dates back to the decade of the eighties, was influenced by a number of factors: a steep reduction in alternative sources of finance such as bank credit in the wake of the debt crisis, the collapse of the Soviet Empire and with it a waning of ideological opposition to capitalism and its institutions, the demonstrable success of the East Asian countries based in part on FDI, and growth in knowledge and understanding of the nature and operations of FDI including its limitations.

This change in attitudes towards FDI on the part of the developing countries has opened up new vistas for research on policy issues. Most developing countries, including those with relatively low volumes of FDI, have for long attempted to regulate the operations of foreign owned firms, including their spheres of operations, their sourcing of inputs, their trade orientation and employment practices. These policies, collectively known as Trade Related Measures (TRIMS) in the jargon of the World Trade Organisation (WTO), have been liberalised considerably in recent years. These developments have inspired a number of studies on the determinants and efficacy of FDI in promoting growth and development.

The celebrated O (ownership advantages), L (location advantages) and I (internalisation) paradigm enunciated by John Dunning (1988) has provided the theoretical framework for the analysis of determinants of FDI in developing countries. The focus of much of the empirical research in this area is on location advantages (L) which encompass a number of factors: natural resource endowments of host countries, availability of relatively cheap but productive labour, endowments of human skills, infrastructure facilities, the system of incentives and regulation of investments in host countries, trade policy of host countries and the economic environment in general as signified by macroeconomic and exchange rate stability. These and other factors determine not only the volume of FDI a country is capable of attracting but also its efficacy in promoting development objectives. There are a number of empirical studies, varying in design and statistical sophistication, on the relative importance of these factors in the volume of FDI the host countries are able to attract. Although the studies have produced a mixed bag of results, they do permit some broad generalisations. First, wage costs in host countries do matter for prospective investors but only when they are adjusted for labour skills. Second, in the absence of a stable economic environment for investment and infrastructure facilities, investment incentives such as tax concessions may not be a factor in the investment decisions of foreign firms. Third, countries following trade policies free of distortions are likely to attract relatively large volumes of FDI. Fourth, stability of policies over time and transparency of rules and regulations, which serve to limit corruption and bureaucratic delays, are important determinants of FDI. It is also argued that prospective host countries have to aggressively promote the attractions of their economies to foreign firms and they should enlist the support of local businesses, political interest groups and the media in their efforts to attract FDI. Yet another issue which is the subject of empirical studies is the impact of regional groupings such as the North American Free Trade Area (NAFTA) on inflows of FDI into member countries. The specific issue here is the relative impact of the twin characteristics of regional groupings – the free trade element and the protectionist element – on inflows of FDI into member countries of the groupings.

There is also a vast array of studies on the efficacy of FDI, including its contribution to diffusion of technology and know-how often referred to as technology spillovers, employment creation, promotion of exports and growth of the national product. Here too the extant empirical studies produce a mixed bag of results – some detect positive spillovers of technology and know-how from the foreign owned firms to the locally owned firms, others find very little spillovers and some even detect negative spillovers, suggesting that the presence of foreign owned firms stifles locally owned firms. There is also a wide-ranging discussion on the prerequisites for positive spillovers and the channels through which such spillovers can be expected to occur. The so-called endogeneity problem introduces additional complications. Does FDI serve to promote growth or do sustained levels of growth attract increased volumes of FDI? Other issues which have surfaced in the recent literature include the contribution of FDI to observed disparities in incomes between regions of host countries and the interrelationship between international labour flows and FDI.

The six papers in this volume provide an analytical review of these and other issues and assess the received wisdom on these issues in the context of the experience of six countries host to FDI. Case studies are likely to shed more light on the role of FDI in the growth process than the ubiquitous cross-country studies based on regression techniques. They permit a detailed analysis of the specific characteristics and policies of each of the countries which have resulted in the volume of FDI they harbour and its impact on their development and growth. In addition, they facilitate cross-country comparisons on a number of facets of FDI with valuable insights for policy formulation.

Each of the six case studies in this volume exemplifies many of the issues on the determinants and impact of FDI discussed in the literature. China has attracted a large volume of FDI in recent years. Annie Wei's survey of the evidence suggests that the large pool of relatively cheap but productive labour in China coupled with the presence of a large market have been factors of some importance in the substantial volumes of FDI China has attracted. The paper also identifies factors specific to China, such as the ethnic ties of the Chinese on the mainland to the Chinese in Hong Kong, Macao and Taiwan, which have facilitated export-oriented FDI from these countries. All this sits well with the conventional wisdom on the determinants of FDI in developing countries.

This thesis though is contested by Yasheng Huang, who argues that institutional factors such as government policy which deprived local firms of access to domestic sources of finance and the acquisition of cash starved state owned enterprises by foreign owned firms account for the large volume of export-oriented and domestic market-oriented FDI in China. Huang's discussion of Wei's paper elaborates on his thesis and suggests that if only domestic firms had access to finance they may have resorted to licensing agreements for their technology requirements and know-how. This line of reasoning suggests that FDI in China may be no more than a substitute for domestic investments. Annie Wei suggests that this explanation may be valid in the case of a few specific investments but it cannot be generalised. Her paper also suggests that FDI has had a positive impact on China's exports and growth, but the precise mechanisms through which foreign investment has contributed to trade and growth remain to be investigated. Huang, building upon his explanation of the determinants of FDI in China, argues that FDI may have promoted labour-intensive exports and growth in China, but the issue is whether domestic firms could have performed as well if they had had access to finance and had been allowed to enter into contractual agreements with foreign firms for their technology requirements. As he puts it "I do not subscribe to the view that foreign firms have some sort of special advantage which Chinese labour-intensive firms do not have and hence the high levels of FDI in China". The lively discussion on these and other issues raised by Wei and Huang is reported in the volume.

Balasubramanyam and Mahambare's paper on India fuels the controversy generated by Wei's paper and Huang's comments on China. The paper raises the issue "what is the optimum volume of FDI a country should aspire to?" Whilst acknowledging the fact that the volume of FDI India has attracted may be below its potential, it questions the policy prescription that India should open all doors to FDI. It argues that the optimum volume of FDI India should aspire to may be well below that which China receives, and in any case, because of the significant differences between the two countries in the structure of their economies, their resource endowments, history of industrialisation and the nature of their institutions, China should not be regarded as a role model for India. It is the quality of FDI a country receives that is important for promoting its development, not the volume.

Sanjaya Lall, commenting on the paper by Balasubramanyam and Mahambare, agrees that the case for an all out open door policy towards FDI advocated by Sachs and Bajpai may be overstated, but parts company with the authors on several other issues. He expresses sympathy for the view that India should adopt a much more aggressive policy to attract FDI and use it to increase competitiveness. India has largely missed out on FDI driven industrialisation centred on labour-intensive activities, mostly because it has not adopted the kind of policies which would promote competitiveness. It is also not true to say that compared with India FDI in China is mostly in low-tech industries. Lall argues that China has rapidly moved up the comparative advantage ladder and is now exporting high-tech products. China has superior endowments of labour skills than India, measured by indicators such as years of schooling and school enrolment rates. This, in fact, may be one of the reasons for the large volumes of FDI China attracts. The two papers on India and China and the discussion on the papers reported in the volume identify several issues for further research.

Nigel Driffield, Roger Clark and Mohd Noor's paper on Malaysia yet again underscores the fact that a country may successfully attract relatively large volumes of FDI, but in the absence of a coordinated trade and investment policy framework FDI may do little to promote technology transfer and domestic capabilities, though it may fuel exports and growth. Malaysia, a country which has attracted relatively high volumes of export-oriented FDI, is regarded as one of the success stories in East Asia. The issue that Driffield and his co-authors address is whether or not domestic industries in Malaysia, especially the electrical equipment industries, where most of FDI is concentrated, have experienced substantial spillovers of technology and know-how from the foreign firms. The paper suggests that there is very little by way of spillovers in Malaysia and the country may have unwittingly ended up with export enclaves with few linkages to the rest of the economy. They attribute this outcome to the sort of policies Malaysia has adopted, most of which are centred on fiscal incentives designed to attract FDI rather than encourage linkages. Indeed, when fiscal incentives are tied to local content requirements linkages are seen to exist. In recent years policymakers appear to have realised that linkages between foreign owned and locally owned firms are weak and that the country needs to adopt broadly based education policies to efficiently utilise FDI in promoting domestically owned industries.

Even so, as Richard Eglin commenting on the paper by Driffield and his colleagues notes, Malaysia faces a very difficult situation. Its protected domestic industries face stiff competition from other countries in the region, its policy of subsidising foreign firms may yield export growth but it does little to promote domestic industries and, in any case, the policy cannot continue forever. The WTO rules prohibit local content requirements and technology transfer requirements. Malaysia cannot also continue with its "Malays First" or the Bhumiputra policy as it is inconsistent with the basic WTO principles of most-favoured nation (MFN) and national treatment. All in all Malaysia faces a difficult transition and it has to redesign not only its investment policies but also its trade policies.

There is a renewal of interest in recent years in the role of geography in trade development. David Griffiths and David Sapsford address the issue in the paper on Mexico. Is the proximity of Mexico to the richest country in the world a factor in the volume of FDI it has attracted and the growth it has experienced? They do find such proximity to be a factor of significance in Mexico's economic performance in recent years. But such proximity alone could not have yielded the gains Mexico has experienced. It is proximity to the richest country in the world coupled with the economic liberalisation policies Mexico initiated in 1985 which appears to be the successful recipe. Indeed, growth of the US manufacturing industry appears to spur inflows of FDI from the US into Mexico. Admittedly Mexico's membership of the NAFTA has also aided Mexico's success, but it appears to have merely consolidated the gains in exports, employment and growth which the country had achieved through extensive economic liberalisation preceding membership of the NAFTA. The paper identifies the impact of high domestic incomes and low efficiency wages in Mexico on inflows of FDI. Surprisingly though, none of the statistical tests, save one, detects a positive impact of FDI on growth. FDI appears to have exerted a significant influence on growth in the post liberalisation period since 1985 but with a lag of two years. The authors, however, note that several other studies have detected positive technological spillovers from foreign owned to locally owned firms. These findings suggest that FDI is beneficial to Mexico.

Frederik Sjöholm in his comment on the paper notes that FDI has been a factor in Mexico's growth and development and the absence of robust statistical support for the proposition in the paper is more than likely due to econometric problems, principally the relatively short period of time to which the data relate. Sjöholm also draws attention to the contribution of FDI to employment generation and the competitive pressures it has generated. He also warns that the contribution of FDI to employment is important and FDI should not always be judged by the spillovers it generates.

The experience of the Republic of Ireland with FDI is not one that immediately springs to mind in discussing the role of FDI in the development process. Its location in the developed world, its membership of the EU, the relatively small size of its population all set it apart from the other case studies in the volume. Even so, the Irish Republic may have several lessons for developing countries which are eagerly seeking FDI. Especially relevant is Ireland's promotion of FDI as a factor of importance in promoting employment and growth. Frances Ruane's scholarly analysis of the role of FDI in the dramatic growth performance of Ireland is instructive in many respects. First, as Ruane graphically describes, during the early years, when both unemployment and emigration were running high, it was easy to sell FDI to employees, employers, diverse political interest groups and even the media. Few could object to inflows of FDI which would create employment opportunities and stem emigration. It is this emphasis of policies towards FDI on employment creation which is one of the attractive features of the Irish experience. Second, Ireland adopted open economy policies towards trade before it sought FDI. This policy facilitated the promotion of export led FDI which would not directly compete with domestic market-oriented locally owned firms. The third is the exemplary managerial skills of the investment and development agency (IDA) which as Ruane notes is probably the world leader in cultivating and promoting potential investors. Fourth, there is the policy of non-discrimination between foreign owned and locally owned firms in matters of tax policies and other incentives. Fifth, there is the consistency of Ireland's policies towards FDI over time. Changes in policy were gradual and all policies were grand-parented in the sense that companies were not affected by policies put into force after they were established. Most of these determinants of FDI are identified in the literature. Ireland appears to have put them to good use and demonstrated their validity.

Peter Buckley commenting on the paper neatly sums up Ireland's success with FDI with an apt acronym – CORCE. C is for consistency of policy, O is for openness, R is for regional (Ireland's orientation towards the EU markets) and E is for environment – the institutional and business environment. Buckley also raises several issues relating to the ability of Ireland to continue with its success, its ability to cope with growing competition, and its ability to contain macro problems such as inflationary pressures. One recurring theme during the discussion of the paper was whether Ireland's experience with FDI had any lessons for developing countries or whether it was unique to Ireland. These and other issues led to lively debate and a detailed reply to the debate by Frances Ruane.

The growth and development performance of the Sub-Saharan African countries abounds with puzzles and paradoxes. Why is the growth and development performance of this group of countries dismally poor compared with that in other developing regions? There are several explanations including their geography, the ethnic composition of their population, external obstacles to their exports and other political economy oriented explanations. The role of FDI in these economies too poses several puzzles. On some indicators, such as the ratio of FDI to GDP and the ratio of FDI to domestic capital formation, the volume of FDI in these countries is not low. But these figures may be misleading. As Mohammad Salisu's paper on FDI in Sub-Saharan Africa argues, the high ratios of FDI to GDP indicate no more than the fact that both GDP and domestic capital formation in most of these countries are low. In other words, FDI accounts for much of the investments and GDP. Also, the exchange rate, as in the case of Nigeria, has depreciated considerably over the years and the ratio of FDI to GDP turns out to be high only because GDP at market exchange rates is low. There are though countries such as Botswana, Mozambique, Uganda, Madagascar and Mauritius which have attracted substantial volumes of FDI and appear to have utilised it efficiently for the promotion of employment and incomes. Admittedly, in most though not all of the African countries FDI is of the resource seeking variety. And such FDI appears to have been a curse rather than a blessing to countries such as Nigeria. Salisu's paper amongst other things identifies lack of transparency of policies and the attendant widespread corruption in most of these countries as a major deterrent to the efficient utilisation of FDI. His estimates of the extent of the black economy in Nigeria and its adverse impact on the growth of the economy shows that in the absence of well-designed policies and efficient mechanisms of governance no amount of FDI can contribute to the welfare of the citizens of host countries. The econometric exercises in the paper identify corruption as the major obstacle to the efficient utilisation of FDI in the African countries. The experience of Botswana and Mozambique is in stark contrast to that of Nigeria in this respect. Nicholas Snowden's comment on the paper elaborates on some of the issues raised in Salisu's paper and discusses the problems associated with statistical tests of the propositions outlined in the paper.

References

Dunning, J. H. (1988), *Explaining international production*, Unwin Hyman/ Harper Collins, London.

2. Foreign Direct Investment in China

Yingqi Annie Wei

2.1 INTRODUCTION

In response to the open-door policy formulated in 1978, inward foreign direct investment (FDI) in China has grown appreciably. By 2002, the cumulative realised values of inward FDI reached US$ 448 billion[1] (UNCTAD, 2003). China is now the largest host to FDI in the developing world. A remarkable development in the contemporary period of globalisation, the opening up of China to FDI has attracted much attention from both the academic and business sectors. A large number of studies have attempted to address the following issues. Why is China so successful in attracting FDI? What role has FDI played in the development process of China? Is China's experience with FDI unique?

This paper examines the evidence on these and other related issues. Section 2.2 of the paper reviews general trends and characteristics of FDI in China. Section 2.3 outlines various determinants of FDI at the national and regional levels in China. Section 2.4 investigates the relationship between FDI and technology transfer, spillovers, foreign trade and economic growth. The last section concludes.

2.2 CHARACTERISTICS OF FDI IN CHINA

China opened up the economy to FDI in 1979 for the purposes of acquiring foreign capital, advanced technologies and management skills required for upgrading the industrial structure and stimulating economic growth. Because of both ideological reasons and lack of experience, China has followed a gradualist policy towards FDI. In the early years since liberalisation in 1978 China could be said to have 'experimented' with FDI; the bulk of it was concentrated in the four special economic zones (SEZs) in Guangdong and Fujian provinces, and foreign enterprise participation was confined to joint ventures (JVs) and export-oriented activities. FDI was then gradually allowed into areas other than the SEZs and into a large number of industrial sectors.

Table 2.1 FDI Inflows into China, 1979-2001

Year	Number of Projects	Contracted FDI (US$ billion)	Realised FDI (US$ billion)
1979-82	920	5.0	1.8
1983	638	1.9	0.9
1984	2166	2.9	1.4
1985	3073	6.3	2.0
1986	1498	3.3	2.2
1987	2233	3.7	2.3
1988	5945	5.3	3.2
1989	5779	5.6	3.4
1990	7273	6.6	3.5
1991	12978	12.0	4.4
1992	48764	58.1	11.0
1993	83437	111.4	27.5
1994	47549	82.7	33.8
1995	37011	91.3	37.5
1996	24556	73.3	41.7
1997	21001	51.0	45.3
1998	19799	52.1	45.5
1999	16918	41.2	40.3
2000	22347	62.4	40.7
2001	26140	69.2	46.9

Source: State Statistical Bureau, China Statistical Yearbook, 2002.

The general trends and characteristics of FDI in China have been reviewed extensively (e.g. Lee, 1997; Hayter and Han, 1998; Sun, 1998a, b; Henley et al., 1999; Wu, 1999; Lemoine, 2000; Huang, 2001, 2003; Wei and Liu, 2001; OECD, 2002). It is recognised that the development path of inward FDI in China has never been even. Table 2.1 shows the number of projects contracted, and the contracted and realised FDI values. Four stages in the development path of inward FDI can be discerned: the experimental stage (1979-83), the growth stage (1984-91), the peak stage (1992-93), and the adjustment stage (1994 onwards).

During the experimental stage, the legal and institutional framework for FDI inflows into China was set up. FDI was mainly directed to the four special economic zones (SEZs) in Guangdong and Fujian provinces. The total volume of FDI was fairly low during this stage, reflecting the cautious attitudes of both the Chinese government and foreign investors. With the seemingly successful experiment with FDI and the satisfactory economic situation nationwide, China took a number of measures and formulated a series of laws and regulations to improve the business environment and facilitate increased FDI inflows during the growth stage. As a consequence, there was a steady and rapid growth of realised FDI inflows at around 20 per cent per annum. Between 1992 and 1993, there was a surge of FDI into China. The figures for contracted and realised FDI exceeded the corresponding figures for the previous 13 years. This was closely associated with a number of events, including Deng Xiaoping's tour of the southern provinces, the nationwide implementation of opening up policies for FDI, and the worldwide rise in FDI flows. From 1994 onwards, however, the investment boom in China seemed to cool down. The growth rates of FDI in terms of number of projects and contracted FDI turned negative in 1994. The growth rate of realised FDI also fell during 1994 and 1999, though there was a recovery in 2000. Since 1994, the Chinese government has closely monitored FDI inflows.

Despite the overall high FDI inflows, its distribution is unbalanced in terms of its sources, types, and regional and sectoral distribution. In the early years, although investors from more than 100 different countries and regions invested in China, the majority of investors were ethnic Chinese. The share of FDI from Hong Kong, Macao and Taiwan reached a peak in 1992, at around 80 per cent (Table 2.2). In recent years, however, the ethnic share in total FDI has decreased while those of US and EU have increased. In 2000, 45 per cent of FDI was from Hong Kong, Macao and Taiwan and 11 per cent from the US and EU, respectively.

It is worth noting here that the Chinese official data on FDI by nationality of source countries may be biased, partly because of the round-tripping problem, and partly because of the diversity of overseas Chinese investors. Hong Kong, Macao and Taiwan were not the only sources of ethnic Chinese investors. Some FDI from other Asian, European, Australian and North American countries was also undertaken by people of Chinese extraction. In addition, FDI from Hong Kong and Macao includes not only investments from Hong Kong and Macao but also investment flows from Taiwan and Southeast Asian countries. This is in part due to political expediency, which appears to have compelled countries such as Indonesia and Taiwan to route their investment through Hong Kong.

According to Wei (1995), inflows of FDI, large though they are, fall short of China's potential, especially those from the US and EU. It is noted that FDI from developed countries is concentrated in capital-intensive and high-tech sectors and that from developing countries is concentrated in labour-intensive and low-tech sectors. The current composition of sources of FDI in China needs to be diversified if China is to gain advanced technologies. There are though several issues associated with this thesis. What sorts of

Table 2.2 Share of Major Source Countries of Realised FDI in China, 1986-2000

Year	Realised FDI (US$ billion)	Share (%)				
		Hong Kong/ Macao	Taiwan	Japan	US	EU
1986	2.2	59.22	-	11.74	14.54	7.96
1987	2.3	69.08	-	9.50	11.36	2.28
1988	3.2	65.60	-	16.11	7.39	4.92
1989	3.4	61.24	4.56	10.50	8.38	5.53
1990	3.5	54.87	6.38	14.44	13.08	4.23
1991	4.4	56.96	10.68	12.20	7.40	5.63
1992	11.0	70.03	9.54	6.45	4.64	2.21
1993	27.5	64.91	11.41	4.81	7.50	2.44
1994	33.8	59.75	10.04	6.15	7.38	4.55
1995	37.5	54.64	8.43	8.28	8.22	5.68
1996	41.7	50.95	8.33	8.82	8.25	6.56
1997	45.3	46.46	7.27	9.56	7.16	9.22
1998	45.5	41.64	6.41	7.48	8.58	8.75
1999	40.3	41.35	6.45	7.37	10.46	11.11
2000	40.7	38.92	5.64	7.16	10.77	11.00

Source: http://www.chinafdi.org.cn/english

advanced technologies does China need? Can they be efficiently absorbed by China or Chinese indigenous firms. These questions will be discussed later in the paper.

The main types of FDI in China are equity joint ventures (EJVs), contractual joint ventures (CJVs) and investments by wholly foreign-owned enterprises (WFOEs). They differ from each other in legal form, the degree of control exercised by foreign firms, and management structure. A WFOE is a limited liability entity solely owned and operated by a foreign investor who receives all of the profits and bears all the costs and risks. An international EJV is defined as a firm where resource commitment, profit distribution, risk sharing, and control and management are based on equity shares of partners rather than defined by contract, a feature of an international CJV.

CJVs were the most important type during the immediate post-1978 years (Table 2.3). Since the late 1980s, EJVs and WFOEs have become predominent and recent years have seen a proliferation of WFOEs. EJV has been a popular entry mode for two reasons. First, the Chinese government believes that EJVs best serve the Chinese objective of absorbing foreign capital, technology, and management expertise. Second, foreign investors

Table 2.3 FDI by Type of Investment, 1979-99

Year	Realised FDI (US$ billion)	Share (%)			
		EJV	CJV	WFOE	Others
1979-84	4.1	14	40	3	43
1992	11.0	56	19	23	2
1993	27.5	56	19	24	1
1994	33.8	53	21	24	2
1995	37.5	51	20	28	1
1996	41.7	50	19	30	1
1997	45.3	43	20	36	1
1998	45.5	40	21	36	2
1999	40.3	39	20	39	2
1979-99	307.7	47	21	30	2

Source: State Statistical Bureau, China Foreign Economic Statistical Yearbook, various issues and http://www.chinafdi.org.cn/english

hope that by engaging in joint ventures the local partners may assist them in penetrating the domestic markets and accessing utilities and critical inputs. The steady and incremental growth of WFOEs as an entry mode, however, suggests that foreign investors have not only gained in confidence over the years but also improved their ability to cope with risks and uncertainties of doing business in China (Luo and Neale, 1998). Deng (2001) notes that many foreign investors in China have chosen WFOEs over EJVs in order to avoid the problems associated with EJVs, mostly caused by uncooperative or incompetent partners, differences in strategic objectives between partners, and the fear of loss of control over proprietary technology and know-how and a loss of long-term competitive advantages.

The regional distribution of FDI in China is very uneven. This is partially due to China's cautious policy towards FDI. In the early years of liberalisation, FDI was restricted to four SEZs. It was then gradually allowed into 14 coastal cities, the traditional industrial or commercial centres, which offered better infrastructure than the inner areas. In recent years, FDI has been encouraged to flow into the inner areas too. Thus regional imbalances were to be expected given the stage and strategy of China's development.

Approximately 87 per cent of the cumulative FDI was located in the coastal (or eastern) regions, 10 per cent in the central regions, leaving the western region with a negligible share during the period of 1985 to 2000 (Table 2.4). However, the proportion of FDI in the central and western regions has increased slightly since the 1990s. Among the eastern regions, there have been changes since the mid-1990s. Though Guangdong continued

Table 2.4 Regional Distribution of Realised FDI in China, 1985-2000

%

Year	1985-89	1990	1995	1997	1998	1999	2000
Eastern Regions	***87.9***	***93.1***	***87.7***	***85.9***	***87.2***	***87.8***	***87.8***
Beijing	9.9	8.1	2.9	3.5	4.8	4.9	4.2
Tianjin	3.6	1.1	4.1	5.6	4.7	4.4	2.9
Hebei	1.5	1.3	1.5	2.5	3.2	2.6	1.7
Liaoning	3.6	7.5	3.8	4.9	4.8	2.7	5.1
Shanghai	9.5	5.1	7.8	9.4	8.0	7.1	7.8
Jiangsu	3.7	3.9	13.9	12.1	14.6	15.2	15.9
Zhejiang	1.6	1.2	3.4	3.3	2.9	3.1	4.0
Fujian	6.9	9.3	10.9	9.3	9.3	10.1	8.5
Shandong	3.5	5.4	7.2	5.6	4.9	5.7	7.4
Guangdong	40.7	46.1	27.6	26.1	26.5	29.2	28.0
Hainan	1.8	3.0	2.9	1.6	1.6	1.2	1.1
Guangxi	1.7	1.0	1.8	2.0	2.0	1.6	1.3
Central Regions	***6.9***	***4.0***	***9.2***	***10.7***	***9.8***	***9.4***	***9.2***
Western Regions	***5.1***	***2.8***	***3.1***	***3.5***	***3.0***	***2.8***	***3.0***
Total	**100**	**100**	**100**	**100**	**100**	**100**	**100**

Source: State Statistical Bureau, China Statistical Yearbook, various issues.

to be the most favoured destination for FDI, its share declined from 46 per cent in 1990 to 28 per cent in 2000. Jiangsu has benefited from its geographic location near Shanghai, Shandong and Fujian, and attracted up to 16 per cent of FDI in China in the year 2000. This is a major achievement for Jiangsu given that its share was less than 4 per cent in the 1980s. Finally, the degree of FDI penetration or dependency in these provinces, measured by the ratio of FDI stock to GDP, varies. Guangdong, Fujian, Tianjin, Shanghai and Beijing appeared to be much more dependent on FDI than Hebei, Zhejiang and Shandong (Lemoine, 2000).

Sectoral distribution of FDI too is highly uneven (Tables 2.5 and 2.6). Much of FDI between 1979 and 1998 was in manufacturing, especially in labour-intensive sectors such as textiles, clothing and the assembly lines of mechanical, electronic and electric products, which were all in line with China's comparative advantage. Foreign firms also participated in capital- and technology-intensive sectors. According to OECD (2002), shares of FDI in terms of value added in labour-intensive, capital- and technology-intensive sectors were 50 per cent, 23 per cent and 27 per cent, respectively, in 1995 and 42 per cent, 25 per cent and 33 per cent, respectively, in 1999. The service sector, especially real estate, was the second leading sector. In the future, especially with China's accession to the WTO and further liberalisation, it is expected that service sectors such as finance, banking and telecommunications will account for increasing volumes of FDI.

FDI has attained increasing importance in the Chinese economy during the last two decades. The contribution of FDI to capital formation in China was more than 10 per cent though there has been a decreasing trend since 1994 (Table 2.7). The share of the industrial output value of foreign invested enterprises (FIEs) in the national total increased from 2 per cent in 1990 to 28 per cent in 1999. Almost half of China's total foreign trade was recently conducted by FIEs, though the net trade effect of FIEs is ambiguous.

Table 2.5 Sectoral Distribution of Realised FDI in China, 1979-98

US$ billion

Sector	1979-86 FDI (%)	1987-91 FDI (%)	1992-94 FDI (%)	1995-98 FDI (%)	1979-98 FDI (%)
Agriculture, forestry, animal husbandry & fishing	0.57 (2.98)	0.80 (2.41)	2.84 (1.13)	5.15 (1.92)	9.355 (1.63)
Manufacturing	7.60 (39.59)	25.66 (77.33)	127.87 (50.70)	177.07 (66.09)	338.20 (59.08)
Construction	0.31 (1.63)	0.56 (1.68)	8.11 (3.22)	8.78 (3.28)	17.76 (3.10)
Transport, warehousing, post & telecommunications	0.28 (1.48)	0.29 (0.87)	5.06 (2.01)	8.23 (3.07)	13.86 (2.42)
Wholesale & retailing, catering	1.42 (7.40)	0.44 (1.33)	9.97 (3.95)	8.93 (3.33)	20.76 (3.63)
Real estate	5.99 (31.21)	4.48 (13.51)	85.71 (33.98)	46.57 (17.38)	142.75 (24.93)
Health care, sports & social welfare	0.07 (0.34)	0.15 (0.46)	2.85 (1.13)	1.48 (0.55)	4.55 (0.79)
Education, culture, arts, broadcasting, film & TV	0.08 (0.42)	0.13 (0.39)	1.16 (0.46)	0.60 (0.22)	1.97 (0.34)
Scientific research & technical services	0.01 (0.05)	0.06 (0.18)	0.92 (0.37)	0.75 (0.28)	1.74 (0.30)
Others	2.86 (14.89)	0.61 (1.85)	7.72 (2.86)	10.37 (3.87)	21.56 (3.77)
Total	19.18 (100)	33.18 (100)	252.21 (100)	267.93 (100)	572.50 (100)

Source: Wei and Liu (2001).

Table 2.6 Share of Foreign Invested Firms in Industries, 1999

Unit: %

Sector	Number of Enterprises	Value Added	Total Capital	Fixed Assets	Sales Revenue
Food Processing	4.0	3.7	2.9	3.1	4.3
Food Manufacturing	3.1	2.6	3.6	2.7	2.5
Beverage Manufacturing	1.6	3.2	4.3	3.4	2.4
Tobacco Processing	0.0	0.1	0.1	0.1	0.1
Textile Industry	7.6	4.8	5.7	5.1	4.9
Garments & Other Fibre Products	10.7	5.1	3.3	3.2	5.1
Leather, Furs, Down & Related Products	4.8	3.2	1.8	2.1	3.6
Timber Processing, Bamboo, Cane, Palm Fibre & Straw Products	1.9	0.8	1.0	1.0	0.9
Furniture Manufacturing	1.5	0.7	0.6	0.6	0.7
Papermaking & Paper Products	2.4	2.0	2.9	2.7	1.9
Printing & Record Medium Reproduction	1.6	1.2	1.2	1.1	0.9
Cultural, Educational & Sports Goods	3.1	1.7	1.4	1.3	1.8
Petroleum Processing & Coking	0.3	0.6	0.5	0.7	0.8
Raw Chemical Materials & Chemical Products	5.2	4.7	5.9	5.5	4.8
Medical & Pharmaceutical Products	2.0	2.5	2.0	2.1	1.7
Chemical Fibre	0.7	2.1	2.3	2.2	1.7
Rubber Products	1.2	1.3	1.6	1.7	1.3
Plastic Products	6.6	3.4	4.1	3.5	3.6

Table 2.6 Continued

Sector	Number of Enterprises	Value Added	Total Capital	Fixed Assets	Sales Revenue
Nonmetal Mineral Products	5.1	3.1	6.2	5.2	2.7
Smelting & Pressing of Ferrous Metals	0.7	1.0	1.6	1.7	1.4
Smelting & Pressing of Nonferrous Metals	1.0	0.9	1.4	1.3	1.3
Metal Products	5.6	3.5	4.2	3.9	4.0
Ordinary Machinery	3.6	3.2	4.4	3.7	2.8
Special Purpose Equipment	2.3	1.4	1.6	1.6	1.4
Transport Equipment	3.0	7.5	7.1	7.8	7.4
Electric Equipment & Machinery	5.9	6.1	6.6	6.1	6.6
Electronic & Telecommunications Equipment	7.2	18.9	10.9	14.9	21.6
Instruments, Metres, Cultural & Office Machinery	1.8	1.9	1.4	1.4	2.2
Production & Supply of Electric Power, Steam & Hot Water	0.9	6.6	7.7	8.4	3.4
Others	0.6	0.4	0.5	0.5	0.4
Total	100	100	100	100	100

Source: State Statistical Bureau, China Statistical Yearbook, 2000.

Table 2.7 Importance of FDI and FIEs in China, 1982-2000

%

Year	Share of realised FDI in fixed asset investment	Share of FIEs in total industrial output	Share of FIEs in total trade	Share of FIEs in import	Share of FIEs in export
1982	0.68		0.79	1.43	0.24
1983	0.88		1.42	1.35	1.49
1984	1.76		0.87	1.46	0.26
1985	1.92		3.39	4.89	1.09
1986	2.14		4.04	5.60	1.88
1987	2.37		5.55	7.81	3.07
1988	2.64		8.12	10.64	5.18
1989	3.19		12.28	14.87	9.35
1990	3.66	2.28	17.43	23.06	12.58
1991	4.15	5.29	21.34	26.51	16.75
1992	7.51	7.09	26.43	32.74	20.44
1993	12.13	9.15	34.27	40.24	27.51
1994	17.08	11.26	37.04	45.78	28.69
1995	15.65	14.31	39.10	47.66	31.51
1996	15.10	15.14	47.29	54.45	40.71
1997	14.79	18.57	46.95	54.59	41.00
1998	13.23	24.00	48.68	54.73	44.06
1999	11.17	27.75	50.78	51.83	45.47
2000	10.30		49.91	52.10	47.93

Source: Wei and Liu (2001) and http://www.chinafdi.org.cn/english

FDI contributes to the creation of employment opportunities both directly and indirectly. The indirect employment effects, e.g. via backward and forward linkages, are difficult to measure. In terms of direct effects, FIEs employed 6.1 million workers, accounting for 2.9 per cent of China's urban employment in 1999. FDI also influences returns to labour. Wu (2000) and Zhao (2001) both argue that FDI can raise the wages of skilled labour relative to unskilled labour in China, which is characterised by segmented labour markets and high labour mobility costs, regardless of whether or not they transfer skill-biased technology. Zhao (2001) also shows that skilled labour earns significantly higher wages in FIEs than in state-owned enterprises (SOEs), while the reverse is true for unskilled labour. The mere entry of FDI brings in competition for skilled labour, which in turn raises returns to skills.

In summary, FDI in China has undergone systematic structural changes (Luo and Neale, 1998). Foreign investors have incrementally increased their commitments to the Chinese market. Many large multinationals such as Motorola, Coca-Cola, Lucent Technologies, General Motor, Ford and Unilever have become "dominant local players" in China. Many more have shown an increasing interest in China. A large number of foreign firms have entered into capital- and technology-intensive sectors and increased their presence in relatively less-developed inland provinces.

2.3 DETERMINANTS OF FDI IN CHINA

The impressive growth of FDI inflows into China has generated a number of empirical studies on the major determinants of FDI in China. They can be broadly categorised into two groups: studies at the national level (why foreign firms invest in China) and those at the regional level (why a foreign firm chooses a specific region within China). Most of these studies are based on the OLI framework, the eclectic paradigm, proposed by John Dunning. In summary, Dunning argues that firms invest abroad because of O (ownership), L (locational) and I (internalisation) advantages. Ownership advantage refers to the multinational's ability to compete with their rivals. Locational advantages relate to the multinational's willingness to invest in one host country rather than in others. Finally, internalisation advantage refers to the ability of the multinationals to internalise the O and L advantages.

2.3.1 National Determinants

Wang and Swain (1995), Wei (1995, 2000), Liu et al. (1997), Dees (1998), Zhang (2000), Hong and Chen (2001) and Wei and Liu (2001) investigate the determinants of FDI at the national level. Most of these studies rely on relatively short period time series data, including Wang and Swain (1995), Hong and Chen (2001) and Zhang (2000), and consequently suffer from the problem of too few degrees of freedom. Our discussion will focus on the results by Wei (1995, 2000), Liu et al. (1997), Dees (1998) and Wei and Liu (2001), in which panel data are used.

The empirical results from all these studies indicate that market size, measured by GDP, GDP per capita, GNP, or GNP per capita, has a significant and positive effect on inward FDI. Rapid economic growth may create large domestic markets and business opportunities for foreign investment and hence bolster investors' confidence to invest in China. The positive relationship between market size and inward FDI is also confirmed by Zhang (2000), who finds that both US and Hong Kong FDI are induced by China's large markets. This reflects the market-seeking motive of US firms and the objective of Hong Kong firms to shift from mainly export-oriented investments towards both the Chinese and international markets.

Liu et al. (1997), Dees (1998) and Wei and Liu (2001) provide evidence to show that China's low labour costs and relatively large volumes of exports play an important role in foreign firms' FDI decisions. Multinationals relocate certain types of manufacturing operations away from their home bases or set up a new business in a host country to exploit international differences in factor prices. Since labour costs are an important part of total costs, especially in labour-intensive manufacturing, the lower the labour costs in a host country, the more attractive the host country is. Zhang (2000) finds that labour costs play a much more significant role in attracting FDI from Hong Kong than that from the US.

Exports may influence FDI in a number of ways. They can integrate home and host country markets. This may enable home country firms to obtain information on investment opportunities in the host market. They may encourage FDI into the host country. In addition, it could be argued that multinationals have an incentive to invest where internalisation provides access to specific sources of comparative advantage in the host country. Comparative advantage can be revealed by trade performance, and FDI could be expected to be positively related to bilateral trade.

Liu et al. (1997), Dees (1998) and Wei and Liu (2001) also investigate the relationship between the exchange rate and FDI inflows. A real depreciation of the host country's currency favours the foreign firms' purchase of the host country's assets and allows foreign investors to take advantage of the relatively cheap labour in the host country. Therefore, depreciation is expected to be positively associated with FDI inflows. Liu et al. (1997) and Wei and Liu (2001) obtain a positive coefficient on the exchange rate variable in the regression equations designed to test the determinants of FDI in China.

The impact of geographical distance on FDI flows is discussed by Wei (1995, 2000), Liu et al. (1997) and Wei and Liu (2001). Geographic proximity of the host to the home country of investors reduces informational and managerial uncertainty, lowers monitoring and transportation costs and reduces the exposure of multinationals to risk. The coefficient of the distance variable is found to be significant in studies on determinants by Wei (1995, 2000) but insignificant in Liu et al. (1997) and Wei and Liu (2001). These contradictory results may be due to differing data samples used in these studies. In Wei (1995, 2000), China is just one of the host countries under investigation, while in Liu et al. (1997) and Wei and Liu (2001) China is the only host country.

It is also found that FDI inflows are positively and significantly influenced by adult literacy rates, a crude measure of average human capital (Wei, 1995), the change in patent registration by foreign invested firms (Dees, 1998), linguistic ties (Wei, 2000) and borrowing costs and imports (Wei and

Liu, 2001). FDI inflows are discouraged by corruption and the regulatory burden (Wei, 2000), and country risk and cultural differences (Wei and Liu, 2001).

2.3.2 Regional Determinants

Quite a number of studies have investigated the regional distribution of FDI in China, including Gong (1995), Chen (1996), Head and Ries (1996), Chen (1997), Wei et al. (1999), Berthélemy and Démurger (2000), Cheng and Kwan (2000), Coughlin and Segev (2000), Zhao and Zhu (2000), Wei and Liu (2001) and Zhang (2001a). The common factors investigated include market size, agglomeration effects, infrastructure, human capital, labour costs and productivity, and investment incentives.

The existing studies seem to agree that regional market size is the principal determinant of FDI. In Wei et al. (1999) and Wei and Liu (2001), a consistent finding is that the growth of regional markets proxied by GDP growth is statistically significant for contracted FDI inflows. Zhao and Zhu (2000) find that the market size of a city significantly induces investment from Hong Kong, Macao, Taiwan, Singapore and other Asian countries, but it does not seem to be important for Japanese, South Korean, US and European firms. Sun et al. (2002) divide the full sample into two sub-samples, 1986-91 and 1992-98 and find that provincial GDP had no significant impact on FDI before 1991, though there is a positive relationship since then. They suggest that this may reflect the shift in the motives of FDI from export-oriented to market-seeking from 1991.

Though different measures are adopted, Gong (1995), Head and Ries (1996), Chen (1997), Wei et al. (1999), Berthélemy and Démurger (2000), Cheng and Kwan (2000), and Kevin Zhang (2001a) provide support to the argument that agglomeration has a significant and positive impact on inward FDI. The agglomeration effect is often associated with externalities. Foreign firms can benefit from the concentration of production and urbanisation. This is because it helps them to enhance their levels of technology and reap economies of scale and scope due to knowledge spillovers, the availability of human capital and the use of joint networks of suppliers and distributors. Foreign firms may also benefit from the presence of their fellow investors, who are either their competitors or suppliers, since this may enable them to obtain valuable information. Firms may also enjoy other positive externalities from agglomeration such as complementarity between industries and experienced local administration.

Infrastructure and human capital (or labour quality) are also important determinants of FDI. Other things being equal, regions with developed infrastructure and high-quality labour tend to be more attractive for foreign investors since they promote profitability in international production. All the studies discussed above except Coughlin and Segev (2000) confirm the positive and significant impact of infrastructure, in one form or another, on inward FDI. Coughlin and Segev (2000) find a positive though insignificant relationship. Empirical support for the importance of human capital (or labour quality) in FDI location decisions is provided by all of the studies with the exception of Cheng and Kwan (2000), in which a positive but statistically insignificant relationship is found. Zhao and Zhu (2000) also find that sound infrastructure and high quality of labour are significant determinants of FDI irrespective of its country of origin.

A dummy variable which differentiates the coastal regions from the non-coastal regions has been introduced in most of the studies analysing determinants of FDI. A consistent finding of these studies is that foreign firms have a significant preference for investing in the coastal provinces. This is not surprising, as the coastal regions are the low information cost areas and they enjoyed preferential treatment during China's early experimentation with FDI.

The studies on the impact of labour costs on FDI, however, produce a mixed bag of results. Cheap factor inputs are obviously a major attraction to foreign investors. Thus, there should be a negative relationship between labour costs and inward FDI. However, a positive relationship between the two is also thought to be possible in the literature, as wage rates could be treated as a proxy for labour quality. Higher wage rates may signify the higher skills that foreign investors seek. It is though inaccurate to say that FDI is attracted mainly by cheap labour. It is the efficiency wage which counts. After controlling for productivity, Chen (1997), Coughlin and Segev (2000), Wei et al. (1999) and Wei and Liu (2001) find that wage rates negatively influence FDI inflows. No significant relationship between FDI and wage costs is found in Head and Ries (1996) and a positive and significant relationship is found in Zhao and Zhu (2000). Sun et al. (2002) provide the evidence to show that wages are positively related to FDI before 1991 but negatively related with FDI since then.

Finally, several studies find a significant relationship between FDI inflows and electricity consumption (Head and Ries, 1996), trade (Wei et al., 1999), the ratio of FDI to domestic investment (Sun et al., 2002), country risk (Sun, et al., 2002) and foreign portfolio investment (Sun et al., 2002). Tung and Cho (2000) indicate that concessionary tax rates and incentives are an effective way of attracting FDI into the designated locations inside China.

In sum, FDI in China has been motivated by several factors. First, market size appears to be one major determinant. China, with the world's largest population of 1.2 billion and a vast and growing middle class, is often regarded as an enormous market that is under-served by multinationals. The

Chinese government's efforts to promote economic growth should help increase the effective market size and thus attract more FDI. Second, foreign trade, which measures the degree of integration of China into the rest of the world, is important in boosting FDI inflows. China has become one of the top ten trading nations in the world since 1997. China's accession to the WTO can be expected to further expand China's foreign trade, which, in turn, may increase the volume of FDI inflows. Third, China has enjoyed an advantage from its endowments of labour in attracting large volumes of FDI. China has abundant supplies of labour, both skilled and unskilled. At the national level, compared with other countries, the low effective wage rate in China is one of her major locational advantages. At the regional level, regions with a low average wage rate, given the productivity level, are in an advantageous position to attract FDI. Research also shows that high labour quality or human capital is essential at the regional level. However, the low-labour-cost advantage of China may not be sustainable as China now faces competition from its neighbouring countries such as Vietnam, Laos and India which are also endowed with cheap labour and have adopted various policies to attract FDI.

As corruption, regulatory burden and country risk at the national level are found to have a negative impact on FDI inflows, China needs a more transparent framework governing FDI and a better business environment. From the late 1970s, China has addressed investors' concerns about political risk by offering protection for FDI. China has also reduced various types of regulatory barriers applicable to FDI. Policies have been designed to shift away from targeting foreign investors towards specific locations and specific sectors to facilitate nationwide and broad-based sector participation. China has also granted various fiscal and financial concessions or incentives to FDI, though the extent of these measures was reduced after 1995 when China made a commitment to national treatment of FDI. China, in recent years, has committed itself to addressing one major concern of large investors – protection of intellectual property rights. After entry into the WTO, China needs to further improve its trade and FDI policy regimes. The findings on infrastructure and agglomeration effects at the regional level suggest that China and her regions need to upgrade the industrial structure and physical, financial and technological infrastructures.

The foregoing empirical studies on the host country and region-specific determinants of overall FDI inflows using aggregate data are a valuable exercise. They provide insights into the types of structural characteristics and macroeconomic policies that may encourage FDI inflows. However, they only capture broad and long-term trends. FDI from different sources may be attracted by different sets of determinants. Tuan and Ng (1995) argue that the heavy investment from Hong Kong has been driven by an international division of labour on the part of multinational enterprises (MNEs). Departments in Hong Kong handle R&D, marketing and management while subsidiaries in China engage in assembly and fabrication processes. Lu and Zhu (1995), based on a survey of 95 Singapore firms in China from 1990 to 1993, claim that Singapore FDI has been determined mainly by firms specific competitive advantages, though business networking and confidence built on ethnic ties and friendly relationship between two nations have also been important. Hou (2002) notes that the Taiwanese investment boom in China is the result of an interaction between China's comparative advantage plus cultural and linguistic affinity across the Taiwan Strait and factors created by the structural changes in the Taiwanese economy. Rong (1999) provides support for the proposition that the unique patterns of Japanese FDI in China can be explained by taking into account the impact of the two countries' historical experience and their love-hate political relationship.

Even FDI from a specific home country can be sector- and project-specific, and may be induced by different factors. Lack of disaggregated data on specific sectors and projects, however, hampers research into these issues. In addition, the possible endogeneity between FDI and GDP growth and between FDI and exports has not been treated adequately in the empirical literature. A rigorous investigation of the determinants and impact of FDI requires this aspect to be taken into account in empirical analyses.

While a fast growing market and a large pool of labour are regarded as the major determinants of FDI in China by mainstream analysts, Huang (2001, 2003) argues that this conventional wisdom is wrong. He suggests that FDI in China can be better explained by an institutional foundation argument. His main proposition is that the absorption of large volumes of FDI by China is not a sign of the strengths of its economy but of its fundamental weaknesses. This view has two components. First, Chinese private export-oriented firms were at a disadvantage when borrowing from banks so that they could do nothing but sell their claims on future cash flows, mainly to ethnic Chinese investors from Hong Kong and Taiwan. This accounts for a large volume of export-oriented FDI from these countries. Second, SOEs had built up a potentially valuable asset base during the reform era, which was financed by a generous infusion of subsidised credit from the banking system. Even so, SOEs have generated a thin or close to negative cash flow, rendering them potential targets for acquisition by foreign firms. It is thus that a large volume of domestic market-oriented FDI has been attracted to China.

No doubt Huang's research is important. He identifies a research area which deserves in-depth investigation. However, further evidence is required to validate this non-conventional view. First, were the Chinese export-oriented firms, as a general rule, private firms with severe liquidity constraints? The traditional view on the rapid growth of labour-intensive products in China is that FDI from Hong Kong and Taiwan was directed to labour-intensive export-oriented projects in the coastal provinces in order to effectively utilise China's large labour force. With the help of capital, simple technology and international marketing skills from ethnic Chinese investors, China's natural comparative advantage of cheap labour was exploited and translated into international competitiveness in the international markets (World Bank, 1994). The importation of machinery by the Chinese to produce and export or the sub-contracting by the ethnic Chinese to Chinese private firms would not be preferred over FDI based on transaction cost economics. Undoubtedly the difficulty in obtaining finance by Chinese private firms may explain some cases of inward FDI, but could this be generalised to cover much of export-oriented FDI in China?

Second, it has not been proved that much of FDI in China takes the form of mergers and acquisitions (M&A) rather than greenfield investments. The fact is that "M&As played a relatively small role in FDI inflows into China – at the most for $2 billion out of a total FDI of $40 billion in 1999" (UNCTAD, 2000, p. 122). This statistic also does not support Huang's argument.

2.4 THE ROLE OF FDI IN CHINA'S ECONOMIC DEVELOPMENT

The role of FDI in the economic development of the host countries has been debated extensively in the literature. Traditionally inward FDI is believed to promote economic development by increasing capital stock and augmenting employment, whereas recent literature points to other effects. Balasubramanyam et al. (1996, 1999) and de Mello (1997, 1999) argue that many of the growth-promoting factors identified by endogenous growth theory can be initiated and nurtured to promote growth through FDI. In most cases, what FDI transfers are not only capital and managerial skills, but also embodied and tacit technologies.

FDI may raise productivity levels among locally owned firms in the industries which they enter by improving the allocation of resources in those industries. Multinationals may develop new products and technologies earlier than local firms, and may exert competitive pressure on them and force them to imitate or innovate. The threat of competition may also spur firms which might otherwise have been laggards to adopt best practice technology. As a result, the presence of multinationals may speed up the process or lower the cost of technology transfer. Multinationals always try to preserve their proprietary rights over knowledge and technology, but spillovers through 'learning by doing' or 'learning by watching' may induce domestic firms to attain higher levels of technical or X-efficiency. Another route for the diffusion of new ideas is the movement of labour from foreign subsidiaries to locally owned firms.

FDI is believed to promote exports, which in turn will promote economic development and growth in the host country. If there are substantial differences in factor endowments between the host and home countries, the capital-abundant country tends to export capital-intensive services (e.g. R&D and marketing) and intermediate inputs to their subsidiaries in the labour-abundant country in exchange for finished varieties of differentiated and homogeneous goods. Thus, FDI generates complementary trade flows. For all these reasons, FDI is recognised as a major source of growth, especially in developing countries (de Mello, 1997; Borensztein et al., 1998).

The unprecedented growth of FDI has been accompanied by China's outstanding progress in foreign trade and economic development. During the period 1978-2000, China achieved an average GDP growth rate of around 8 per cent. Foreign trade also expanded dramatically. In the world league tables for international trade, China ranked 32nd in 1978. However, it moved up to become the seventh largest trading country in 2000.

2.4.1 Technology Transfer and Spillovers from FDI

Although FDI is regarded by the Chinese government as a prominent vehicle of technology transfer, there is very little research on the issue. The existing studies of technology transfer through FDI are mainly case-study based. Chen et al. (1995) indicate that technology transfer from FDI is relatively low. The majority of FDI projects in the industrial sector are relatively unsophisticated, involving, at best, the transfer of low and intermediate technologies. However, inward FDI has transferred important managerial "software" and export marketing technology so crucial for the development of a market economy. Chen et al. argue that FDI's less than satisfactory contribution to high technology transfer to China is partially explained by the fact that China relied on Hong Kong and Taiwan as its principal sources of FDI.

Based on a case study of FDI in the coastal city of Dalian, Young and Lan (1997) also suggest that the extent of technology transfer is fairly limited but at the level to be expected given that China is a developing country with low technological capabilities. More specifically, the problems associated with technology transfer to China through FDI include: (1) many investors are not genuine sources of technology; (2) local partners have distorted motives and limited absorptive capabilities; (3) moderate technology gap, an incomplete technology package and the excessive inflows of hardware hamper advanced technology transfer; and (4) most direct technology transfer is conducted in EJVs but there was only a small difference between the technology gap and technology transferability in many JVs.

Huang (2001, 2003) is quite sceptical about technology transfer given that the dominant source of inward FDI is ethnic Chinese FDI from Hong Kong and Taiwan. He argues that the evidence on "hard technology transfer" associated with FDI is thin. In addition, it is implausible to argue that the organisational know-how is present in all the FDI projects. Bennett et al. (2001) investigate 20 EU industrial firms operating in China and Zhang and Taylor (2001) examine the process of technology transfer in the context of learning by doing in the Chinese automotive industry. They conclude that there are transfers of low and intermediate technologies to Chinese indigenous firms via various means. Based on a case study of 84 Hong Kong garment firms in China, Thompson (2002) finds that there is technology transfer and inter- and intra-industry spillovers from Hong Kong to China. Hong Kong's FDI plants in China are of a similar level of technological advancement as their Hong Kong plants. More specifically, the findings from Thompson (2002) support the proposition that FDI within geographical industry clusters transfers technology and facilitates knowledge spillovers more than FDI that is geographically dispersed. Li and Yeung (1999) conduct two company case studies in Shanghai: Shanghai Volkswagen Automotive Company Ltd (SVW) and Shanghai Bell Telephone Equipment Manufacturing Co Ltd. They report that in both cases, there are inter-firm technology transfer and knowledge spillovers. Tan (2002) finds that, in the case of a specific product (stored programme controlled switch), because of technology transfer and spillover effects of FDI, China has successfully transited from the status of an importer to one where foreign and domestic manufacturers of the product account for 57 per cent and 43 per cent of total sales respectively, in the year 2000.

In sum, there is only evidence on low and intermediate technology transfers, mainly from investors from Hong Kong and Taiwan. Of course, it is arguable that technology consists of many things. What is appropriate depends on the stage of development of the host country. If the prime objective is employment, Hong Kong technology is ideal. If more advanced technologies are to be transferred and absorbed, Chinese government policy needs to be refined and the technical capabilities of Chinese indigenous firms need to be enhanced.

Apart from the research on technology transfer, there are also econometric studies on productivity spillovers in China. Fan and Warr (2000) find that FDI only promotes total factor productivity (TFP) growth in low and medium technology industries. They argue that productivity spillovers from FDI depend on the technology gap between domestic and foreign firms. Spillover effects increase with the gap up to a certain critical level. Beyond this threshold level, local firms will generally have little ability to absorb advanced technology.

Liu et al. (2001) and Wei and Liu (2001) examine the impact of FDI on labour productivity in the Chinese electronics industry. Both studies show that foreign presence is associated with higher labour productivity in the industry. Li et al. (2001) estimate a system of three equations for foreign-invested firms (FIEs), state owned enterprises (SOEs) and other locally owned enterprises (OLOEs) respectively. Their results indicate that the extent to which spillovers occur varies with different types of ownership. While productivity gains of SOEs largely come from competition with FIEs, OLOEs benefit from demonstration and contagion effects from foreign presence. Productivities of local and foreign firms are jointly determined.

2.4.2 Impact of FDI on Foreign Trade

As both inward FDI and foreign trade have increased dramatically since the late 1970s, several empirical studies have recently examined the relationship between both means of international integration. Chen (1999), Zhang and Song (2000), and Sun (2001) investigate the issue using panel data at the provincial level. Chen (1999) and Zhang and Song (2000) conclude that FDI has a positive and significant impact on provincial export performance. Sun (2001) confirms that increased levels of FDI has a positive impact on exports in the coastal and central regions of China. However, its impact on the western region was positive and significant during the period of 1984-96, but negative and insignificant during the period of 1984-97.

Using monthly time series data for the years 1986 to 1999 and cointegration/error correction modelling techniques Zhang and Felmingham (2001) find bi-directional causal links between inward FDI and exports for China as a whole. They also adopt a panel data approach to the examination of the FDI-trade relationship at the provincial level and conclude that bi-directional causality applies in both the coastal and western areas, and that exports Granger cause FDI in the case of medium level FDI recipients in central China. Liu et al. (2001) focus on the country of origin of the inward FDI and the destination of exports from China. They examine the causal relationship between FDI and trade based on a panel of bilateral data for China and 19 home countries/regions over the period 1984-98. They show a virtuous procedure of development for China: the growth of China's imports causes the growth in inward FDI from a home country/region, which, in turn, causes the growth of exports from China to the home country/region. The growth of exports causes the growth of imports.

It seems that the national and provincial data largely support a bilateral positive relationship between inward FDI and China's exports, in particular, or foreign trade, in general. The evidence on FDI determinants reported earlier is confirmed here. However, as the FDI-trade relationship can be industry- or even firm-specific, the use of firm-level data may be more appropriate.

2.4.3 FDI and Economic Growth

There are a number of studies which examine the relationship between inward FDI and economic development or growth in China. Some are largely descriptive, supported by simple statistical or enterprise survey data, while others are based on econometric analyses. This subsection focuses on the direct relationship between FDI and economic growth. Among the descriptive studies, the preliminary discussion of Huang (1995) suggests that FDI has induced China's economic growth and introduced advanced operation and management experiences, especially advanced and applied technologies, as well as speeded up the renovation of old enterprises.

Based on the Porter-Dunning diamond model of international competitiveness (Porter, 1990; Dunning, 1990, 1993), Liu and Song (1997) argue that FDI promotes China's economic growth via its influence on the demand and supply conditions, business strategy and competition. The economic reform and open-door policy has enabled China to translate its natural comparative advantage into economic growth and international competitiveness in a wide range of labour-intensive commodities. In this process, the industrial restructuring of Asian newly industrialising economies (NIEs) and their FDI in China has played a very important role. China needs to link its economy more closely not only to the Asian NIEs but also to other economies, especially those of the triad (Japan, EU and North America) and develop higher order competitiveness ahead of the current factor endowments.

One interesting development relating to studies of the impact of FDI on growth in China is that it has spurred econometric analysis of the phenomenon. Several recent studies seem to have arrived at a consensus that FDI, together with other explanatory variables, helps promote regional or industrial economic growth.

Wei (1994) is probably the first attempt on the subject using econometrics. However, one problem with Wei's (1994) study is that he treats FDI as an exogenous variable in the regression equations. In fact, this is a common problem in most studies for China, including Chen et al. (1995), Chen and Fleisher (1996), Mody and Wang (1997), Sun (1998b), Dayal-Gulati and Husain (2000), Sun and Parikh (2001), Kevin Zhang (2001b), Wei Zhang (2001) and Zhang and Felmingham (2002). As discussed in the previous section, China's rapid economic growth may have induced large volumes of FDI into China as it has rendered China attractive to foreign investors. Empirically, Zhang (1999) and Shan et al. (1999) find a bi-directional causation between FDI and economic growth. Failure to consider the endogeneity issue may lead to ambiguous results.

Taking explicitly into account the two-way relationship between FDI and growth, Berthélemy and Démurger (2000) estimate a simultaneous equation model. They confirm that FDI has played a fundamental role in China's economic growth, though the magnitude of FDI is rather small. One special feature of Wei et al. (2001) and Wei and Liu (2001) is that they have carried out unit root tests and confirm the existence of a long-run positive relationship between FDI and economic growth.

One merit of Dayal-Gulati and Husain (2000) and Kevin Zhang (2001b) is that they attempt to identify possible structural variations over time through conducting panel and/or cross-sectional studies for three sub-periods. Dayal-Gulati and Husain (2000) argue that it seems that FDI had a much more positive and significant impact on China's economic growth during 1993-97 than during 1983-87, but had no significant effects during 1988-92. In Kevin Zhang (2001b), over the periods of 1984-88, 1989-93 and 1994-98, the impact of FDI on growth appeared to increase, with growth in FDI.

Mody and Wang (1997), Berthélemy and Démurger (2000) and Kevin Zhang (2001b) all report complementarity between human capital and FDI, i.e. sectors or provinces with a higher level of human capital seem to have benefited more from FDI than others. This is because availability of human capital is essential for absorbing technologies, managerial techniques and other spillover effects of FDI. Mody and Wang (1997) establish that industrial sectors can benefit from FDI only if the secondary school enrolment rate in the region in which they locate exceeds a threshold level of 16 per cent.

Wu (2000) takes a different approach, the stochastic frontier method, to the investigation of how efficiently FDI was utilised in China's ten coastal regions over the period of 1983-95. He shows that the utilisation of FDI by all regions experienced a learning process, i.e. FDI's productive efficiency initially declined and after a period of time it increased.

Despite different approaches and methodologies adopted by various studies, the central message from the above discussions is clear. FDI has significantly benefited the Chinese economy as a whole, although the coastal regions seem to have gained more than the rest of the country. However, one important limitation of the aforementioned empirical studies is that the utilization of aggregate data can only capture the net effects of FDI. Some negative effects cannot be identified by using aggregate data sets. Moreover, there is a lack of precision in identifying the mechanisms through which FDI promotes knowledge spillovers, exports and economic growth.

It is established in the literature that FDI from developed countries is mostly concentrated in the high-tech and capital-intensive sectors with vertically differentiated goods, while that from developing countries, particularly NIEs, is mostly in the low-tech and labour-intensive sectors with horizontally differentiated or homogeneous goods. It is also argued that the local economy benefits more from EJVs than from WFOEs. However, in the context of China, there is no solid evidence on how FDI from different source countries or through different entry modes impact on economic development.

2.5 CONCLUSIONS

China initiated economic reform in 1979, with the introduction of FDI as one of its key development strategies. Despite the substantial literature on the determinants and impact of FDI in China, there is no systematic review of the existing studies. This survey is an attempt in this direction.

A number of factors are recognised to be critical in firms' foreign investment location decisions. At the national level, FDI inflows are positively influenced by China's relative market size and economic integration through exports and imports, and negatively influenced by China's effective real wage rates, corruption, red tape, country risk, and cultural differences. At the regional level also the positive and significant determinants of FDI include market size and economic integration, as well as human capital, infrastructure, and the availability of information and investment incentives. Effective wage rates are negatively associated with FDI inflows into the Chinese regions. These empirical studies indicate that sustained efforts to promote political, economic and social development have contributed to the success of China in attracting a substantial volume of FDI. It is important to note that China is unique in attracting FDI in so far as much of FDI has been contributed by ethnic Chinese.

There is also evidence in support of the proposition that FDI leads to transfers of low and intermediate technologies, imparts positive productivity and knowledge spillovers to Chinese indigenous firms, promotes foreign trade, and exerts a positive impact on economic growth in China. FDI, foreign trade and economic growth are closely inter-related. Thus, China seems to follow a virtuous process of development: the policy of economic reform and opening to the outside world accelerates economic development, foreign trade and FDI inflows, which in turn speed up economic growth in China.

China's experience of FDI is unique in the sense that a substantial proportion of total FDI is from the Chinese Diaspora. However, Diaspora investments can be explained by conventional wisdom. Most critiques of FDI in China ignore its contribution to China's growth, but their arguments belittling such investments do not stand up to scrutiny. The introduction of low and intermediate technologies by FDI is associated with the limited technical knowledge possessed by most foreign investors in China, and with the limited capabilities of technology absorption of Chinese indigenous firms. FDI has contributed to growth in China though it has had some adverse consequences for development.

Given China's goal of modernising industry, agriculture, national defence and science technology, the introduction of only low and intermediate technologies from FDI is necessary though not sufficient. FDI from sources other than the Asian NIEs should be encouraged. In the meantime, domestic economic reforms, R&D expenditure and human capital accumulation are important for enhancing the technological capabilities of indigenous firms so that advanced technologies and knowledge spillovers via FDI can be absorbed.

While the existing studies help us in understanding the determinants and impact of FDI in China, several issues need to be taken into consideration in future research. Few theoretical models designed especially for the Chinese case have been constructed, although a number of empirical studies with sound methodology have been undertaken. Another problem that has often been ignored or not properly dealt with in the empirical literature is the arbitrary choice of explanatory variables. Existing data limitations necessitate caution in analysing the results based on empirical estimations and studies at the disaggregated industry and sector level are yet to be undertaken.

NOTE

1. The volume of FDI in China reported by official agencies may be an overestimate, partly because of the overvaluation of capital equipment contributed to joint ventures by foreign investors, and partly because of 'round-tripping' investment. Huang (1998) estimates round-tripping capital at 23 per cent of China's FDI inflows. But even after netting out this type of investment, China's FDI inflows are relatively high. With recent improvements in statistical methods and national treatment accorded to foreign investors, the magnitude of the problem should be reduced. However, as noted by Huang (2001), China defines FDI at the level of at least 25 per cent of a firm's equity, which is much higher than the threshold level set in OECD countries, which is 10 per cent. This is likely to cause FDI in China to be understated. For these reasons, it is difficult to identify the direction of bias in the data. Most studies acknowledge the problem and urge caution in interpreting it. This caveat also applies to this study.

References

Balasubramanyam, V.N., M. Salisu and D. Sapsford (1996), 'Foreign Direct Investment and Growth in EP and IS Countries', *Economic Journal*, 106, 92-105.

Balasubramanyam, V.N., M. Salisu and D. Sapsford (1999), 'Foreign Direct Investment as an Engine of Growth', *Journal of International Trade and Economic Development*, 8(1), 27-40.

Bennett, D., X. Liu, D Parker, F. Steward and K. Vaidya (2001), 'Technology Transfer to China: A Study of Strategy in 20 EU Industrial Companies', *International Journal of Technology Management*, 21(1/2), 151-182.

Berthélemy, J.C. and S. Démurger (2000), 'Foreign Direct Investment and Economic Growth: Theory and Application to China', *Review of Development Economics*, 4(2), 140-155.

Borensztein, E., J. de Gregorio and J.W. Lee (1998), 'How Does Foreign Investment Affect Economic Growth?' *Journal of International Economics*, 45, 115-135.

Broadman, H.G. and X. Sun (1997), 'The Distribution of Foreign Investment in China', *World Economy*, 20, 339-61.

Chen, Chien-Husn (1996), 'Regional Determinants of Foreign Direct Investment in Mainland China', *Journal of Economic Studies*, 23(2), 18-30.

Chen, Chunlai (1997), 'Provincial Characteristics and Foreign Direct Investment Location Decision within China', Chinese Economy Research Unit Working Paper No. 97/16, University of Adelaide.

Chen, Chunlai (1999), 'The Impact of FDI and Trade', in Wu, Y. (ed.), *Foreign Direct Investment and Economic Growth in China*, Edward Elgar.

Chen, Chung, Lawrence Chang and Yimin Zhang (1995), 'The Role of Foreign Direct Investment in China's Post-1978 Economic Development', *World Development*, 23(4), 691-703.

Chen, Jian and Belton M. Fleisher (1996), 'Regional Income Inequality and Economic Growth in China', *Journal of Comparative Economics*, 22, 141-164.

Cheng, L. K. and Y. K. Kwan (2000), 'What are the Determinants of the Location of Foreign Direct Investment? The Chinese Experience', *Journal of International Economics*, 51, 379-400.

Coughlin, C. C. and E. Segev (2000), 'Foreign Direct Investment in China: A Spatial Econometric Study', *World Economy*, 23(1), 1-23.

de Mello, L. (1997), 'Foreign Direct Investment in Developing Countries and Growth: A Selective Survey', *Journal of Development Studies*, 34, 1-34.

de Mello, L. (1999), 'Foreign Direct Investment Led Growth: Evidence from Time-Series and Panel Data', *Oxford Economic Papers*, 51, 133-151.

Dayal-Gulati, Anuradha and Aasim M. Husain (2000), 'Centripetal Forces in China's Economic Take-off', IMF Working Paper WP/00/86.

Dees, S. (1998), 'Foreign Direct Investment in China: Determinants and Effects', *Economics of Planning*, 31(2/3), 175-194.

Deng, Ping (2001), 'WFOEs: The Most Popular Entry Mode into China', *Business Horizons*, July-August, 63-72.

Dunning, J.H. (1990), 'Dunning on Porter', Paper presented at the Annual Meeting of the Academy of International Business.

Dunning, J.H. (1993), *The Globalization of Business*, Routledge: London and New York.

Fan, Xiaoqin and Peter G. Warr (2000), 'Foreign Investment, Spillover Effects and the Technology Gap: Evidence from China', Working Paper in Trade and Development No. 00/03, The Australian National University.

Gong, H. (1995), 'Spatial Patterns of Foreign Investment in China's Cities, 1980-1989', *Urban Geography*, 16, 198-209.

Gray, H.P. (1998), 'International Trade and Foreign Direct Investment: The Interface', in Dunning J.H. (ed.) *Globalization, Trade and Foreign Direct Investment*, Elsevier, Oxford.

Hayter, R. and S. S. Han (1998), 'Reflections on China's Open Policy towards Foreign Direct Investment', *Regional Studies*, 32(1), 1-16.

Head, K. and Ries, J. (1996), 'Inter-City Competition for Foreign Investment: Static and Dynamic Effects of China's Incentive Areas', *Journal of Urban Economics*, 40, 38-60.

Henley, John, Colin Kirkpatrick and Georgina Wilde (1999), 'Foreign Direct Investment in China: Recent Trends and Current Policy Issues', *World Economy*, 22(2), 223-243.

Hong, Mao and Luoshou Chen (2001), 'Quantitative and Dynamic Analysis of the OLI Variables Determining FDI in China', *Review of Urban and Development Studies*, 13(2), 163-172.

Hou, Jack W. (2002), 'China's FDI Policy and Taiwanese Direct Investment (TDI) in China', http://china-ces.org/HK2002Paper/Jack%20W%20HOU.pdf

Huang, Fanzhang (1995), 'China's Utilisation of Foreign Capital and the Related Policies', *Journal of Asian Economics*, 6(2), 217-232.

Huang, Yasheng (1998), 'FDI in China: An Asian Perspective', Institute of Southeast Asian Studies, Singapore.

Huang, Yasheng (2001), 'Internal and External Reforms: Experiences and Lessons from China', *Cato Journal*, 21(1), 43-64.

Huang, Yasheng (2003), *Selling China: Foreign Direct Investment during the Reform Era*, Cambridge University Press, New York.

Lee, Chyungly (1997), 'Foreign Direct Investment in China: Do State Policies Matter?' *Issues and Studies*, 33(7), 40-61.

Lemoine, F. (2000), 'FDI and the Opening up of China's Economy', *CEPII Working Paper*, No. 00-11, June.

Li, Xiaoying, Xiaming Liu and David Parker (2001), 'Foreign Direct Investment and Productivity Spillovers in the Chinese Manufacturing Sector', *Economic Systems*, 25(4), 305-321.

Li, Xiaojian, and Yue-man Yeung (1999), 'Inter-firm Linkages and Regional Impact of Transnational Corporations: Company Case Studies from Shanghai, China', *Geografiska Annaler Series B: Human Geography*, 81(2), 61-72

Liu, X. and H. Song (1997), 'China and the Multinationals: A Winning Combination', *Long Range Planning*, 30(1), 74-83.

Liu, X. H. Song, Y. Wei and P. Romilly (1997), 'Country Characteristics and Foreign Direct Investment in China: A Panel Data Analysis', *Weltirtschaftliches Archiv*, 133(2), 313-329.

Liu, X., C. Wang and Y. Wei (2001), 'Causal Links between Foreign Direct Investment and Trade in China', *China Economic Review*, 12(2), 190-202.

Liu, X., D. Parker, K. Vaidya, and Y. Wei, (2001) 'Impact of Foreign Direct Investment on Labour Productivity in the Chinese Electronic Industry', *International Business Review*, 10, 421-439.

Lu, Ding and Gangti Zhu (1995), 'Singapore Foreign Direct Investment in China: Features and Implications', *ASEAN Economic Bulletin*, 12(1), 53-63.

Luo, Yadong and O'Connor Neale (1998), 'Structural Changes to Foreign Direct Investment in China: An Evolutionary Perspective', *Journal of Applied Management Studies*, 7(1), 95-109.

Mody, Ashoka and Fang-Yi Wang (1997), 'Explaining Industrial Growth in Coastal China: Economic Reforms … and What Else?' *World Bank Economic Review*, 11, 293-325.

Ng, Linda F. Y. and Chyau Tuan (2001), 'FDI Promotion Policy in China: Governance and Effectiveness', *World Economy*, 1051-1074.

OECD (2002), *China in the World Economy: The Domestic Policy Challenges*, OECD

Page, John (1994), 'Comment', in Takatoshi Ito and Anne O. Krueger (eds.), *Growth Theories in Light of the East Asian Experience*, Chicago: University of Chicago Press.

Porter, M. (1990), *The Competitive Advantage of Nations*, Macmillan, New York.

Rong, Xiaomin (1999), 'Explaining the Patterns of Japanese Foreign Direct Investment in China', *Journal of Contemporary China*, 8(20), 123-146.

Shan, Jordan, Gary Tain and Fiona Sun (1999), 'Causality between FDI and Economic Growth', in Wu, Y. (eds.), *Foreign Direct Investment and Economic Growth in China*, Edward Elgar.

Shi, Yizheng (2001), 'Technological Capabilities and International Production Strategy of Firms: The Case of Foreign Direct Investment in China', *Journal of World Business*, 36(2), 184-204.

Sun, Haishun (1998a), *Foreign Investment and Economic Development in China, 1979-1996*, Aldershot, Ashgate Publishing Company.

Sun, Haishun (1998b), 'Macroeconomic Impact of Direct Foreign Investment in China', *World Economy*, 21(5), 675-694.

Sun, Haisun and Ashok Parikh (2001), 'Exports, Inward Foreign Direct Investment (FDI) and Regional Economic Growth in China', *Regional Studies*, 35(3), 187-196.

Sun, Q., W. Tong and Q. Yu (2002), 'Determinants of Foreign Direct Investment across China', *Journal of International Money and Finance*, 21(1), 79-113.

Sung, Yun-Wing (1994), 'Comment', in Takatoshi Ito and Anne O. Krueger (eds.), *Growth Theories in Light of the East Asian Experience*, Chicago: University of Chicago Press.

Tan, Zixiang Alex (2002), 'Product Cycle Theory and Telecommunications Industry – Foreign Direct Investment, Government Policy, and Indigenous Manufacturing in China', *Telecommunications Policy*, 26, 17-30.

Thompson, Edmund R. (2002), 'Clustering of Foreign Direct Investment and Enhanced Technology Transfer: Evidence from Hong Kong Garment Firms in China', *World Development*, 30(5), 873-890.

Tseng, Wanda S. and Harm H. Zebregs (2002), 'Foreign Direct Investment in China: Some Lessons for Other Countries', IMF Policy Discussion Paper No. 02/3. http://www.imf.org/external/pubs/ft/pdp/2002/pdp03.pdf

Tuan C. and L.F.Y. Ng (1995), 'Hong Kong's Outward Investment and Regional Economic Integration with Guangdong: Process and Implications', *Journal of Asian Economics*, 6(3), 385-405.

Tung, Samuel and Stella Cho (2000), 'The Impact of Tax Incentives on Foreign Direct Investment in China', *Journal of International Accounting, Auditing and Taxation*, 9(2), 105-135.

United Nations Conference on Trade and Development (UNCTAD) (2000), *World Investment Report 2000*, United Nations, New York and Geneva.

United Nations Conference on Trade and Development (UNCTAD) (2003), *World Investment Report 2003*, United Nations, New York and Geneva.

Wang, Zhenquan and Nigel J. Swain (1995), 'The Determinants of Foreign Direct Investment in Transforming Economies: Empirical Evidence from Hungary and China', *Weltwirtschaftliches Archiv*, 131(2), 359-382.

Wei, Shang-Jin (1994), 'The Open Door Policy and China's Rapid Growth: Evidence from City-Level Data', in Takatoshi Ito and Anne O. Krueger (eds.), *Growth Theories in Light of the East Asian Experience*, Chicago: University of Chicago Press.

Wei, Shang-Jin (1995), 'Attracting Foreign Direct Investment: Has China Reached Its Potential?' *China Economic Review*, 6(2), 187-199.

Wei, Shang-Jin (2000), 'Sizing up Foreign Direct Investment in China and India', Centre for Research on Economic Development and Policy Reform, Working Paper No. 85, Stanford University.

Wei, Y. and Liu, X. (2001), *Foreign Direct Investment in China: Determinants and Impact*, Edward Elgar.

Wei Y., X.Liu, D. Parker and K. Vaidya (1999), 'The Regional Distribution of Foreign Direct Investment in China', *Regional Studies*, 33(9), 857-867.

Wei, Y., X. Liu, S. Song, and P. Romilly (2001), 'Endogenous Innovation Growth Theory and Regional Income Convergence in China', *Journal of International Development*, 13(2), 153-168.

World Bank (1994), *China: Foreign Trade Reform*, World Bank.

Wu, X. (2000), 'Foreign Direct Investment, Intellectual Property Rights, and Wage Inequality in China', *China Economic Review*, 11, 361-384.

Wu, X. (2001), 'The Impact of Foreign Direct Investment on the Relative Return to Skill', *Economics of Transition*, 9(3), 695-715.

Wu, Yanrui (1999), *Foreign Direct Investment and Economic Growth in China*, Edward Elgar.

Wu, Yanrui (2000), 'Measuring the Performance of Foreign Direct Investment: a Case Study of China', *Economics Letters*, 66(2), 143-150.

Young, Stephen and Ping Lan (1997), 'Technology Transfer to China through Foreign Direct Investment', *Regional Studies*, 31(7), 669-679.

Zhang, Kevin Hongli (1999), 'How does FDI Interact with Economic Growth in a Large Developing Country? The Case of China', *Economic Systems*, 21(4), 291-304.

Zhang, Kevin Hongli (2000), 'Why is US Direct Investment in China so Small?' *Contemporary Economic Policy*, 18(1), 82-94.

Zhang, Kevin Hongli (2001a), 'What Attracts Foreign Multinational Corporations to China?' *Contemporary Economic Policy*, 19(3), 336-346.

Zhang, Kevin Hongli (2001b), 'How does Foreign Direct Investment Affect Economic Growth in China?' *Economics of Transition*, 9(3), 679-693.

Zhang, Kevin Hongli, Shunfeng Song (2000), 'Promoting exports: The role of inward FDI in China', *China Economic Review*, 11(4), 385-396.

Zhang, Qing and Bruce Felmingham (2001), 'The Relationship between Inward Direct Foreign Investment and China's Provincial Export Trade', *China Economic Review*, 12(1), 82-99.

Zhang, Qing and Bruce Felmingham (2002), 'The Role of FDI, Exports and Spillover Effects in the Regional Development of China', *Journal of Development Studies*, 38(4), 157-178.

Zhang, Wei (2001), 'Rethinking Regional Disparity in China', *Economics of Planning*, 34(1/2), 113-138.

Zhang, Wei and Robert Taylor (2001), 'EU Technology Transfer to China: The Automotive Industry as a Case Study' *Journal of the Asia Pacific Economy*, 6(2), 261-274.

Zhao, Hongxin and Gangti Zhu (2000), 'Location Factors and Country of Origin Difference: An Empirical Analysis', *Multinational Business Review*, 8(1), 60-73.

Zhao, Yaohui (2001), 'Foreign Direct Investment and Relative Wages: The Case of China', *China Economic Review*, 12, 40-57.

COMMENTS

Yasheng Huang

I shall briefly summarise Annie Wei's paper and then comment on some of the salient characteristics of FDI in China. Patterns of FDI in China differ from that in other countries. My explanation of these patterns of FDI in China is an institutional one. I began work on FDI about four years ago; before that I was working on transition strategies and institutional issues in transitional economies. I use FDI to illustrate institutional dynamics in a socialist economy. Most of my thoughts on FDI in China are based on my book on China published by Cambridge University Press.

The paper by Annie Wei is a comprehensive survey of the literature on FDI in China. Because it is a survey article it is difficult to comment on the overall theme of the piece. I shall first comment on some of the observations in the paper and then comment on some of the approaches used by commentators on FDI in China.

First is Annie's comment that the regional distribution of FDI in China is very uneven. This is a common view in China. The statistical basis for the statement is the data percentage distribution of FDI across regions. Here there is a theoretical issue and an empirical issue. The theoretical issue is what does unevenness mean? Is it uneven relative to theoretical expectations? I would argue that what is far more striking is how even the FDI distribution is in China. Evenness here is defined by the fact that the interior provinces of China also get a lot of FDI, not just coastal regions. It is true that only 13 per cent of FDI is in the interior regions, as the paper argues, but remember, China between 1990-2000 got an enormous amount of FDI. The absolute volume was huge, about $300 billion. So 13 per cent of $300 billion is a lot of money, especially so relative to the size of the economies in the interior provinces. These are poor provinces so their GDP is small, so relative to the size of these economies 13 per cent of 300 billion is a substantial sum. By way of illustration, the 14 interior provinces, between 1992-98, got $33 billion by way of FDI. Compare this with FDI in other countries. The total FDI stock by the end of 1997 for India was $11 billion, for Argentina $36 billion, for Chile $25 billion. So many of the interior provinces got somewhat more or the same volume of FDI as these economies. It is even more striking if you compare the ratio of stock of FDI to GDP; it is quite high. For 1998, it is about 11 per cent for these provinces, much the same as North America, Central and East Europe and Southeast Asia. These are stock and not flow figures. I am not saying these somewhat mechanical comparisons are accurate, but there are strong indicators which suggest that there is a substantial amount of FDI in the interior provinces.

The paper also suggests that the sectoral distribution of FDI in China is highly uneven. This is an empirical issue. My own research shows that what is striking about FDI sectoral distribution in China is that it is highly even. We know from Peter Buckley's work that FDI tends to be concentrated in industries with high transaction costs. Peter Buckley in an article observes that we need to be specific about the meaning of the term transaction costs. He specifies that vertically integrated industries, knowledge and communication intensive industries are subject to high strong transaction costs. FDI in most countries is concentrated in these industries and this is how it should be.

Look at the empirical patterns. In China the empirical pattern shows that FDI distribution is quite even. If you look at investments from Hong Kong in Indonesia, Malaysia, Taiwan and China, the top three manufacturing industries account for the largest volume of FDI. In Indonesia these three industries – textiles, chemicals and metal products – account for about 79 per cent of the total Hong Kong FDI. In Malaysia, three industries – textiles, food manufacturing, and electrical and electronics – account for about 75 per cent of total. In Taiwan three industries – chemicals, electronics and electrical appliances, and garments and footwear – account for 86 per cent of FDI. And in China the top three industries – electronics, plastic products and textiles – only account for 47 per cent. What is unusual about China is how even FDI distribution is. In my book, *Selling China: Foreign Direct Investment during the Reform Era*, published by Cambridge University Press, I have statistics at the more disaggregated industry level and it shows much the same thing.

Now let me turn to the issue of determinants of FDI discussed in the paper. My impression is that a lot of the empirical research on determinants in China concentrates on macro variables such as GDP growth and labour costs. But much of the theoretical literature is on micro drivers and micro mechanisms such as ownership advantages and internalisation. Very little of the literature in China focuses on these micro mechanisms. There is a mismatch between the empirical approach and the underlying theoretical ideas.

The other major area of research is on the effects of FDI. Annie Wei summarises this research brilliantly. There are two issues that researchers on China pay attention to. Has FDI promoted exports and economic growth in general and second is labour-intensive FDI beneficial even though it is low-tech. China receives a high proportion of its FDI in labour-intensive industries. This is a pattern different from that of other economies. In other economies domestic firms enter into contractual arrangements with foreign firms to produce for overseas markets; in China FDI is an equity approach. The issue is not whether FDI promotes growth or exports but whether it promotes growth and exports in excess of the costs of attracting FDI. In many countries, in China in particular, governments confer several benefits or afford incentives to foreign firms. The literature does not address this issue.

The second issue is whether or not foreign firms promote growth and exports in excess of what domestic firms do. This is an issue that has to do with spillovers. If there are spillovers the incentives are justified. But to my mind there is not much evidence in favour of spillovers. This is worrying because China has had thirty years of experience with FDI. As Annie's paper suggests the evidence is at best mixed.

The other issue has to do with the kind of benefits associated with labour-intensive FDI. It provides market access and provides for quality control. The issue then is whether or not the kinds of benefits have to be obtained through equity FDI rather than a contractual form of foreign participation. This is the central issue; it is not so much whether labour-intensive FDI has brought about market access. It definitely has, but is this benefit uniquely associated with FDI? Here there is room for debate. This dominance of the equity approach in China requires an explanation.

Let me present some evidence to show that FDI in labour-intensive industries is unusual. Many theories argue that many of these industries are perfectly competitive, search costs are low as there are many alternative suppliers and there is a high geographic concentration of producers. In my interviews with Hong Kong traders and distributors of garments, I learnt that over the years they have developed a very sophisticated business technique to minimise supply disruptions. What they do is, if I have 100 orders for shoes, some for highly fashionable ones and others for plain standardised ones, I place orders for both types of shoes with a number of producers, I do not place orders exclusively for one type or the other with a single producer. If there is a sudden change in fashions none of the producers suffers much. Typically buyers of shoes contract out production to several producers to minimise risk and disruption of production.

The other issue has to do with quality control. From my researches in Taiwan and Hong Kong I know that quality control can be imposed in contractual arrangements too, not just FDI. There are quality control inspectors who do the job efficiently.

In China FDI in labour-intensive sectors is quite high. They dominated cross-border alliances of other sorts. In 1995 foreign firms accounted for 60 per cent of Chinese garment exports. In Taiwan it was about 6 per cent. In Indonesia it was about 33 per cent by the mid-nineties. Hong Kong relied mainly on contract production with foreign firms in labour-intensive industries; it did not rely on FDI.

Why does China rely so heavily on FDI instead of other contractual forms of importing technology and know-how? It has to do with the sort of institutional conditions facing Chinese entrepreneurs. They are private entrepreneurs and face credit constraints. They cannot borrow from banks. In Taiwan a garment or food producer gets an order and opens a credit line with a bank. In China this mechanism doesn't work, because there is systematic political discrimination against private entrepreneurs. They can't get finance. The statistics here are striking. In 1998 about 1 per cent of Chinese credit went to private entrepreneurs. China has one of the world's highest savings rates. In fact, China was a net capital exporter every year during the nineties except in 1996. This is a country with a low per capita income, but it is rich in capital and yet it doesn't allocate capital to the private entrepreneurs.

Between 1980 and 1990 there were 800 garment producers with FDI; 500 were set up between 1988-1990 and the reason was that most private firms in these years were starved of capital and the conservative central government systematically went after private firms. A number of private firms failed. Those which survived had to seek FDI to secure legal protection and property rights.

China depends on FDI substantially. In the 1990s, ratio of FDI to fixed assets was 13 per cent. In China much of the investment was done by the SOEs. If you now deduct SOE investments and compare FDI in non-state owned fixed assets, the ratio of FDI to fixed assets increases to 28 per cent. For Malaysia it is 24 per cent. Malaysia also has high levels of SOE investments and FDI. In Singapore the figure is around 30 per cent and here also SOE investments and FDI are both high. These are the two economies with high levels of FDI as a proportion of total private investments.

This is the institutional side of the story of FDI in China which is not emphasised in the literature. There are three institutional drivers behind FDI. One is the severe credit and legal constraints on private firms imposed purely for political and not economic reasons. This is one reason for low levels of contract production because it requires local financing. In the presence of local credit constraints FDI financed labour-intensive firms are the only method of getting markets and know-how. Hong Kong and Taiwan didn't need much FDI because local financial markets were more efficient than in China in the 1990s. The other institutional factor is that the SOEs are on the verge of insolvency. Many of the SOEs have a good asset base but their profitability is negative. In any other market economies, these types of firms will be targets for acquisition. These have survived by attracting FDI.

The third factor to note is that China's economy is fragmented. Domestic capital does not move easily across regions, but foreign capital is not constrained; it moves across regions. It is thus that many of the provinces in China are far more dependent on FDI than domestic investments.

Let me illustrate the acquisitions story. Annie Wei cites a figure to show that out of $40 billion FDI only $2 billion has gone into mergers and acquisitions. But many of the joint ventures (JVs) set up in China are acquisitions. This is a different kind of acquisition. Let me illustrate with a story about my interview with a manager of an SOE which formed a joint venture with Phillips in 1994. All these desks and chairs you see here, he said, were purchased after 1994, the JV took everything away. After 1994 the manager of the JV in China sat on a cardboard box for a chair and used another for a desk. This is how ruthless the market economy is. The SOE capitalises all the operating assets including office furniture as equity stakes in the JV. SOEs have all sorts of assets including hospitals, cafeterias, housing facilities and dormitories. They are essentially social service providers rather than a producer of goods. This sort of JV where assets of SOES have been acquired by foreign firms is significant in China.

Let me raise some of the implications of this sort of analysis of FDI in China. I shall argue that there is a need for firm-level analysis rather than regression analysis of regional data and country-level data for China. We need to understand micro level mechanisms better. The other implication is why does labour-intensive FDI occur and why know-how has to be transferred through this mechanism. Here we have to understand the L in John Dunning's OLI paradigm deeply before we begin to know why this kind of FDI occurs in the first place. I do not subscribe to the view that foreign firms have some sort of special advantage which Chinese labour-intensive firms do not have and hence the high levels of FDI in China.

Reference

Huang, Yasheng (2003), *Selling China: Foreign Direct Investment during the Reform Era*, Cambridge University Press, New York.

DISCUSSION

John Dunning drew attention to the fact that most of the work on FDI by Chinese authorities, principally the Ministry of Foreign Trade and Economic Cooperation (MOFTEC) as opposed to that by academics was very micro-oriented in its whole approach. He agreed with Annie Wei's argument that contractual relationships would be better than FDI in labour-intensive industries. A large proportion of the output of labour is exported and therefore the multinationals have control over where they want the products to be exported as well as the quality of the product exported. John thought there was a degree of consistency in terms of the transactions cost model between control and labour cost operations if (a) they are part of an integrated value chain and (b) there was a need to control export markets and some times import markets too. So control spreads beyond the value chain as such. John also had a question about data. Sometimes foreign investors set up new joint ventures and sometimes existing ventures are taken over to form joint ventures. He was not clear how these activities are treated in the data. If multinationals are buying up quite a large number of small companies would it all amount to a large volume of joint-venture-type investments?

Frederik Sjöholm thanked Annie Wei for a good paper and agreed with her that transaction costs and constraints on domestic finance explain FDI in China. He was though not aware of any literature which talks about competition between provinces in China for FDI. He wished to know if FDI was endogenous in the sense that foreigners come into China and then force through changes to the FDI regime. This lowers transaction costs and encourages a second wave of FDI from Western countries rather than from Hong Kong.

In reply to Frederik Sjöholm, Annie Wei said that there was no evidence of the sort of endogeneity in policy regime. The government had targeted the overseas Chinese in the early years, who then demanded increased liberalisation of the economy. Yasheng Huang thought that this was all a part of the story. The big push for FDI was from the policy makers to finance the SOEs which had been hurt by the austerity programme. Private firms were not big in the early nineties and the only growth point the authorities could see was FDI.

Yasheng Huang also added that the growth of joint ventures was due to privatisation and there was a transfer of existing operating assets from the SOEs to the joint ventures.

Peter Buckley had two related observations. A lot of work on FDI from the theory of the MNE starts at the stage when the entry mode decision is made. It leaves out issues behind the choice mode and treats both L and I in the OLI framework too lightly. The other point is that we are missing a comparative perspective here. In Vietnam the biggest employer after the government is Nike. And Nike employs nobody; it is all contract manufacturing.

Nicholas Snowden was of the view that it was not at all obvious to him why China should choose the technology level of her industries and be ahead of her static comparative advantage. China has abundant labour and why should it go for high technology, which doesn't create jobs. Annie may have to justify her case for high technology.

Nigel Driffield concurred with Snowden and wondered why China was not explicitly interested in more jobs, albeit at low wages.

Reply by Annie Wei

I think Professor Huang's presentation is very informative. I quite agree with some of the points raised. But there are a few things which I certainly disagree with. First of all, let me comment on your theoretical explanation for the unevenness of regional distribution and sectoral distribution of FDI in China. You are right in the sense that it depends on how you define evenness. I said that FDI is unevenly distributed in China because most of FDI is located in the coastal areas and in labour-intensive sectors. Professor Huang correctly notices that "China receives a high proportion of its FDI in labour-intensive industries". Even in the knowledge and communication-intensive industries, much of FDI is concentrated in low-tech labour-intensive sub-sectors such as ordinary telephone sets. Thus, these sectors are not subject to high transaction costs. Therefore, we can still say that the sectoral distribution of FDI in China is highly uneven despite transaction-cost consideration.

With regard to the comment on macroeconomic variables, there are limitations in current research. China opened up only 20 years ago. Data at the firm level are rare. Therefore, research using firm-level data is limited. My paper only reviews what has been done in the literature. Possibly, using micro-level data, you may get different answers. However, I strongly believe that some variables identified in the current literature as the determinants of FDI can also be applied at the firm level. It doesn't matter, in fact, which level of data is used. For example, even when you look at case studies, many authors argue that labour costs are one of the main determinants of FDI in China. Similarly, market size is another main determinant. However, I do acknowledge that, at the moment, current research cannot answer the question about how large the market size is. A province is an isolated market. So how large is the market? Many investors didn't really think about this question before they went into China. So this variable probably will become insignificant at the firm level. However, generally speaking, labour cost, especially effective labour costs, i.e. labour costs adjusted for productivity, is the most important variable.

Yasheng Huang also discussed why many firms chose FDI rather than a contractual entry mode. Yes, you are quite right in the sense that you can use supervisors to control quality. You also talked about the switching cost which you believe is low. Is this really the case in China? In the beginning of the opening up, there were very few private firms. Most firms were state-owned. Was it easy to find someone else if you were not happy with your existing suppliers? I believe that transaction costs were very high, though they may show a decreasing trend. Recently I read a case about a British firm doing business in China. Because the Chinese market is segmented, it has to have separate plants in different locations in China. They believe this is the right strategy in China though they use a contractual mode in Taiwan and other East Asian countries. They tried a contractual mode in China before, which proved to be very costly. Their first enterprise in China was a joint venture but later on they turned it to a wholly owned subsidiary because their partner was incompetent. If you look at entry mode, much of FDI in China now chooses wholly owned subsidiaries instead of joint ventures to minimise transaction costs.

With regard to the degree of the contribution of FDI to the Chinese economy, as I discussed in my paper, the empirical results are mixed. However, my own research shows that FDI contributes less than domestic investment to the economy, though it is still significant. I believe that there are spillover effects that are difficult to quantify. Chinese are different from people in Malaysia. Chinese are more willing to run their own enterprises after they learn from foreign firms. Therefore, there are spillovers due to labour mobility. There are also spillovers from backward and forward linkages. Although these spillovers are mainly in low-tech sectors, there are spillovers in certain high-tech sectors as found by Li and Yeung (1999). Given the recent phenomenon of FDI in China, there is a demand for more research on the impact of FDI. Yasheng also discussed the high concentration of suppliers in China. In fact, this confirms the possible spillovers because of agglomeration.

In terms of your comments on private entrepreneurs, I agree with you that there may be credit and legal constraints that create difficulties for their choice of a contractual entry mode. However, the number of private firms has grown substantially during the past few years. According to the *People's Daily*, nearly one third of China's GDP was contributed by non-state-owned enterprises. Now, there are still constraints on private firms' activities, but such constraints are being relaxed. I do know of some cases where private firms use foreign firms to secure funding. However, is it a general rule? I am not very sure.

Finally, with regard to mergers and acquisitions, you argue that SOEs' assets were undervalued in the process. To what extent were the assets undervalued? Price is determined by demand and supply. How do we know that SOEs' assets were undervalued?

With regard to the objectives of China's FDI policies, it is true that China had a huge population and it needed labour-intensive technologies. However, political objectives dictated the development of high-tech industries. The government also had defence and other national security objectives in promoting high-tech industries with the help of foreign-invested firms.

3. Foreign Direct Investment in India

V.N. Balasubramanyam and Vidya Mahambare[1]

3.1 INTRODUCTION

There has been a considerable change in policies and attitudes towards foreign direct investment (FDI) on the part of most developing countries in recent years. Distrust and suspicion of FDI in the past appears to have yielded place to a newfound faith in its ability to foster growth and development. This change in attitudes is due to a number of factors: a steep reduction in alternative sources of finance such as bank credit in the wake of the debt crisis, the demonstrable success of the East Asian countries based in part on FDI, and growth in knowledge and understanding of the nature and operations of multinational enterprises, the principal purveyors of FDI.

In the year 1991, India too liberalised its highly regulated FDI regime, in place for more than three decades. Arguably it took an economic crisis for India to liberalise its trade and FDI regime rather than a fundamental change in attitude towards the role of FDI in the development process. Nonetheless, the 1991 reforms marked a major break from the earlier dirigiste regime with its regulation of the spheres of foreign enterprise participation and its modes of operation. And the policy framework was opaque with implementation of policy based on bureaucratic consideration of each case on its merits.

The 1991 economic reforms were to change all this. Along with the virtual abolition of the industrial licensing system, controls over foreign trade and foreign investment were considerably relaxed, including the removal of ceilings on equity ownership by foreign firms. The reforms did result in increased inflows of FDI during the decade of the nineties. Even so, the volume of FDI in India is relatively low compared with that in most other emerging economies. The relatively low volume of FDI in India, especially so in comparison with that in China, has attracted widespread comment. If China, with its newfound faith in capitalism, can embrace and attract substantial volumes of FDI, why can't India which is blessed with western institutions and capitalist organisations? The advocates of increased volumes of FDI argue that "in terms of foreign investment, it is the direct investment that should be actively sought for and doors should be thrown wide open to FDI. FDI brings huge advantages (new capital, technology, managerial expertise, and access to foreign markets) with little or no downside" (Bajpai and Sachs, 2000). Admittedly, FDI is a potent instrument of development. But sweeping generalisations such as that FDI brings huge advantages, it has no downside, and that throwing doors wide open would necessarily attract increased volumes of FDI are suspect.

The case for attracting large volumes of FDI into India requires an analysis of the determinants and impact of FDI in the Indian context. Why has the liberalisation of the FDI regime failed to attract increased flows? Does the experience of China with FDI provide any lessons for India? Would increased volumes of FDI alone necessarily accelerate growth and development? This paper addresses these and other issues drawing upon the extant literature on FDI in general and on FDI in India in particular. Section 3.2 reviews the determinants of FDI, section 3.3 analyses the efficacy of FDI in promoting development. Section 3.4 examines policies, and section 3.5 concludes.

3.2 DETERMINANTS

Why do firms go abroad? Why do they choose to invest in specific locations? The literature on these issues emphasises three main elements which guide the foreign investment decision process of firms. Dunning (1973) neatly synthesises these elements in the well-known eclectic paradigm or the OLI explanation of FDI. For a firm to successfully invest abroad it must possess advantages which no other firm possesses (O), the country it wishes to invest in should offer location advantages (L), and it must be capable of internalising operations (I). Internalisation is synonymous with the ability of firms to exercise control over operations essential for the exploitation of ownership and location advantages.

It is location advantages which form the core of much of the discussion on the determinants of FDI in developing countries. The two other attributes necessary for FDI are taken as given from the perspective of developing countries. Dunning's (1973, 1981) analysis set in train a number of econometric studies designed to identify the main determinants of FDI. (Agarwal, 1980; Root and Ahmed, 1979; Levis, 1979; Balasubramanyam and Salisu, 1991). The main conclusions of these studies can be briefly summarised.

- Host countries with sizeable domestic markets, measured by GDP per capita, and sustained growth, measured by growth rates of GDP, attract relatively large volumes of FDI.

- Resource endowments of host countries including natural resources and human resources are a factor of importance in the investment decision process of foreign firms.
- Infrastructure facilities including transportation and communication net works are an important determinant of FDI.
- Macroeconomic stability, signified by stable exchange rates and low rates of inflation, is a significant factor in the foreign investment decisions of firms.
- Political stability in the host countries is a significant factor in the investment decision process of foreign firms.
- A stable and transparent policy framework towards FDI is attractive to potential investors.
- Foreign firms place a premium on a distortion-free economic and business environment. An allied proposition here is that a distortion-free foreign trade regime, which is neutral in terms of the incentives it provides for import-substituting (IS) and export industries (EP), attracts relatively large volumes of FDI compared with either an IS or an EP regime.
- Fiscal and monetary incentives in the form of tax concessions do play a role in attracting FDI, but these are of little significance in the absence of a stable economic environment.

India fares well on the attributes relating to market size and growth. Its growth rate of around 6 per cent per annum since the nineties is substantial if not dramatic. India's overall record on macroeconomic stability, save for the crisis years of the late eighties, is superior to that of most other developing countries. And judged by the criterion of the stability of policies it has displayed a relatively high degree of political stability.

It is, however, India's trade and FDI regimes, which are major impediments to increased inflows of FDI. Admittedly the 1991 reforms considerably relaxed the dirigiste regime, which prevailed for more than four decades. Even so, the product and factor market distortions generated by the earlier policy regime continue to persist. And liberalisation of the economy has not progressed much since the 1991 reforms. Also there seems to be a wide gap between the intent and practice of policies towards FDI.

Two distinct phases can be identified in India's foreign trade and investment regimes – the pre-1991 reforms phase and the post-1991 phase. The pre-1991 phase, which stretches over four decades, is well worth reviewing in some detail for two reasons. First, although the regime was marked by extensive regulation of trade and investment, it did not shun foreign enterprise participation in the economy. Second, the pattern and industrial composition of foreign enterprise participation it gave rise to seems to have endured and may be a factor in the observed volume and pattern of FDI in India in recent years.

The cumbersome and complex nature of the regulatory framework during these years has been extensively analysed (Kidron, 1965; Kumar, 1994). The specification of sectors in which both foreign financial and technical participation were allowed, those in which only technical collaboration was permitted, and those in which neither technical nor financial participation was allowed, reflects the desire to restrict foreign ownership and control to sectors of the economy in which its contribution was deemed to be essential. A preference for technical collaboration agreements as opposed to foreign equity ownership reflects the desire to promote the twin objectives of preserving freedom from foreign control over operations and at the same time gaining access to foreign technology and know-how. There were though bouts of liberalisation, as in the mid-fifties and the eighties, mostly though not entirely dictated by foreign exchange shortages. The growth in the number of foreign collaboration agreements approved over the years (Table 3.1) and foreign equity participation in Indian industry reflect these swings in policy.

Table 3.1 Foreign Collaboration Approvals, 1948-2003

Period	Number of collaborations	Those with foreign equity		Foreign investment (Rupees billions)
		Number	% in total	
1948-58	500	n.a.	n.a.	n.a.
1959-66	2079	756*	36	n.a.
1967-79	2904	468	16	0.6
1980-90	6587	1554	24	10
1991-95	8137	4183	51	594
1996-00	10782	7867	73	1873
2001	2270	1982	87	269
2002	2273	1966	86	114
Jan.-Apr. 2003	580	467	81	12

Notes: n.a. = not available, * based on figures for 1961-66.

Source: Kumar (1994).

India's reputation for hostility towards foreign economic participation though is mostly due to the restrictions on equity participation and export obligations imposed on foreign firms during the 1970s. The Foreign Exchange Regulation Act (FERA) of 1973 was Prime Minister Indira

Gandhi's response to the economic crisis that bedevilled most years of her premiership. Her economic policy initiatives were mostly driven by political exigencies rather than an objective strategy with specific goals. Hostility to private enterprise, especially foreign private enterprise, headline grabbing initiatives such as the nationalisation of banks along with increased state control of economic activity were all part of an orchestrated strategy to please the electorate. The FERA required foreign firms to dilute their equity holdings to less than 40 per cent or export a substantial share of their total output. In response to these regulations, some multinationals such as IBM and Coca Cola chose to close down their operations in India, some fell in step with the requirement that foreign firms should shed equity in favour of Indian nationals, others such as Unilever diversified their production base in order to fulfil export obligations stipulated by the FERA in return for retaining majority equity ownership. During the period 1967-79 the number of collaboration agreements per year reached an all-time low of 242, and the proportion of agreements with foreign equity participation fell from 36 per cent during the years 1959-66 to 16 per cent over the years 1967-79 (Kumar, 1994). During the eleven-year period 1966-79 the total amount of foreign capital approved by the government amounted to only $0.6 billion and the net inflow (net of dividends and repatriation of capital) was negative (Lall and Mohammad, 1983).

The mid-1980s saw a considerable though not a radical relaxation of the dirigiste trade and investment regime, with a relatively benign attitude towards foreign enterprise participation. Prime Minister Rajeev Gandhi with his penchant for science and technology, mirroring that of his grandfather Nehru, appears to have been much more sanguine about foreign enterprise participation in the economy than his predecessor. The total number of collaboration agreements approved per year increased from 242 during the period 1967-79 to 658 during the period 1980-90.

One of the major consequences of the policy regime during the pre 1991 phase was a significant change in the pattern of foreign investment in India, away from plantations, minerals and petroleum towards the manufacturing sector. By the end of the decade of the eighties manufacturing accounted for nearly 85 per cent out of a total stock of FDI of about Rupees 28 billion. Within the manufacturing sector the high technology intensive industries such as machinery and machine tools, transport equipment, electrical equipment and chemicals including pharmaceuticals accounted for the bulk of foreign capital (Table 3.2).

Although there are a number of estimates of foreign presence in Indian industry, they differ from each other depending on the data and concepts they employ. Kumar (1994) estimates that at the end of the decade of the eighties the foreign share in assets or sales of the organised private corporate sector in

Table 3.2 Sectoral Distribution of the Stock of FDI in India

Rupees billions and percentages

	Mar. 1964	Mar. 1974	Mar. 1980	Mar. 1990	Approvals 01/08/91 - 30/04/03
	Value (%)	Value (%)	Value (%)	Value (%)	Value (%)
I. Plantations	1.1 (19)	1.1 (12)	0.4 (4)	2.6 (10)	n.a. (n.a.)
II. Mining	0.1 (1)	0.1 (1)	0.1 (1)	0.1 (0.3)	43 (2)
III. Petroleum	1.4 (25)	1.4 (15)	0.4 (4)	0 (0)	775 (27)
IV. Manufacturing	2 (41)	6.3 (68)	8 (87)	23 (85)	1780 (62)
Food and beverages	0.3 (13.2)	0.5 (8.3)	0.4 (5)	1.6 (7.0)	98 (3.4)
Textiles	0.2 (7.2)	0.4 (5.7)	0.3 (4)	0.9 (4.0)	35 (1.2)
Machinery and Machine Tools	0.2 (6.8)	0.4 (6.7)	0.7 (9)	3.5 (15.4)	55 (1.9)
Transport and Transport Equipment	0.2 (6.5)	0.3 (5.1)	0.5 (6.3)	3 (12.3)	212 (7.5)
Metal and Metal Products	0.3 (14.4)	1 (14)	1.2 (14.6)	1.4 (6)	112 (4.0)
Electrical Equipment and Communication (incl. of Software)	0.2 (8)	0.7 (11)	1.0 (12)	3.0 (13)	846 (30.0)
Chemicals and Allied Products	0.6 (26.2)	2.0 (32.6)	3.0 (37.2)	7.7 (33.4)	113 (3.7)
Miscellaneous	0.4 (17.6)	1.1 (16.7)	1.0 (12.3)	2.0 (8.8)	309.2 (10.8)
V. Services	1 (14)	0.4 (4)	0.4 (4)	1.4 (5)	262 (9)
Total	6 (100)	9 (100)	9 (100)	27 (100)	2859 (100)

Notes: Figures may not exactly add up due to rounding. n.a. = not available.

Sources: Kumar (1994), Secretariat for Industrial Assistance Newsletter, Government of India (May 2003).

India was around 23 per cent. The share of foreign firms in individual industries, within the manufacturing sector, however, varies widely from a high of 98 per cent in leather products to a low of 7 per cent in textile machinery. In the case of 11 industries, including processed foods, cigarettes, leather goods, pharmaceuticals and automotive components, the share of foreign firms was 66 per cent of total sales; in 15 others including electrical lamps, electric machinery, paints and varnishes and automobile components foreign share in total sales ranged between 34 to 66 per cent. More recent estimates suggest that over the period 1970-94 foreign controlled firms accounted for between a third and a quarter of gross sales of India's manufacturing sector (Athreye and Kapur, 2001).

These estimates, especially those relating to individual industries, suggest that foreign control over Indian industry during the pre 1991 phase was not low; in fact, it was significant in a number of consumer goods and technologically intensive industries. Whist the regulatory phase may have limited the absolute volume of foreign capital in India relative to that in some of the Latin American and East Asian countries, it may not have limited the extent of control exercised by foreign firms in individual industries and the manufacturing sector in general.

The size of markets in India, especially for consumer goods with well known brand names, India's industrialisation policies with emphasis on science and technology oriented industries, the generally stable macroeconomic environment, and India's endowments of human capital were all factors in the volume and pattern of FDI and technology licensing agreements in the economy during the period 1950-90. And foreign presence in a wide variety of industries appears to have been sizeable despite the complex regulations. This pattern of FDI in India does not appear to have changed during the post 1991 phase. All this suggests that the attraction of India for foreign firms resides in the profitable domestic markets for branded goods and high-tech products and India's endowments of human capital, especially its trained scientists and engineers.

3.2.1 The Post 1991 Phase

Relaxation of controls over FDI constituted a significant element of the wide-ranging economic reforms introduced in 1991. The three main elements of the reform were the abolition of the licensing requirements governing domestic investment, reduction in tariffs on imports and relaxation of controls over FDI. The principal changes in the foreign investment regime included automatic approval of FDI up to 51 per cent of equity ownership by foreign firms in a group of 34 technology intensive industries, a case by case consideration of applications for foreign equity ownership of up to 75 per cent in nine sectors, mostly relating to infrastructure, and the streamlining of procedures relating to approval of investment applications in general.

Relaxation of controls over the extent of foreign ownership of equity signals a major departure from the earlier regime, although foreign ownership of equity over and above 50 per cent was subject to the requirement that the investors should balance all outgoings of foreign exchange on account of their operations with export earnings over a seven year period.[2] The reform package in general heralded a departure from the earlier dirigiste regime. And FDI flows appear to have responded to the new initiatives; foreign inflow approvals increased from around Rupees 10 billion (around $384 million) during the late eighties to around Rupees 2.5 trillion ($3 billion) during the late nineties (Table 3.1).

Even so, inflows of FDI are low relative to the size of the economy, they account for only 5 per cent of gross domestic capital formation, actual inflows are much less than approvals (around 21 per cent of approvals amounting to $54 million between the years 1991-98), and the volume of FDI India has attracted shades into insignificance compared with the sizeable volume of FDI China has attracted in recent years (Table 3.3).

Table 3.3 Realised FDI in China and India

US$ billion

	China	India
1979-1990	20.6	1.5
1991	4.4	0.1
1992	11.0	0.1
1993	27.5	0.3
1994	33.8	0.6
1995	73.3	1.3
1996	41.7	2.1
1997	45.3	2.8
1998	45.5	3.6
1999	40.4	2.5
2000	40.8	2.2
2001	46.9	2.3*
2002(P)	52.7	3.9*

Notes: Financial year for India is from April-March. *While FDI statistics in China, as per the IMF definition, include equity capital, reinvested earnings and other capital (inter-corporate debt transaction between related entities), Indian data includes only equity capital. Recent RBI data (2003), revised to reflect the international definition, estimates that FDI in India was $4 billion and $6 billion in 2001 and 2002 respectively.

Sources: China – PRC Ministry of Foreign Trade and Economic Cooperation; India – 1979-90 World Bank database, 1991 onwards Economic Survey 1/02.

Comparisons between India and China seem irresistible, mostly because of their size, their geographical location and their economic liberalisation policies. It is though arguable whether China is a role model for India in its efforts to attract FDI. An analysis of the comparative experience of India and China in relation to FDI may therefore be instructive for policy formulation.

3.2.2 FDI in India and China

Is it likely that China's FDI policy framework is much more liberal than that of India and hence the large volumes of FDI it attracts? In fact, India's FDI regime may be much more liberal than that of China. It is reported that China does not allow wholly owned foreign enterprises in 31 industries and in 31 others Chinese partners are required to hold a majority of the equity (Nagaraj, 2003). India's regime allows 51 per cent of equity participation by foreign firms with automatic approval and in several sectors such as airports and mass transport systems foreign firms are allowed to hold 100 per cent of the equity (WTO, 2002). According to official sources, these and other measures designed to streamline foreign investment approval procedures place India's FDI policy framework amongst the most liberal of investment regimes (WTO, 2002).

The reasons for India's poor performance in attracting FDI relative to that of China may have to be sought elsewhere other than in its policy framework. These have to do principally with the differing sources of FDI in the two countries, differences in the implementation of policies as opposed to the policy framework in place and the differing composition of FDI in the two countries.[3]

The differences in the sources of FDI is a factor in the relatively high volumes of FDI China attracts. A large proportion of FDI in China, around 40 per cent of the total annual inflows of around $46 billion, is on account of investments from its Diaspora, chiefly from those resident in East Asian countries including Hong Kong. There are several reasons for the high proportion of FDI in China by its Diaspora. First, there is their familiarity with the culture, institutions and business practices in China. Second, faced with increasing wage costs in East Asian countries such as Taiwan and Malaysia, Chinese expatriates in these countries have sought relatively low wage cost locations for their investments in China.

But India too has its Diaspora. Why haven't they sought to invest in India? The differing composition of the Chinese and Indian Diaspora provides one reason for the differences in the volume of FDI from their Diaspora the two countries have attracted. Although there are no precise data on the size and composition of the Chinese and Indian Diaspora, available evidence suggests that whilst the Indian Diaspora are located mostly in the US, the UK and other western countries, the Chinese Diaspora are mostly located in East Asia. And while the Indian Diaspora, especially so in the US, mostly belong to the professions, including education, health services and science and engineering oriented professions, the Chinese Diaspora are business oriented. The opening up of China to trade and investment appears to have provided the Chinese Diaspora with an opportunity to extend and/or shift their business interests to the mother country and take advantage of its relatively low cost labour and land. The Indian Diaspora with their lack of business interests have for long opted for the portfolio variety of investments, principally bank deposits, the sudden withdrawals of such investments was one of the proximate causes for the economic crisis India experienced in 1991.

The one notable exception here is the participation of India's Diaspora in the Silicon Valley in the spectacular growth of India's export oriented software industry. The Indian software engineers and entrepreneurs in the Silicon Valley appear to have successfully utilised India's endowments of highly trained but relatively cheap engineering talent (Balasubramanyam and Balasubramanyam, 2000).

Another explanation for the differing volumes of FDI in India and China relates to the composition of FDI in the two countries. A substantial proportion of FDI in India is located in the high technology end of the spectrum of industries and in services, whereas investments in China are mostly located in the low technology end of the spectrum including electronics, which mostly relates to assembly operations (Table 3.4). This fact too reflects the differences in the stage of industrialisation and local market conditions in the two countries. The relatively high volume of FDI in the technologically oriented industries in India reflects the attraction of a sheltered domestic market for the products of these industries, a consequence of the import-substituting industrialisation strategy the country followed for more than four decades. So too is the sizeable foreign enterprise participation in branded consumer goods including food products. Most of the consumer goods sector, even after the 1991 reforms, enjoys not only protection from import competition, but also access to imports of equipment at relatively low rates of tariffs resulting in high rates of effective protection. Foreign firms facing a liberalised FDI regime have taken advantage of these high rates of protection and a sizeable domestic market for these goods. The volume of such tariff jumping domestic market-oriented FDI, however, would be relatively low for a variety of reasons. These include the product and factor market distortions typical of an import substituting industrialisation strategy, the artificial nature of incentives provided by the strategy and the capital and technology intensive nature of such investments (Balasubramanyam et al., 1996) In contrast, export oriented investments designed to exploit cheap labour, as in the case of China, tend to be sizeable.

Table 3.4 Composition of FDI in Manufacturing in India and China

	China 1995	India Aug 91-Apr 03
Low Technology Intensive Industries		
Food and Beverages	10.5	5.5
Textiles	8.9	2.0
Garments and Footwear	6.0	n.a.
Paper and Paper Products, Printing	4.7	2.0
Leather and Related Products	3.6	0.3
Total	**33.7**	**10.0**
High Technology Intensive Industries		
Chemical and Chemical Products*	3.4	9.0
Rubber Products	1.8	0.8
Plastic Products	5.1	n.a.
Non Metal Mineral Products	7.7	n.a.
Metal and Metal Products	5.5	6.3
Machinery Manufacturing	4.0	3.0
Special Purpose Equipment	1.9	0.2
Transport Equipment	5.9	12.0
Electrical Equipment and Machinery	6.6	14.0
Electronics and Communication	9.6	33.5
Instruments	1.8	0.1
Other Manufacturing		11.0
Total	**47.3**	**90.0**

Notes: * including pharmaceuticals. n.a. = not available.

Sources: Huang (2003), Secretariat for Industrial Assistance Newsletter, Government of India (May 2003). Published data for the sectoral distribution of FDI in China are not available for recent years.

It is also possible that India may not need the sort of FDI which is attracted to low wage and low skill intensive export oriented sectors. Indigenous entrepreneurs, with long years of experience with industrialisation and a history of exporting labour-intensive products such as textiles and clothing, may be able to exploit export opportunities in low wage and low skill intensive products. India's overall policy framework, however, appears to dissuade and constrain them from doing so. It dissuades them because of the distinct anti-export bias of India's trade polices, which has not been entirely eliminated by the 1991 reforms (WTO, 2002). Average levels of tariffs on imports at around 32 per cent continue to be high, much higher than that in other emerging economies such as Indonesia (8.8%), Malaysia (10.2%), Thailand (17%) and the Philippines (9.7%). Tariffs on imports of capital goods and intermediates are low relative to that on final goods thereby providing high effective rates of protection for the final goods manufacturing sectors. The protection afforded to domestic market-oriented sectors by these and other policies dissuades investors from investing in the export oriented sectors. There are also policies which constrain firms from investing in labour-intensive sectors. These include the policy which reserves production of a vast array of labour-intensive products to small-scale industries, and labour laws in the organised sector which limit the ability of firms to hire and shed labour in response to market conditions. These laws serve to increase wage costs and provide an incentive for firms to substitute capital for labour.

Also relevant in this context is the thesis that the relatively large volumes of FDI in China are a consequence of China's policy framework, which discriminates against domestic firms and favours foreign firms in the provision of fiscal and monetary incentives (Huang, 2003). The suggestion here is that FDI may be no more than a substitute for domestic investments which are denied the sort of incentives foreign firms enjoy. In the case of India the rules and regulations relating to labour laws and reservation of sectors to small-scale industries apply to both foreign and domestic firms. As a consequence, both sorts of firms appear to have been deterred from exploiting the vast export potential that India's endowments of low-skill and low-wage labour provides. And both types of investors appear to have opted for the relatively capital-intensive high-tech industries mostly oriented towards the protected domestic markets. As suggested earlier, for various reasons FDI in these protected industries tends to be relatively low. It is though likely that if India were to remove the various product and labour market distortions, both foreign and locally owned firms would invest in labour-intensive export-oriented sectors. And locally owned firms may be able to compete effectively with foreign owned firms in these sectors and India may not be compelled to woo foreign firms into these sectors.

For all these reasons China may not be a role model for FDI in India. The structure, stage of development, sources of FDI and historical factors set India apart from China. The optimum level of FDI a country should aspire for is a function of the structure, stage of development, sources of FDI it has access to and the volume of co-operant factors it possesses. For these reasons econometric exercises (Wei, 1999) which regress current FDI flows into specific countries on variables such as growth rates, per capita incomes and corruption indices, and suggest that not even China let alone India has fully exploited its potential for inward FDI seem vacuous. These sorts of exercises are vacuous because they fail to recognise the interdependence between FDI and growth, they ignore the composition and quality of FDI countries are able to attract, their stage of development, the co-operant factors they are endowed with, and above all they rely on dubious estimates of levels of corruption.

In sum, India has the potential to attract increased volumes of FDI. It can do so with a set of policies which are in the interests of not only foreign investors but also domestic investors. It is though a bit far fetched to argue that FDI is a panacea for the development problem and India should throw all doors wide open to FDI. It would also be a folly to woo FDI only because China attracts relatively high volumes of FDI.

3.3 EFFICACY

The one principal characteristic of FDI which distinguishes it from other sorts of capital flows is its ability to transmit technology and know-how, broadly defined to include managerial and marketing know-how. Technology spillovers constitute the major contribution of FDI to development, apart from employment and the foreign exchange earnings it promotes.

There are several channels through which such spillovers occur. These include imitation, acquisition of skills, competition and enhanced export intensity of locally owned firms (Görg and Greenaway, 2001). Imitation of the products produced by the foreign firms through reverse engineering, an activity which enables local firms to copy the processes and design of new products, is a recognised channel for spillovers. Acquisition of skills occurs mainly through the movement of skilled labour employed by the foreign firms to locally owned firms. Such internal migration of labour, trained by foreign firms, is a significant channel for spillovers. Labour employed in the foreign firms may wish to set up their own establishments with the experience and skills gained from their sojourn in the foreign firms. Also, foreign firms may, either in response to trade related investment measures (TRIMS) imposed by the host country or because of distinct cost advantages, train or establish local suppliers of components and parts. This too would be a channel for spillovers.

Another potent channel for spillovers, or more to the point growth of productive efficiency, is competition. The theory here is that the entry of foreign firms increases competition in the market place and locally owned firms are compelled to increase their productive efficiency. This is the sort of efficiency recognised in the literature as X-efficiency rather than allocative efficiency. Finally, locally owned firms may learn marketing techniques and methods of penetrating export markets from export oriented foreign firms.

These propositions have been extensively tested in the context of FDI in developed and developing countries (for a survey of the empirical literature see Görg and Greenaway, 2000; Blomstrom and Kokko, 1998). These econometric studies have produced a mixed bag of results; some identify positive spillovers from the presence of foreign owned firms in the manufacturing sectors, and others find them to be either negligible or negative.

Ever since the 1991 reforms and the relatively mild bout of reforms in the mid-eighties, a number of studies have investigated the impact of reforms on FDI and its efficacy in India's manufacturing sector. A study on the mid-eighties liberalisation efforts finds that both domestically owned and foreign owned firms in the chemicals and machinery industries increased their investments, their imports of capital goods, their in house R&D expenditures and imports of technology. There was, however, no such growth of investments by foreign firms in the pharmaceuticals industry, mostly because of the absence of protection of intellectual property legislation in India at that time (Siddharthan and Pandit, 1998). A variant of this finding is that over the period 1980-94, which includes both the liberalisation episodes, there were technology spillovers in the pharmaceutical industry of India, but only between multinational firms themselves, with little impact on domestic firms (Feinberg and Majumdar, 2001). Here again weak protection of intellectual property is seen as the reason for the spillovers, which were confined to MNEs themselves in the pharmaceuticals sector.

There are also studies which identify positive spillovers. A study based on stochastic frontier analysis, utilising data for 368 medium and large sized firms in India's manufacturing sector, finds that there were positive spillovers from FDI in science based industries, but only in the case of domestic firms which possessed significant R&D capabilities. In the sub-group of 'non-science' industries, presence of foreign owned firms had compelled domestic firms to increase their productive efficiency (Kathuria, 2000). In addition to these econometric studies, there are also case studies of linkages and technology transfer between foreign owned and locally owned firms relating to specific MNEs in India and specific industries such as India's truck manufacturers (Lall, 1980, 1983). These studies, shorn of the statistical and methodological problems which beset most econometric studies, identify spillovers and more specifically linkages which are undertaken by MNEs with a view to promoting productive efficiency and minimising costs.

Another recent study (Mahambare, 2001), based on a sample of 2417 firms in the manufacturing sector for the period 1988-89 to 1997-98, notes that foreign firms in chemicals, drugs and non-electrical machinery sectors increased their exports in the post-reform period. There is also evidence to show that the reforms have had a favourable impact on the productivity of foreign firms. Mahambare also notes an improvement in the efficiency of foreign firms in the post-reform period. The analysis, which is based on Data Envelope Analysis technique, reports that 61 per cent of foreign firms showed an improvement in efficiency after the reforms compared to 35 per cent of locally owned firms. Changes in the pattern of financing, namely a decline in the debt-equity ratio in the post-reform period, also appears to exert a positive impact on efficiency of foreign owned firms in chemicals, inorganic chemicals, drugs, computer hardware, and software industries.

As stated earlier, the statistical studies on spillovers yield a mixed bag of results. But they do identify a number of factors which are likely to promote spillovers of technology and know-how from foreign owned firms to the locally owned firms. First, the magnitude of spillovers tends to be high in industry segments where the gap in technological capabilities between foreign owned and locally owned firms tends to be narrow. Second, spillovers are likely to be high when the competition in the market place between locally owned and foreign firms tends to be intense. Third, the extent and magnitude of spillovers differ between industries and host countries. Fourth, several studies show that spillovers are proportional to the magnitude of foreign presence, measured by shares of foreign firms in total equity or sales of the relevant industry groups. Fifth, local capabilities including R&D and human skills sustain high levels of spillovers. Finally, analogous to the last proposition, is the suggestion that liberalisation of foreign trade, increased competition and development of local infrastructure all promote spillovers.

The message of all this is clear. Externalities or spillovers of technology are significant sources of growth and technical change, and FDI is a major engine of such spillovers. Increased volumes of FDI alone, however, are unlikely to generate widespread spillovers. In the absence of competition and co-operant factors such as local R&D and human skills, spillovers from FDI may be limited. Put another way, FDI is a catalyst of technical change and growth; it cannot be expected to be the prime mover. Indeed empirical research suggests that FDI is most effective as an agent of change in economies which possess a threshold level of human capital and skills and in those economies which have attained a threshold level of growth (Balasubramanyam et al., 1999; Blomstrom et al., 1994).

In sum, in the absence of the necessary ingredients and co-operant factors large volumes of FDI alone may be ineffective in promoting growth and may even be counter-productive. For these reasons the exuberance relating to the role of FDI in the growth process and exhortations that India should adopt an open door policy towards FDI should be tempered by a recognition of the conditions necessary for the effective utilisation of FDI.

3.4 POLICY FRAMEWORK

The 1991 reforms considerably relaxed the FDI regime. The issue though is how much further should India go on the road to liberalisation and what are the specific policies it should adopt to reach the official target of £10 billion of FDI inflows per annum. The policy proposals may be divided into two broad sets. The first set would include general policies designed to remove product and factor market distortions of various sorts, policies designed to promote infrastructure facilities and growth of human capital and policies designed to promote R&D and competition in the economy.

The second set includes specific policies designed to attract FDI such as transparency of rules and regulations, abolition of red tape and delays in the approval of foreign investment projects, removal of ceilings on the amount of equity foreign firms are entitled to hold and the establishment of export processing zones (EPZs) designed to attract FDI.

The evidence from statistical studies and theoretical literature strongly endorse the proposition that the first set of general policies listed above are conducive to both increased flows of FDI and its efficacy in promoting development objectives. Liberalisation of the foreign trade regime, for instance, may remove product market distortions which bias investments in favour of protected domestic markets and promote exports. Liberalisation of the foreign trade regime does not imply an all out export promotion strategy with attendant export subsidies and various other incentives for exports. As suggested by Bhagwati (1978) a distortion free regime is a neutral regime which does not favour either the export oriented industries or the import substitution industries, but allows comparative advantage to determine the allocation of investments between the two groups. There is some statistical evidence in support of the proposition that such a neutral regime attracts both relatively large volumes of FDI and promotes its efficacy (Balasubramanyam et al., 1996). Again the elimination of stringent labour laws and abolition of policies which restrict entry of firms into areas reserved for small scale industries would also remove distortions in the economy and promote competition and productive efficiency. Policies which emphasise investments in human capital and R&D would be attractive to both foreign and locally owned firms and promote spillovers of technology and know-how from foreign owned firms to locally owned firms.

The second set of policies which are specific to FDI may be a bit more problematic than the first set. The exception here is the need to eliminate the red tape and delays associated with the administration of the FDI regime. These delays and cumbersome bureaucratic procedures are a factor in the relatively low volumes of FDI in India It is reported that it takes 10 permits to start a business in India against six in China, while the median time it takes is 90 days in India against 30 days in China. And a typical foreign power project requires 43 clearances at central government level and another 57 at state level (Financial Times, 4 April 2003).

The suggestion that the present policy which requires government approval for projects which involve foreign share of equity in excess of 51 per cent should be scrapped in favour of automatic approval up to 100 per cent of equity except in the case of selected projects is controversial. (Bajpai and Sachs, 2000). It is arguable if such automatic approval of 100 per cent foreign owned investments would necessarily increase competition in the market place and serve consumer interests. It may result in the establishment of foreign owned monopolies and eliminate nascent domestic firms with a potential for growth. The belief underlying this suggestion of a wide-open door policy for FDI is that relatively large volumes of FDI necessarily promote growth and development objectives. It is not the volume of FDI but its quality and the environment in which it operates that determines its contribution to development.

As stated earlier, FDI is a superb catalyst of development not an initiator and it can effectively function as a catalyst only in the presence of cooperant factors such as a threshold level of human capital, and the ability of indigenous firms to adapt and restructure the know-how and technology provided by foreign firms to suit local factor and product markets. In the absence of these factors the social rates of return to foreign investments may be low although private rates of return to foreign firms on their investments may be relatively high.

Establishment of export processing zones (EPZs) is another policy popular with most developing countries. India too has established a variety of such zones including EPZs, export oriented units and more recently special economic zones (SEZs). Although the zones are not restricted to foreign owned firms one principal objective of these zones is the promotion of FDI. It is the belief that foreign owned firms would be attracted to the zones which permit duty-free imports of materials and intermediates and place no restrictions on exports of final goods. These zones, with the exception of export-oriented units, also provide infrastructure facilities, telecommunication facilities and exemptions from local taxes to the firms located in the zones. The record of these zones in promoting exports and attracting FDI appears to be poor. Whist there are no data on the volume of FDI in these zones, it is unlikely that they have attracted large volumes as the total volume of FDI in the country as a whole is relatively low. The total absolute value of exports from these zones is reported to have increased from Rupees 48 billion in 1997/98 to Rupees 86 billion in 2001, but their share of total exports increased only marginally from 3.7 per cent in 1997/98 to 4.2 per cent in 1999/00 (WTO, 2002).

This poor performance of the zones is in part due to the cumbersome red tape and regulations associated with the operations of these zones. The problem with EPZs, however, may be much more general, residing in the nature of these institutions. They are in effect designed to offset the distortions of various sorts present in the economy which bias resource allocation in favour of specific sectors. In an economy which is rife with tariffs and non-tariff barriers to imports, both domestic and foreign resources would be attracted to the protected domestic market-oriented sectors away from the export-oriented sectors. EPZs are designed to offset this bias against exports, with the provision of various sorts of incentives including duty-free imports and fiscal incentives for production of goods and services destined for the export markets. They are in the nature of small islands of free trade resident in a sea of protectionism. EPZs may be successful in promoting exports and FDI if they are able to attract resources over and above those which already exist in the economy. It is, however, possible that resources from elsewhere in the economy would be diverted to the zones with very little addition to existing resources. Labour-intensive export-oriented investments elsewhere in the economy may be relocated to the zones because of the various sorts of incentives they provide. In such cases, there would be very little addition to the total volume of exports of the economy, merely a reallocation of existing exports, achieved at a cost in terms of the incentives the zones provide. Such relocation of exports may occur even in the presence of fresh inflows of FDI into the zones. Foreign firms may successfully attract labour from export industries located elsewhere in the economy by paying relatively high wages. The increased wage payments paid by the foreign firms would be a gain to the economy, but this gain should be set against the payments in the form of dividends and profits the foreign firms earn.

Such relocation may explain the observed fact that the absolute volume of exports from the zones in India have grown but the share of the zones in the total value of exports of the country has hardly increased. In this context the suggestion that the sluggish exports of the EPZs in India are "partly because some EPZs have accounted for a large share of the total export earnings of EPZs, while the share of others has fallen; this superior export performance may be related to infrastructural and locational advantages provided by some of the EPZs rather than the incentives themselves" (WTO, 2002). The implication of this statement is that there may be a relocation of exports between the zones themselves, and it is location and infrastructure facilities which promote exports rather than incentives such as tariff and tax concessions. In any case, EPZs are an attempt at offsetting distortions present elsewhere in the economy but not their removal. As Panagariya (2000) cogently argues, the correction of one distortion by another distortion may not be any more efficient than leaving the original distortion in place. This is because the introduction of the corrective distortion, such as EPZs, which are essentially export promotion measures, not only adds to the existing distortions but also reduces the pressure to eliminate the existing distortions in place.

It could, however, be argued that contrary to India's experience EPZs have been successful in promoting exports and attracting FDI in other developing countries such as China. Arguably FDI and growth of exports in China may not have been any less than what it is now in the absence of EPZs. Here again it is the location and infrastructure facilities China provides and not EPZs *per se* which may account for China's superior performance. There also other reasons specific to China, discussed earlier, which explain China's superior performance.

The relatively low volumes of FDI India has attracted are to be attributed to the overall economic policies of the country, which amongst other things have failed to remove the pervasive distortions in the economy. These include not only the stringent labour laws and array of subsidies and incentives designed to cater to special interest groups but also the relatively high tariffs and restrictions on imports. In sum, policies which provide level playing fields for both domestic and foreign firms are much more likely to both attract increased volumes of FDI and promote its efficacy than specific policies geared to the foreign firms.

3.5 CONCLUSIONS

FDI is a superb conduit for the transfer of technology and know-how to developing countries. This message has not been entirely lost on India's policy makers. The 1991 economic reforms, a watershed in India's economic development strategy, signalled a major departure in the highly regulated FDI policy framework of earlier years and removed many of the restraints on ownership and composition of FDI. These policies have had an impact on inflows of FDI; annual inflows since 1991 are appreciably higher than that during the pre-reform years. Even so, the volume of FDI in India is much lower than that in other developing countries and is well below the government's target of $10 billion of FDI inflows per annum.

This paper has argued that the reasons for the relatively low volumes of FDI India attracts are to be sought in the pervasive factor and product market distortions generated by the overall policy framework and not entirely due to the FDI policy regime in place. The operation of the regime in practice, however, appears to be riddled with excessive delays and red tape, with attendant opportunities for rent-seeking. The paper has no quarrel with the advocacy of policies designed to remove various sorts of distortions in product and factor markets, reform of labour laws and promotion of infrastructure and the growth of human capital. These are policies which should be adopted in the interests of both domestic and foreign investment.

Indeed, a level playing field for one and all may be a much better bet than specific policies geared to the promotion of FDI.

The country needs to put its house in order if it is to attract increased volumes of FDI. In the absence of an overall policy framework designed to remove the pervasive product and factor market distortions in the economy, throwing all doors wide open to FDI is unlikely to be successful.

The paper has also argued that for a variety of reasons China and its spectacular success in attracting FDI may not be the role model for India. In any case, large volumes of FDI alone are not a panacea for the development problem. Advocacy of FDI should be tempered by the recognition that it is a superb catalyst of growth and not an initiator. Its efficacy in promoting development objectives is conditioned by the presence of co-operant factors in the host economies and it is most effective in countries which possess a threshold level of human capital and infrastructure facilities. The optimum level of FDI a country should aspire to is conditioned by the history and the stage of its industrialisation, the sources of FDI it has ease of access to, and its endowments of co-operant factors and the sort of institutions it possesses to facilitate and monitor the operations of foreign firms.

NOTES

1. An earlier version of this paper is published in *Transnational Corporations*, Vol. 12, No. 2, pp. 45-72.
2. These export-balancing requirements have been relaxed in recent years.
3. It is frequently argued that inflows of FDI into China are overstated because of accounting procedures which differ from those of India and also because FDI in China includes the so called round-tripping variety of capital inflows or monies taken out of China and brought back into the country to take advantage of tax and tariff concessions accorded to foreign investors. Whilst these factors may account for some of the FDI in China, they cannot account for the huge differences in the volume of FDI in the two countries.

References

Agarwal, J. (1980), 'Determinants of Foreign Direct Investment: A Survey', *Weltwirtschaftliches Archiv*, 116, 739-773.

Athreye, S. and S. Kapur (2001), 'Private Foreign Investment In India: Pain or Panacea', *World Economy*, 24, 399-424.

Bajpai, N. and J.D. Sachs. (2000), 'Foreign Direct Investment in India: Issues and Problems', Development Discussion Paper No. 759, Harvard Institute For International Development.

Balasubramanyam, V. N. and M. Salisu, (1991), 'Export Promotion, Import Substitution and Direct Foreign Investment in Less Developed Countries' in Koekkoek, A. and Mennes, L. (eds.) *International Trade and Global Development*, London: Routledge.

Balasubramanyam, V. N., M. Salisu and D. Sapsford (1996), 'Foreign Direct Investment and Growth in EP and IS countries', *Economic Journal*, 106, 92-105.

Balasubramanyam, V. N., M. Salisu and D. Sapsford (1999), 'Foreign Direct Investment as an Engine of Growth', *Journal of International Trade and Economic Development*, 8, 27-40.

Balasubramanyam, V.N. and A. Balasubramanyam (2000), 'The Software Cluster in Bangalore' in Dunning, J.H. (ed.) *Regions, Globalisation and the Knowledge - Based Economy*, Oxford University Press, London.

Bhagwati, J. N. (1978), *Anatomy and Consequences of Exchange Control Regimes*, Balinger Publishing, New York.

Blomstrom, M., R.E. Lipsey and M. Zejan (1994), 'What Explains Growth in Developing Countries', NBER Discussion Paper, No1924.

Blomstrom, M. and A. Kokko (1998), 'Multinational Corporations and Spillovers', *Journal of Economic Surveys*, 12, 2.

China-PRC Ministry of Foreign Trade and Economic Cooperation (2003), http://www1.moftec.gov.cn/moftec_en/

Dunning, J.H. (1973), 'The Determinants of International Production', *Oxford Economic Papers*, 25, 289-336.

Dunning, J.H. (1981), 'Explaining the International Direct Investment Position of Countries: Towards a Dynamic or Developmental Approach', *Weltwirtschaftliches Archiv*, 117, 30-64.

Feinberg, S. and S.K. Majumdar (2001), 'Technology Spillovers From Foreign Direct Investment in the Indian Pharmaceutical Industry', *Journal of International Business Studies*, 32(3), 421-437.

The Financial Times (2003), 'India's Slowing Growth; Why a Hobbled Economy Cannot Meet the Country's Needs', London, Friday, April 4.

Görg, H. and D. Greenaway (2001), 'Foreign Direct Investment and Intra-Industry Spillovers: A Review of the Literature', Research Paper Series No, 137, Centre for Research on Globalisation and Labour Markets Programme, School of Economics, Nottingham University.

Huang, Y. (2003), *Selling China: Foreign Direct Investment During the Reform Era*, Cambridge University Press, New York.

Kathuria, V. (2000), 'Productivity Spillovers from Technology Transfer to Indian Manufacturing Firms', *Journal of International Development*, 12, 343-369.

Kidron, M. (1965), *Foreign Investments In India*, London, Oxford University Press

Kumar, N. (1994), *Multinational Enterprises and Industrial Organization: The Case of India*, New Delhi: Sage

Lall, S. (1980), Vertical Inter-firm Linkages In LDCs: An Empirical Study, *Oxford Bulletin of Economics and Statistics*, 42, 203-226

Lall, S. (1983), *Technological Change, Employment Generation and Multinationals: A Case Study of a Foreign Firm and a Local Multinational In India*, International Labour Office, Geneva.

Lall, S. and S. Mohammad (1983), 'Foreign Ownership and Export Performance in the Large Corporate Sector in India', *Journal of Development Studies*, 20, 56-67

Levis, M. (1979), 'Does Political Instability in Developing Countries Affect Foreign Investment Flows? An Empirical Examination', *Management International Review*, 19.

Mahambare, V. (2001), *Economic Reforms in India: Impact on Savings and Productivity of the Manufacturing Sector*, PhD Dissertation, International Business Research Group, Department of Economics, Lancaster University.

Nagaraj, R, (2003), 'Foreign Direct Investment in India in the 1990s; Trends and Issues', *Economic and Political Weekly*, April 26, Bombay.

Panagariya, A, (2000), 'Evaluating the Case for Export Subsidies', World Bank Policy Research Working Paper 2276, World Bank, Washington D.C

Reserve Bank of India (2003), 'Revised data on Foreign Direct Investment', Press Release, Mumbai, June 30.

Root, F. and A. Ahmed (1979), 'Empirical Determinants of Manufacturing Direct Foreign Investment in Developing Countries', *Economic Development and Cultural Change*, 27, 751-68.

Secretariat for Industrial Assistance (2003), SIA Newsletter, Government of India (May)

Siddharthan, N.S. and B.L. Pandit (1998), 'Liberalisation and Investment: behaviour of MNES and Large Corporate Firms in India', *International Business Review*, 7, 535-48

Wei, S.J. (1999), 'Can China and India Double their Inward Foreign Direct Investment', Working Paper, Kennedy School of Government, Harvard University.

World Trade Organization (2002), *Trade Policy Review India 2002*, Geneva.

COMMENTS

Sanjaya Lall

This is an excellent paper, well written, and informative. It strikes a nice balance between being provocative and analytical.

Balasubramanyam has chosen to present the paper on two themes: the China-India comparison and a critique of Sachs and Bajpai's analysis of FDI in India. I think the paper would have been better if he had taken a slightly different approach, say by comparing India not only with China but also with the more successful countries in the neighbourhood of southeast India. By these international benchmarks, can we say that India has done well in attracting foreign investment, coping with globalisation and using FDI to develop the kinds of export industries that drove the growth of many Asian Tigers? I think the answer is clearly 'no'. India has been left behind in globalisation, at least in manufacturing industry, where it remains very uncompetitive. Software is a major exception, and in many ways the reasons for its success illustrate why manufacturing is so weak in India. It is not dependent on traditional infrastructure; labour unions are not a problem; red tape is minimal because the government has recognised its need for free operations.

In terms of manufacturing, India is one of the most uncompetitive economies of all the newly industrialising countries, despite the size, depth and diversity of its manufacturing sector. Its handicaps lie in technological lags, exacerbated by poor infrastructure, cumbersome labour practices and excessive bureaucratic interference – and a trade regime that still favours the domestic market. In sum, 'business costs' are still too high in India to attract export-oriented FDI. Foreign investors could well have helped India to overcome some of its handicaps in technology, export marketing and advanced management skills, but the other deterrents have till now been too powerful to allow this to happen. Balasubramanyam mentions several of these handicaps in his paper, and I agree fully with his analysis of high business costs, red tape, corruption and weak infrastructure.

Indian policy makers acknowledge much of this. Take one benchmark, FDI per capita. China, with a much bigger population, receives FDI of $30 per capita while India gets less than $4. Another measure is the share of FDI in gross domestic investment. In India it has gone up from 0.1 per cent to about 2.5 per cent. In China, at the end of the year 2000 it was around 11 per cent and is likely to be higher today. I calculated a revealed comparative advantage index for FDI for UNCTAD's *World Investment Report 2002*. This was a simple measure, a country's share in global FDI inflows divided by its share in global GDP: India's index value was 0.1 in 1990 and 0.2 in 2000, while for China the index values were 0.9 and 1.2, respectively.

It is difficult to avoid the conclusion that India under-performs grossly in attracting FDI. Why does China do so much better? Balasubramanyam provides several explanations. 'Round tripping' is certainly one, though it may not be of sufficient magnitude to explain the difference with India. Investment by the Chinese diaspora is another investment, and this does account for a significant part of FDI in China; India does not have three large, dynamic economies offshore populated by its people willing to invest in it and take advantage of its low wages.

Balasubramanyam also makes a point about the different composition of FDI between the two countries, with FDI in India concentrated in high technology industries. I am not convinced. Balasubramanyam argues, correctly, that part of this is due to India's capital-intensive industrialisation process over the years, but he seems to understate the complexity of China's industry and FDI structure. China is the world's largest exporter of low-tech products but it is also now the developing world's largest exporter of high technology products. Its export structure has upgraded very quickly over time and rapidly conquered global market shares. FDI has played a significant role in this process, not only by final assembly of imported components but also by setting up advanced manufacturing facilities in industries like telecommunications to serve both domestic and international markets. China is, in other words, exploiting its comparative advantage in cheap labour but is quickly moving beyond this in terms of raising local content and R&D. We visited the Motorola factory in Tianjin a few months ago and found that the company is setting up a huge R&D centre and has very high local content. Analysts claim that this is fairly representative of much of FDI in China, and that there are highly efficient clusters of high technology suppliers and subcontractors emerging in the more developed regions like Shanghai.

China's move up the technological ladder is difficult to explain simply in terms of labour and capital intensity. We have to move beyond 'factor endowments' and look at such factors as cumulative skill and capability building, with strong agglomeration advantages and targeted industrial policy thrown in. China has realised that it has to move quickly up the comparative advantage ladder if it is to sustain competitiveness. China's exports of high-tech products are about $45 billion, about as large as India's total merchandise exports, and totally overshadow Indian hi-tech exports (that consist largely of pharmaceuticals). Chinese high technology exports are the most dynamic element in its total manufactured exports and there is a rapid structural shift from low to high technology products. India is, by contrast, rather stagnant in terms of the technology structure of its exports. As I noted above, FDI accounts for a very large share of China's hi-tech exports, while such activity is conspicuously absent in India. All these facts lead me to qualify somewhat Balasubramanyam's analysis of the differences in FDI composition between China and India.

Moving on from the China-India comparison, I would have liked to see Balasubramanyam paint on a larger canvas and compare India with other industrialising countries. He could have talked about the role of mergers and acquisitions (M&As) in promoting FDI, which figure hardly at all in India's case. I know little about the Indian government's attitude towards M&As and would have liked to learn more. In Latin America, M&As account for a very significant proportion of FDI, not just in the privatisation of public utilities but also in the private sector.

Low levels of skills in India may be another deterrent to FDI. This may seem surprising since India is now regarded as well endowed with skills. However, India comes out poorly on any measure of skill formation such as years of schooling and enrolment rates. China is also poor at high levels (tertiary enrolments), though it has been improving very rapidly; at the primary and secondary levels, however, China is far ahead of India. It has universal literacy and, something enrolment figures cannot show, a very disciplined and hard-working labour force. This makes China the most efficient place to produce manufactured products today. Surely this explains why it gets so much more FDI than India, at least in competitive manufacturing. Yet this factor is not cited in Balasubramanyam's paper.

Let me return briefly to export performance. In 1985 India's exports were a few billion dollars larger than China's; today China's exports are over $300 billion while India's exports are about $30 billion. India has missed out on the export boom for two reasons. First, many domestic enterprises are not competitive and India has not adopted the kind of strategies that would make them competitive quickly. Second, it has missed out completely on the FDI driven industrialisation, the fragmentation of the global production system that has dynamised South East Asia. Even textiles and clothing, still India's main export industry, would have done better if India had allowed FDI in these industries. India has simply not used FDI to increase competitiveness.

I agree with Balasubramanyam that Sachs and Bajpai overstate their case. There *is* a downside to FDI, but I have considerable sympathy for their position. I agree with them that India should have a much more aggressive policy to attract FDI and to use it to increase competitiveness. The blame does not lie with FDI but with domestic policy. Attracting FDI requires strong competition policy, low business costs and a much more efficient and supportive public sector. It does not, however, need 'distortion free' policies in the sense that FDI flows should be left to free markets. The most successful countries are not distortion free; on the contrary they have pervasive government interventions in resource allocation, both by domestic firms and by foreign investors. Efficient and targeted FDI promotion is increasingly essential to attracting FDI, particularly in export-oriented activities.

India is lagging badly in investment promotion. It needs to persuade and entice prospective investors to set up in India, at the same time removing the irritants that stop them considering India as a base for global sourcing. It needs to do more. It has to create the kinds of skill, infrastructure and technical advantages that would attract high value FDI. The Indian government is certainly aware of the need for better investment promotion, but it still has to set up an agency that can match global best practice in this respect. This is not 'distortion' but an essential part of efficient industrial strategy.

DISCUSSION

John Dunning was of the view that it is difficult to estimate the optimum level of FDI a country should have when there are imperfections and distortions in the system. His gut reaction was that if there was a reasonably open door policy to FDI, equally if not more importantly with infrastructure facilities for all kinds of investment, there would have been more investment in India than there is now. But at the moment for a whole set of reasons this has not happened.

It seems difficult to answer Balasubramanyam's question: what is the optimum level of investment? But if one moved to more open door policy there might be occasion to estimate what the optimum might be. One other point about negative spillovers – the adverse effect on firms that might be competing with foreign firms. The firms that might be adversely affected because of the superior efficiency of foreign firms, that is the relatively inefficient firms can be deployed elsewhere. This of course depends on appropriate government policy. So when one looks at these negative and positive spillovers one must be cautious. It depends on whether one is looking at it from a partial or general equilibrium point of view.

Yasheng Huang said that he agreed with Sanjaya Lall's analysis on most issues, but wondered if Sanjaya Lall was understating the achievements of India in comparison with China. On the revealed comparative advantage (RCA) indices on FDI for China and India, India comes out lower than China. But this is not important. We don't care about whether FDI share or exports share in world totals is large; what we care about is GDP growth. All the others are mechanisms to generate GDP growth. One can argue India is able to generate a higher growth with less FDI. It can use FDI more efficiently; that is one interpretation. In the last five years India has generated about 80 per cent of China's GDP growth rate at a fraction of FDI as compared with China. It has about 10 per cent of China's FDI and 50 per cent of Chinese savings rate. India's savings rate is about 20 per cent, China's savings rate is about 40 per cent.

Annie Wei commented on the observation about China's high-tech exports. China is an above average exporting country. However, if one looks at the sub-categories within the high-tech industries, China's exports are mostly at the low-tech end of the high-tech industries.

4. Inward Foreign Direct Investment and the Industrial Development of Malaysia

Nigel Driffield, Roger Clarke and Abdul Halim Mohd Noor

4.1 INTRODUCTION AND BACKGROUND

Industrialisation in Malaysia[1] was formally pursued after the country achieved her independence from Britain in 1957. Pre-independence Malaysia was a primary-commodity-based economy, reliant on rubber and tin. Import-substitution strategies for developing the manufacturing sector were implemented immediately after independence and were aggressively pursued until the late 1960s. However, the limitations of such policies were soon realised, and a new policy based on semiconductors was formulated. This was founded on the expectation that there would be a relocation of the international semiconductor industry in the 1970s from developed countries to developing countries. Thus, policies towards FDI (and indeed towards industrialisation more generally) became more export-oriented. The manufacturing sector, especially the electrical and electronic components sub-sector, became the catalyst for the country's economic growth.

Tables 4.1 and 4.2 present a historical summary of Malaysia's industrialisation phases. Table 4.1 illustrates Malaysia's five policy-led phases of industrial development, highlighting various issues such as factors that determined why a particular strategy was chosen, economic objectives, types of industries and MNEs, impact on the economy and major policies that have characterised each phase. Table 4.2 provides selected statistics for various years. Up to the financial crisis of the late 1990s, Malaysia generally achieved a high average growth rate of real GDP. Table 4.2 also illustrates the growing contribution of the manufacturing sector to the economy.

Table 4.1 Industrial Phases in Malaysia

	Pre-Independence	ISI (1957–late 1960s)	EOI (late 1960s onward)	Second round ISI (1980 onward)	Renewed EOI (late 1980s onward)
Factors contributing to the chosen industrial strategy	Extractive economic policies	High dependence on primary commodities and import bills	Relocation of the international semiconductor industry	High import of intermediate goods. Government-led strategies	Revert to a more market-oriented approach.
Main objectives	To increase the production of primary commodities	To diversify the economy, reduce imports and generate employment	To diversify the manufacturing sector, create linkages and employment	To create linkages in the manufacturing industry. To reduce imports of intermediate goods	To increase manufacturing linkages, competitiveness and to achieve other socio-economic objectives
Main industries	Processing of rubber and tin	Perishable consumer goods, light industries	Electronic, electrical and textiles	Heavy industries such as automobiles, steel, cement	Electrical and electronic goods – priority given to higher value added product

Table 4.1 Continued

	Pre-Independence	ISI (1957–late 1960s)	EOI (late 1960s onward)	Second round ISI (1980 onward)	Renewed EOI (late 1980s onward)
MNEs	Mostly British-based	Mostly British-based and the beginning of investments of US-based MNEs.	US-based MNEs were the pioneers in electronics. Japanese-based MNEs followed suit.	State-owned enterprises, mostly joint-ventures with Japanese and Korean MNEs.	Emergence of NIC-based MNEs. Especially from Korea and Taiwan.
Impacts	An economy overly dependent on rubber and tin. Manufacturing industries were not developed.	ISI achieved the desired objectives. However, linkages to the economy were weak due to MNEs importing most of their raw materials and intermediate goods.	EOI significantly increased employment opportunities. Linkages to the economy were still weak. Imports of intermediate goods were still high.	Suffered heavy losses initially, partly due to the 1985 recession. Linkages to the economy not fully materialised. Supporting industries not yet fully developed.	Rapid growth experienced in the first half of the 1990s. Increased focus on technology and technological capability.
Major policies	None	Pioneer Industries Ordinance Act 1958	Investment Incentive Act Free Trade Zone Act Industrial Coordination Act	IMP1 1986-1995 Promotion of Investment Act 1980	IMP2 1996-2005.

Table 4.2 Key Economic Indicators for Selected Years

%

State's emphasised industrialisation strategy	None Pre-Independence	ISI (1957 to late 1960s)		EOI (late 1960s onward)		Second round ISI (1980s onward)		Renewed EOI (late 1980s onward)		
Average annual growth rate of real GDP		1957-67		1968-73	1974-78	1979-85		1989-94	1995	1998[8]
	n.a.	6.1		8.5	8.4	5.5		8.6	9.4	-4.8
Investment as share of GDP		1960	1965	1970	1975	1980	1985	1990	1995	1998[8]
Private	n.a.	10.0	9.1	12.5	14.5	20.2	18.0	22.0	31.8	21.4
Public	n.a.	2.6	7.3	5.9	8.8	12.1	15.9	12.1	16.1	11.3
Share of industrial sectors in GDP	1955	1960	1965	1970	1975	1980	1985	1990	1995	1998[8]
Manufacturing	8	9	10	13	14	20	19	27	33	35
Agriculture	40	38	32	31	29	23	20	18	14	12
Services	n.a.	n.a.	n.a.	n.a.	48	n.a.	46	41	44	42
Others[1]	52	53	58	56	5	n.a.	15	14	9	11
Structure of Exports	1955	1960	1965	1970	1975	1980	1985	1990	1995	1998[8]
Manufacturing[2]	-	8.5	12.2	11.9	21.4	21.8	34.6	58.8	79.6	81.2
Electrical and Electronics	-	n.a.	n.a.	6.0	n.a.	9.2	14.2	33.3	52.3	54.9
Agriculture[3]	80.3	66.1	54.5	59.2	52.8	48.5	31.9	22.3	13.1	10.7
Minerals[4]	17.7	22.2	30.0	25.9	22.6	26.4	24.2	18.3	5.8	7.1
Other	1.9	3.2	3.3	3.0	3.2	4.5	4.3	0.6	1.5	0.9

Table 4.2 Continued.

State's emphasised industrialisation strategy	None Pre-Independence	ISI (1957 to late 1960s)	EOI (late 1960s onward)		Second round ISI (1980s onward)	Renewed EOI (late 1980s onward)		
Structure of Imports (%)	1955	1961	1970	1975	1980	1988	1993	1998[8]
Consumption goods[5]	46.9	46.7	28.0	20.0	18.4	23.6	16.0	13.5
Investment goods[6]	12.4	28.4	26.6	31.9	29.9	29.2	40.9	39.6
Intermediate goods[7]	19.6	17.1	36.4	43.4	49.9	46.2	42.7	46.1
Others	20.7	7.8	9.0	4.7	1.7	1.0	0.5	0.8

Notes: 1. Includes services for 1955, 1960, 1965 and 1970. 2. SITC 1+5+6+7+8. 3. Mainly rubber and palm oil. 4. Mainly petroleum and tin. 5. Mainly food, beverages and tobacco, consumer durables and others. 6. Refers to finished goods used for investment purposes such as plant and machinery. 7. Unfinished and semi-finished goods used for the production of other goods, including products which have to undergo further processing, assembly and transformation. 8. Estimates from January to July by the Ministry of Finance.

Sources: Economic Report (ER), 1996/97; ER, 1998/99; Third Malaysia Plan (3MP), 1975; 4MP, 1981; 5MP, 1985; 6MP, 1990; 7MP, 1995; Malaysia, 1996e; Corden and Ritcher (1963).

The following section will outline these policy initiatives and the progress of FDI, with subsequent sections paying particular attention to the electrical and electronics (EE) industry. The EE industry continues to be the most important sector of the Malaysian economy, in terms of not only FDI, but also exports, employment and growth.

4.2 FDI AND DEVELOPMENT IN MALAYSIA

Like most colonies of the former British Empire, the Malayan economy was a resource-based economy. Rubber and tin were the main commodities. Mostly British-based, MNEs exerted a dominant presence in the production of both commodities. Output from British rubber plantations and tin mining corporations contributed more than three-quarters of the country's exports. The manufacturing sector was not very significant in the economy during the colonial era. British colonial economic policies dominated the shape and nature of the Malayan economy. Emphasis was on the production of export-oriented raw materials and British manufactured imports. Local industry was confined to processing raw materials for exports and producing certain items for local consumption (World Bank, 1955, p. 422). Following independence, the path towards development that Malaysia has taken has been heavily dependent on inward FDI, especially in the export-orientated phases of development. Indeed, the stages of Malaysia's development can be traced in terms of a series of policy initiatives aimed at attracting inward investment, and basing the development of the economy on this investment.

In 1971 foreign-owned firms accounted for 63.3 per cent of share capital (at par value) of limited companies in Malaysia. Figure 4.1 illustrates foreign ownership in the corporate sector. The value increased ten times between the years 1971 to 1995 although the share fell until the mid-1980s and then increased slightly.

4.2.1 The First Phase of Import-Substitution Industrialisation (ISI): 1957-

Inward investment was seen in this period as a means of addressing the trade imbalance. Foreign firms which had marketed their products locally, were encouraged (largely through tariffs) to set up production lines, and assembling and packaging plants, to supply finished goods. Between Independence (1957) and 1970 value added in the manufacturing sector more than doubled. To encourage this industrial development, infrastructure was developed, manufacturers were indirectly subsidised and the domestic market was protected. However, most MNEs sourced their inputs abroad, and local activities were restricted to minor assembly operations and packaging and as a result, imports of intermediate goods increased dramatically. MNEs with their technological advantages were able to capture their respective local markets and consequently, in general, linkages between foreign and local firms were weak.

Figure 4.1 Foreign Ownership of the Corporate Sector in Malaysia

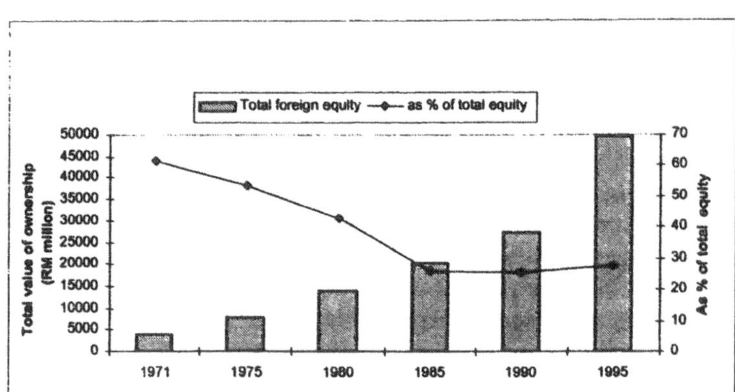

In addition, there have been numerous joint ventures in Malaysia. The formation of Malayawata Steel Mill, a joint venture between Japan and Malaysia, founded in 1961, was the beginning of the development of heavy industry in Malaysia. However, the inception of the Heavy Industries Corporation of Malaysia (HICOM)[2] in 1980, with an authorised capital of RM 500 million, marked the first major Malaysian thrust into heavy industry. It also marked direct government involvement in the market. The capital requirement of large scale projects, a high level of technological requirement (which local firms lacked), and long gestation periods with low returns necessitated government involvement in establishing heavy industry in Malaysia. To obtain the requisite technology and expertise in these industries, the state set up joint venture enterprises with foreign firms, mainly from Japan and South Korea. MNEs such as Mitsubishi, Nippon Steel and Hyundai were invited to form joint venture firms with state-owned enterprises. The main heavy industries in Malaysia are petroleum and chemicals, steel, cement, shipbuilding and automotive assembly.

4.2.2 Export-Oriented Investment: 1968-

From the 1960s onwards Malaysia has sought to take advantage of the international relocation of MNEs' production to developing countries. MNEs from the US and Japan sought locations with an abundant workforce, lower wages and inward investment incentives. Two instruments that played a major role in attracting foreign investors were the Investment Incentive Act (IIA) of 1968 and the Free Trade Zone (FTZ) Act of 1971. The IIA was specially formulated to encourage export-oriented foreign firms. The incentives included investment credits, tax concessions for exports and tax exemptions, preferential treatment for import permits and other infrastructural facilities. The FTZ Act of 1971 also provided a very attractive package for MNEs. FTZs are areas especially designed for manufacturing companies that produce or assemble products mainly for export. The objective of providing FTZ facilities to export-oriented industries is to enable them to enjoy minimum customs formalities and the duty-free import of raw materials, component parts, machinery and equipment required in the production process, together with minimal formalities in the export of their finished products. Currently there are 19 FTZs in Malaysia (MIDA, 1998). The export-orientated industrialisation (EOI) gave new impetus to Malaysia's industrial growth and the EOI phase of the 1970s marked the second phase of industrialisation.

4.2.3 The First Phase of Import-Substitution Industrialisation: 1980-

Malaysia's economy suffered a recession in the mid-1980s. The performance of the state-owned enterprises was poor, and productivity growth was slow. However, with export growth still being generated by the foreign-owned sector, the government determined to attract further investment. Table 4.3 highlights the importance of foreign investment, which comprised 53.0 per cent of total capital investment for the five year period 1991 to 1995.

Table 4.3 lists the value of approved projects according to the respective industries. Foreign investment was concentrated in the EE, chemicals, and petroleum industries. These three industries made up more than 55 per cent of foreign investment for the period. Included in the chemical and chemical products were production of chemical inorganic products, plastic resins, cosmetics, soaps and detergents, while investment in the petroleum sector was mostly concentrated in offshore exploration and refineries. Foreign investment in the petroleum sector was nearly four times larger than domestic investment, implying a strong reliance not only on foreign capital but also on foreign technology. The scenario was similar in the EE sector with foreign investment four times greater than domestic investment. The Ministry of International Trade and Industry (MITI) Report of 1994 reported that these industries were heavily dependent on foreign R&D and suffered serious shortages of skilled personnel (Malaysia, 1994, p. 181-185).

Table 4.3 Approved Manufacturing Projects, 1991-95

RM millions

Industry	No. of projects	Domestic investment	Foreign investment	Total investment
Resource-based	*1908*	*33,466.3*	*34,057.2*	*67,523.5*
Food manufacturing	216	1,467.2	954.8	2,422.0
Beverages & tobacco	21	169.6	330.6	500.5
Wood & wood products	333	3,887.7	2,942.5	6,830.2
Furniture & fixtures	182	457.2	355.8	813.0
Paper, printing & publishing	150	1,710.9	514.0	2,224.9
Chemical & chemical products	271	5,571.8	8,007.2	13,579.0
Petroleum refineries/ products	18	3,248.3	13,198.6	16,446.9
Natural gas	2	5,909.0	1,722.0	7,631.0
Rubber products	149	638.6	470.1	1,108.7
Plastic products	310	1,358.2	1,020.0	2,378.2
Non-metallic products	256	9,047.5	4,541.6	13,589.1
Non-resource based	*2,297*	*20,863.0*	*27,318.7*	*48,181.7*
Textiles	311	959.2	3,728.0	4,687.2
Leather	27	76.7	56.7	133.4
Basic metal products	182	11,300.6	5,791.5	17,092.1
Fabricated metal products	225	1,173.9	2,403.1	3,577.0
Machinery manufacturing	193	511.3	1,085.7	1,597.0
Electrical & electronics products	1,131	3,805.0	12,703.2	16,508.2
Transport equipment	198	2,995.2	1,321.6	4,316.8
Scientific & measuring equipment	30	41.1	228.9	270.0
Miscellaneous	*92*	*236.2*	*221.3*	*457.5*
Total	**4,297**	**54,565.5**	**61,597.2**	**116,162.7**

Notes: Based on the number of projects approved by the MITI. Obviously not all of these projects were realised. It is estimated that about 20 per cent were not realised, mainly due to changes in economic circumstances which made them non-viable.

Source: Seventh Malaysia Plan, 1996-2000, Table 9.5.

4.2.4 The Current Situation

In 2001, RM 24,718.8 million worth of projects were approved by Malaysia's Ministry of Industrial Trade. Foreign investment contributed 74.2 per cent of the total approved investment, although 2001 saw a slight decline of 7.6 per cent in foreign investment on the previous year. There is also a significant downturn in new entry, as most of the foreign investment was allocated for expansion or diversification of existing projects.

EE remains the main sector that attracted foreign investment despite the fact that some firms have been affected by the downturn and ongoing restructuring and consolidation in the global industry coupled with growing competition from China. Foreign investors accounted for 90 per cent of the approved investment. This has been acknowledged as owing to the continuing attractiveness of Malaysia as the investment destination for MNEs especially in high value-added products and activities.

The US, with investment mainly in the EE industry, remains the largest investor in Malaysia in 2001 (RM 3,305.4 million). This is followed by Japan, (RM 3,286.5 million), also mainly in the EE industry. Eighty per cent of the total Japanese investments were for diversification or expansion of existing projects. China and Singapore were the third and fourth largest investors, respectively. China's participation is in a single large-scale project for pulp, printing and writing paper.

Malaysia, with its strong manufacturing base, has been successful in attracting investment in high value-added products and activities such as optoelectronics and photonics, other high-end electronics, R&D and virtual manufacturing.

There will be significant challenges for Malaysia to maintain the momentum given the intense competition from China and other countries in the region. The government has put in place several policies to ensure Malaysia remains competitive. Policies will be fine-tuned to attract quality investments and special incentive packages will be designed for targeted sectors. These are some of the efforts taken to ensure Malaysia remains cost-competitive and a viable location for both foreign and domestic investors. There are, however, signs that Malaysia is still able to attract new large-scale investments. Dyson have announced plans to relocate from the UK to Malaysia, citing a 30 per cent reduction in production cost, and the ease of sourcing components from elsewhere in South East Asia as the motivating factors. Also, Motorola plans to relocate some of its Hong Kong semiconductor operations to Malaysia. This will likely lead to more high quality semiconductor products being produced in Malaysia than has previously been the case. Table 4.4 provides an indication of the sources of inward investment in recent years.

The discussion now turns to the electronic and electrical sector in Malaysia and the level of FDI that it has experienced. Table 4.5 below illustrates the importance of the EE sector to the Malaysian economy.

Table 4.4 Sources of Foreign Investment in Approved Projects, 1997-2001

No. of projects	1997	1998	1999	2000	2001
US	39	45	36	48	36
Japan	100	127	112	118	157
Singapore	118	145	129	145	153
UK	19	24	13	17	20
Germany	25	10	17	30	23
Taiwan	63	74	66	92	88
Korea	18	15	6	14	21
FDI (RM millions)	1997	1998	1999	2000	2001
US	2,397	6,433	5,159	7,492	3,405
Japan	2,164	1,867	1,006	2,881	3,359
Singapore	1,281	968	902	1,778	2,222
UK	207	479	192	771,	122
Germany	1,811	152	187	1,665	2,593
Taiwan	1,345	1,001	267	916	1,127
Korea	678	76	35	722	1,696
Total	11,473	13,065	12,273	19,756	18,820

Note: Currently the Malaysian Ringgit (RM) is pegged to the US dollar at US$1.00 = RM 3.80.

Source: Malaysia Industrial Development Authority (MIDA).

Table 4.5 The Contributions to GDP of Malaysia's Industrial Sectors

Industry	Value Added (RM Million in 1987 prices)		Share of Value Added (%)		Annual Growth Rate, 1996-2000
	1995	2000	1995	2000	(%)
Textiles, wearing apparel and leather	2,311	2,451	5.1	3.5	1.2
Basic metal	513	1,049	1.1	1.5	15.4
Metal products	1,551	3,182	3.4	4.6	15.5
Manufacturing of machinery, except electrical	2,675	3,434	5.9	4.9	5.1
Electronics	10,288	19,460	22.8	27.9	13.6
Electrical machinery	832	1,507	1.8	2.2	12.6
Transport equipment	4,136	7,356	9.2	10.5	12.2

Source: Eighth Malaysia Plan, 2001-2005, p. 236.

4.3 DEVELOPMENT OF THE ELECTRICAL AND ELECTRONICS INDUSTRY

Early electrical and electronics (EE)[3] industries were labour-intensive, based on the manual assembly of semiconductors. There has been a massive influx of inward investment in this sector from the US, Japan and the EU. This phenomenon is relatively easy to explain: low wages, a trainable workforce and incentives, particularly FTZs, were the main attractions for these multinationals. Other factors, such as the depreciation of the Malaysian Ringgit, the government becoming more sympathetic towards private enterprise and the introduction of new incentives to promote exports through the Promotion of Investment Act (PIA) of 1986, contributed significantly to renewing the commitment to inward investment. Furthermore, favourable external market conditions such as the appreciation of the Yen and the new Taiwanese dollar, and the removal of the Generalised System of Preference (GSP) status from NIC countries[4] in February 1988 made Malaysia an excellent choice for investors from these countries (UNIDO, 1991: 114). As expected, the EE industry was the main beneficiary with many EE firms from NICs relocating to Malaysia.

However, over time, especially in the late 1980s and early 1990s, Malaysian electrical and electronics industries became highly capital-intensive processes and highly automated, generating increasingly sophisticated tasks, so that more highly skilled workers were required. Most of the firms, especially foreign firms, provided training to upgrade the skills of their staff. However, as the number of firms grew more rapidly than the supply of skilled labour, firms began to experience a shortage of labour. This situation became more readily apparent in the fourth phase of Malaysia's industrialisation.

In terms of output, Malaysia has emerged as one of the world's largest exporters of EE products. Evidence presented in Lall (1995) shows it is the world's largest exporter of semiconductors and among the world's largest exporters of disk drives, telecommunications apparatus, audio equipment, air-conditioners, calculators, colour televisions and various other household appliances. EE exports account for more than half of Malaysia's total manufactured exports. Electrical and electronics components such as microcircuits, transistors, diodes, other conductor devices and electrical appliances were the dominant growth areas. Textiles followed a distant second, the further growth of the textile sector being hampered by the Multifibre Agreement (MFA), which imposed quotas on the export of textiles and apparel from developing countries to the US, EU and Canada (Malaysia, 1994, p. 48).

Japan was the largest source of investment in Malaysia. Japanese investment was mainly in the manufacturing sector, producing a wide range of products of varying levels of technology, such as electronic components and electrical appliances (including air-conditioners, radio-cassette players, stereos, television sets, etc.), textiles and basic metals. Japanese investment in Malaysia, as noted in one study, occurred in 'waves' (Phongpaichit, 1990: 29). Three waves of Japanese investment in Malaysia have been identified:

i) Resource-based MNEs in the 1960s;
ii) Non-resource based MNEs, especially in the electrical and electronics industry in the 1970s and the 1980s;
iii) Subcontractors from Japan operating in Malaysia to supply large MNEs in the late 1980s and early 1990s (Phongpaichit, 1990).

US-based MNEs were pioneers in the electronics industry, relocating their production facilities to the country as early as 1970 (Narayanan and Rasiah, 1989: 2). Firms from the EU include Audio Electronics (the Netherlands), Robert Bosch and Grundig (both from Germany), Thompson Audio (France) and Lucas Automotive (from the UK)[5].

Evidence is also emerging of this sector becoming increasingly research intensive. Intel, for example, has located a design centre for microprocessors for hand-held equipment in Malaysia, while Motorola has established an R&D centre in Malaysia and designated it as a corporate design centre for cordless telephones for Motorola world-wide (Hobday, 1996). Komag US, the world's largest producer of thin-film disks, also has its own R&D centre in Malaysia as does Matsushita with an R&D centre for air-conditioners (Mohd Noor, 1999). These developments highlight the fact that foreign firms are willing to locate research activities in host-countries, with the benefits to local countries that this may imply.

The electrical and electronics industry (EE) is the main manufacturing sector in Malaysia, in terms of output, export earnings and employment. In 1995, the industry employed 345,000 people, or 16.8 per cent of total manufacturing employment. In 1998, EE exports contributed 55 per cent of the nation's total exports (Table 4.2). Output growth in this sector was 32.6 per cent for 1993 and 16.9 per cent for 1992.

The high growth performance of the EOI sector has strengthened the importance of manufactured exports in the economy. However, foreign firms contribute most of the manufactured exports. This reinforces the crucial role of MNEs in the industrialisation of Malaysia. For example, the electrical and electronics industry, which contributes more than half the exports of manufactured goods, comprises mostly foreign-owned multinationals.

4.4 LINKAGES BETWEEN THE FOREIGN AND DOMESTIC SECTORS

Apart from employment creation, possibly the major reason for developing (and more developed) countries seeking to attract FDI is that MNEs may develop links with the domestic economy. Such links may then support technology transfer, the transfer of skills to the local workforce, and generate investment and employment multipliers from FDI. Successive policies designed to reduce imports and stimulate exports through FDI, however, appeared to have done little to foster linkages between MNEs and the local economy. Growth of manufacturing exports was offset by growth in imports of intermediate goods. Most MNEs, especially in the electrical and electronics (EE) industry, operate from FTZs and export most of their products. This enclave factor and access to duty-free importation of raw materials and intermediate inputs has resulted in weak linkages with local firms. Linkages were especially weak in the EE industry with the heavy concentration on semiconductor and components manufacturing, which mostly comprised of simple assembling and testing activities based on imported materials. This offered limited scope for local linkages (UNIDO, 1990).

O'Brien (1993) and Warr (1989) also note a distinct technology gap between foreign and local firms. Foreign firms that utilised advanced technology have to source their inputs from elsewhere due to the low and unreliable quality of products produced by local firms. Furthermore, most manufacturing processes of MNEs were based on imported technologies on a turnkey basis which aggravated the dualistic nature of Malaysia's industry – foreign firms with modern technologies existing side-by-side with traditional local firms using low level technologies (Onn, 1986). In many cases inputs were supplied by sister subsidiaries of foreign firms most recently located in Malaysia. In 1988 and 1989, for example, Japanese affiliates reported an increase in local procurement of 77 per cent and 60 per cent respectively. Locally procured goods amounted to 23.7 per cent of total non-labour inputs by value of Japanese MNEs in 1989 (Aoki, 1992). The data, however, can be misleading, as Aoki also reports that locally owned firms supplied only half of these inputs by value, the rest being supplied by foreign subcontractors. A survey undertaken by the Malaysia American Electronics Industry (MAEI) reported a much lower usage of locally sourced inputs. In 1994, the MAEI firms reported that their local sourcing was only 9 per cent of total value of output produced.[6] Athukorala and Menon (1996) and Hobday (1996) attribute the low level of local linkages to the inability of local firms to meet appropriate quality standards, and to compete with global components prices.

Guyton (1995) reports that the lack of local linkages was due to MNEs' sourcing practices, which gave preference to home country firms.

Although these linkages are weak when viewed from an MNE perspective, they appear to be considerable when viewed from a local firm perspective. Driffield and Mohd Noor (2000) report that there are significant linkages between foreign investors and domestic firms in Malaysia viewed from this perspective. However, it is also true to say that these linkages, to borrow a phrase from Turok (1993), are of the 'dependent' nature rather than 'developmental'. It is also clear that general subsidies do little to stimulate these linkages, as they simply encourage "branch plant" organisation by the MNE, or plants, which merely assemble imported components for export. There is evidence, however, that such linkages have strengthened and developed over time, and that older technology is transferred more readily to the domestic sector. This is important, as it is indicative of the problem faced by many developing economies. Such countries are able to attract and assimilate older foreign technology, by virtue of being able to facilitate large scale labour-intensive production. However, their ability to gain access to newer foreign technology is distinctly limited, as only MNEs that employ older technology foster local input linkages with domestic suppliers.

The traditional explanations for the lack of local input linkages within MNEs have often focused on the extent to which the MNE is simply unwilling to engage local suppliers, and the degree to which such behaviour is then detrimental to the development of the host country. Driffield and Mohd Noor (2000) have, however, argued that such an approach is not valid, and that the differing costs of local *vis-à-vis* source country suppliers, including transaction cost differences, is the overriding factor. To this end, it is important to note that to the extent that MNEs employ local labour in technical or managerial positions will quickly reduce the transaction costs associated with MNEs buying from local firms, and lead to an increase in local input linkages. From a policy perspective, inward investment policies which provide incentives to foreign firms should seek to reduce the transaction costs associated with local inputs. For example, while it is generally assumed that MNEs operating in Malaysia will employ high proportions of locally recruited manual workers, the employment of local people in managerial or technical positions is seldom stipulated as one of the conditions for a foreign firm to qualify for an investment subsidy. It is suggested that this is a policy initiative that should be considered by development agencies, with a view to promoting developmental rather than dependent linkages, which would result in technology transfer and other spillovers from FDI.

Driffield and Mohd Noor (2000) suggest that policy initiatives could be fruitful in generating linkages. Their results concerning the relationship between the various policy initiatives and local input linkages provide some clear policy implications. In the most general terms, firms that simply received a subsidy, either in the form of an investment tax allowance, or training or R&D subsidies, seem to generate very little in terms of local input linkages, and as such technology transfer is limited. Equally, firms that have been attracted to Malaysia simply to avoid import restrictions are likely to engage in branch plant activity, and again the local development from FDI is limited. However, there is evidence that investment incentives which are targeted at specific outcomes, and require certain commitments on the part of the recipients, are more effective in fostering local input linkages. For example, to an extent the *Pioneer Initiative* takes the form of a tax allowance, but places several conditions on the recipient, one of which is a local content requirement. There is evidence that this policy has been effective, not only in generating local input linkages, but also in fostering technology transfer. The same can be said, perhaps more surprisingly, of export incentives. One thinks of export incentives as being designed to attract MNEs who simply want to export assembled components that have previously been imported. Linkages in export industries, one imagines, are dependent on the extent to which the technology employed in the assembly operation is modified for local conditions, which again encourages local input linkages.

There is little evidence that joint ventures encourage local input linkages. This is contrary to the apparent belief of policy makers that JVs 'internalise' the technology and encourage the involvement of local firms. This however does not appear to occur, possibly because the imported technology is not disseminated beyond the local partner.

Finally, it is often claimed that Japanese MNEs are least likely to foster local input linkages, preferring to use Japanese firms with whom they have vertical relations elsewhere. While there is no specific evidence of this, there is evidence that US firms have higher local input linkages than other firms, possibly a function of the distance between Malaysia and the home country compared with firms from other parts of South East Asia.

4.5 FDI AND TECHNOLOGICAL DEVELOPMENT

Foreign firms' R&D is concentrated in the manufacturing sector with 80 per cent of this in the EE industrial sector. Inward foreign direct investment provides Malaysia's domestic firms with access to advanced technologies through subcontracting and other supply arrangements and there is evidence that foreign investors train some local employees to high scientific and technical standards. Further, some foreign firms appear willing to spin-off certain activities to firms under local ownership (Mohd Noor, 1999). Malaysia is attracting many high-tech MNEs. Intel, for example, had a cumulative investment of RM 4.4 billion in Malaysia by 1996 and plans to continue investing more than RM 1 billion annually. Intel Malaysia is the firm's largest manufacturing site outside the US. It assembles Intel's flagship products such as the Pentium and Pentium II processors. Additionally, Advanced Micro Devices (AMD) has made its Malaysian plant its global manufacturing centre. The presence of these firms and numerous others such as Motorola, Sony, Phillips and Mitsubishi present many valuable opportunities for technological development of local firms. While the available evidence suggests that MNEs in Malaysia are engaging in R&D and other forms of technological effort, some suspicion remains that these are rather isolated events compared with the general pattern. It is important therefore to understand the causes in the variation in levels of technological effort across foreign MNEs in the Malaysian EE sector.

It has been argued that MNEs are likely to undertake technological activities if operating for a large domestic market (Kumar, 1996; Odagiri and Yusada, 1996). The activities undertaken usually take the form of R&D, supporting the manufacturing activities of local affiliates. Other activities will include the necessary adaptation of the product if MNEs are to maintain or increase their local market share. Thus, if MNEs have a strong presence in the local market, this could indicate a greater likelihood of undertaking technological effort. With the rapid advancement of technologies and increasingly globalised operations, however, export-oriented subsidiaries have undergone a widening of their functions. The complexity of production and the need to lower costs has made it necessary for MNEs to undertake increased technological effort on site. Locating R&D units close to the production site enables efficient communication and monitoring of production to be undertaken.

Adaptation may also be required. Here it is envisaged that MNE affiliates undertake some form of technological activity in order to cater for necessary modification to the production process. Assuming that the technological level of many host countries is low, such technological activity may make an important contribution to domestic productivity as well. Adaptation by MNEs can also be identified through changes in plant design and production methods. It is argued that increasing adaptation will increase the need for technological activity by MNEs. This, in turn, will generate productivity growth, and allow the firm to be more responsive to market changes (Hobday, 1996).

Additionally, evidence of significant technological competition between MNEs in Malaysia is emerging. In a developing country, subsidiaries of MNEs often compete on a global scale, which gives them strong incentives to undertake R&D. Results reported in Clarke et al. (2002) suggest that export-oriented MNEs in Malaysia are engaging in local R&D and other forms of technological effort. In general, however, this is limited to the larger subsidiaries.

In terms of technology acquisition, there is a strong link between technological modification and the technology transfer process (Clarke et al., 2002). This may be encouraging for the government since it suggests that technological development and transfer will take place, in addition to other, initial, benefits of FDI. Equally there is evidence that even the relatively small foreign owned plants, while not engaging in R&D, do engage in other forms of technological effort. The literature on the benefits of FDI to developing countries makes much of the "technological gap" that exists between foreign and local firms, and the extent to which this "gap" hampers technology transfer. The fact that the smaller foreign subsidiaries are engaging in the more basic forms of technological effort is likely to be an important part of the technology transfer process.

4.6 CONCLUSION: INFORMING FUTURE POLICY

Foreign direct investment has been a major feature of the industrial development of Malaysia. Following independence in 1957, the Malaysian government has made major efforts to increase and widen the industrial base in Malaysia. An important part of this process has been the encouragement of FDI. In 1998, 81 per cent of all exports from Malaysia were made from the industrial sector and 55 per cent from the EE sector. This compares with just 12 per cent of all exports from the industrial sector in 1970, and 6 per cent from the EE industry. Total capital investment in non-resource-based industries was RM 48.2 billion in 1991-95 of which RM 16.5 billion (34.2 per cent) was made in EE industries and RM 12.7 billion (77.0 per cent) by foreign-owned firms. The industrial sector as a whole accounted for 35 per cent of Malaysian GDP in 1998 compared to just 13 per cent in 1970. The EE industries themselves accounted for 13.2 per cent of manufacturing employment and 3.8 per cent of total employment in Malaysia.

Development of FDI in the EE industry took place during two periods associated with the export-orientated industrialisation (EOI) policies adopted by the Malaysian government. Evidence for this is shown in Table 4.6.

The first arrivals took place at the time of the first EOI policy between 1969-80. In this period, most of the arrivals were Japanese or US firms seeking to switch production abroad to take advantage of lower labour and material costs. The Malaysian government also provided strong incentives for foreign firms in the form of licensed manufacturers' warehouses and free-trade zones. In the second phase (1988-), further incentives were given to foreign firms. During this period Japanese firms were again prominent in setting up production facilities in Malaysia as were a wider range of other

MNEs including those from newly industrialising countries such as Taiwan and Korea.

Table 4.6 Foreign Firm Arrivals in the EE Industries, 1957-98

	First ISI (1957-68)	First EOI (1969-80)	Second ISI (1981-87)	Second EOI (1988-)	Total
Japan	-	5	2	16	23
US	-	5	-	2	7
Taiwan	-	1	2	3	6
S. Korea	-	-	-	3	3
EU	1	2	-	1	4
Joint ventures	-	-	-	2	2
Total	1	13	4	27	45

Source: Mohd Noor (1999), Table 5.14.

In realising the acute competition for FDI and the importance of local firms in developing the manufacturing sector, as shown by NICs, particularly Taiwan and South Korea, further impetus has to be given to developing local firms. In fact, the importance of developing local firms, especially SMEs, has been recognised in every major Malaysian economic plan. In the Second IMP 1996-2005, for example, the thrust of the Plan includes the increased participation of local firms in a broad range of activities, especially in areas that have been identified as being strategically important in the future development of the manufacturing sector (Malaysia, 1996e, p. 11). Indeed, there was an increase of 21 per cent (RM 546.9 million) in the spending allocated for SMEs' development in the Seventh Malaysian Plan, compared within the Sixth Malaysian Plan.

From the outset, MNEs have played a major role in Malaysia's industrialisation process. MNEs not only contribute to providing employment for the growing population, but also provide access to global markets, and encourage local firms to undertake technological activities and development. This scenario will remain for the foreseeable future. However, in light of the competition for FDI and following the Asian financial crisis, Malaysia's industrial development may have to depend more on local firms. To cater for this probable eventuality, it is necessary to increase the manufacturing performance of local firms and at the same time make full use of the presence of MNEs.

This paper has identified two key issues that need to be properly addressed and acted upon if Malaysia is to maximise the benefits of inward FDI. First, the apparent weak linkages in the EE industry. Despite the impressive growth and development of the manufacturing sector, most of it is MNE driven. With the exception of a few, involvement of local firms has been mostly restricted to supplying low value added components and services to MNEs. As yet, there is not a significant pool of local firms that can act as an anchor to a locally owned EE industry.

It is also clear that the policies hitherto employed by Malaysia will not be permitted under WTO rules. As such, if Malaysia wishes to further base its development on its ability to attract inward investment, policies other than simply offering greater and greater subsidies will be required. From this perspective, a more fundamental concern is the low technological capability of local firms, suggesting that linkages between the foreign and domestic sectors are unlikely to strengthen significantly. Low technological capability is also evident on a national level as highlighted in various official documents. This, as argued in some studies, is a result of inadequate local technological activity. Most technologies have been imported thus leading to dependency. Increasing technological capability, in the long term, will require strengthening local absorptive capacity and more effective utilisation of foreign technology.

The latest (eighth) industrial plan seeks to address these problems, and outlines the following objectives.

- Positioning industries to take advantage of the opportunities arising from globalisation
- Strengthening the manufacturing base by developing strong industrial clusters
- Sustaining the momentum of growth by strengthening manufacturing related services
- Providing more focused incentives for high value added industries
- Increasing the use of technology and developing strong domestic capability
- Enhancing the local production of capital and intermediate goods to reduce import intensity and foster industrial development
- Enhancing competitiveness through productivity improvement
- Developing new initiatives in export promotion
- Increasing the use of Information and Communications Technology (ICT)
- Developing resilient SMEs

While much of this statement may be interpreted as the commonly used phrases from development "mission statements" it is clear that the government appreciates the link between inward foreign direct investment and the technological development of domestic industry. Many governments are seeking to target inward investment more carefully than has been the case and it seems that Malaysia is no exception.

NOTES

1. Formerly known as Malaya, Malaysia consists of 13 states and 3 federal territories: Penang, Kedah, Perlis, Perak, Selangor, Negeri Sembilan, Malacca, Johor, Trengganu, Kelantan, Pahang, Sabah, Sarawak and the Federal Territory of Kuala Lumpur and Labuan. Sabah and Sarawak joined Malaya in 1963 to form Malaysia. Singapore seceded from the union in 1965.
2. Initially, HICOM was wholly government-owned. It was later privatised with the government still holding a substantial share of the company. However, in 1996, the government sold its entire share of (RM 1.7 billion) to the private sector. The HICOM group of companies comprise: HICOM, Kedah Cement, Perwaja Trengganu (steel mill), HICOM-Properties, PROTON, HICOM-Yamaha Manufacturing, HICOM-Honda Manufacturing, HICOM-Suzuki Manufacturing, and Petro-Pipes Industries.
3. The Malaysian EE industry essentially consists of two related industries. The electronics industry is defined as the production of "*equipment whose functioning is based on the manipulation of electrical signals/impulses and/or components of such equipment*". The electrical industry produces equipment which "*generates, stores and transmits electrical power or transforms electrical energy into other forms of energy*". Source: UNDP (1990).
4. Taiwan, South Korea and Singapore.
5. Evidence from Mohd Noor (1999).
6. Malaysian-American Electronics Industry (1995) *Annual Survey 1994/1995*, Hay Management Consultants, Kuala Lumpur, 5-6.

References

Aoki, T. (1992), 'Japanese FDI and the Forming of Networks in the Asia-Pacific Region: Experience in Malaysia and Its Implications.' in Tokunaga, Suminari. (ed.) *Japan's Foreign Investment and Asian Economic Interdependence*, University of Tokyo Press, Tokyo.

Athukorala, P. and J. Menon (1996), 'Foreign Investment and Industrialization in Malaysia: Exports, Employment and Spillovers', *Asian Economic Journal*, 10(1), 29-44.

Clarke, R., N.L. Driffield and Abdul Halim Mohd Noor (2002), 'Technological Effort of MNEs in Developing Countries: Evidence from the Electronics and Electrical Industry in Malaysia', mimeo.

Driffield, N.L. and Abdul Halim Mohd Noor (2000), 'Foreign Direct Investment And Local Input Linkages In Malaysia', *Transnational Corporations,* 8(3), 1-25.

Guyton, L.E. (1995), 'Japanese FDI and the Transfer of Japanese Consumer Electronics Production to Malaysia', *Journal of Far Eastern Business*, 1(4)

Hobday, M. (1996), 'Innovation in South-East Asia: Lessons for Europe?' *Management Decision*, 34/9, 71-81.

Kumar, N. (1996), 'Intellectual Property Protection, Market Orientation and Location of Overseas R&D Activities by Multinational Enterprises', *World Development*, 24, 673-688.

Lall, S. (1995), 'Malaysia: Industrial Success and the Role of the Government', *Journal of International Development*, 7(5).

Mohd Noor, H.M. (1999) Technological Effort: a Study of the Influencing Factors in MNCs and Local Firms in the Electronics and Electrical Industries in Malaysia. PhD thesis, Cardiff University.

Narayanan, Suresh and Rajah Rasiah (1989), 'The Electronics Industry in Malaysia: the First Decade in Retrospect", in Suresh Narayanan, Rajah Rasiah, Mei Lin Young and Y.B. Jong (eds.), *Changing Dimensions of the Electronics Industry in Malaysia*, Malaysian Economic Association, Kuala Lumpur.

O'Brien, L. (1993), 'Malaysian Manufacturing Sector Linkages', in Jomo, K.S. (ed.) *Industrialising Malaysia*, Routledge, London.

Odagiri, O. and H. Yusada (1996), 'The Determinants of Overseas R&D by Japanese Firms: an Empirical Study at the Industry and Company Levels', *Research Policy*, 25, 1059-1079.

Onn, F.C. (1986), *Technological Leap: Malaysian Industry in Transition*, Oxford University Press, Singapore.

Phongpaichit, P. (1990), *The New Wave of Japanese Investment in ASEAN: Determinants and Prospects*, Institute of Southeast Asian Studies, Singapore.

Turok, I. (1993), 'Inward Investment and Local Linkages: How Deeply Embedded is 'Silicon Glen'?, *Regional Studies*, 27, 401-417.

UNDP (1990), *Dynamic Input-Output Analysis and Sectoral Projections of the Manufacturing Sector 1990 - 2000: Electronics and Electrical Industry*, Kuala Lumpur, Malaysia.

Warr, P.G. (1989), 'Export Processing Zones and Trade Policy', *Finance and Development*, 26(2), 34-36.

COMMENTS

Richard Eglin

What interests me is where Malaysia sits in policy terms with regard to further liberalisation particularly of foreign investment. Its position in the WTO is firmly launching multilateral negotiations on an investment agreement. This is in contrast to Mexico, Taiwan, Korea, and Ireland. Only India is more strongly opposed.

My question is: why this opposition? It is an interesting question because in Malaysia you have an economy that has benefited enormously from integration into the international economy in the past 20 years, through both trade and investment. It has grown rapidly on the basis of high inflows of FDI and very strong exports.

I think some of the answers to the question are to be found in Malaysia's policies, which have resulted in two parallel manufacturing sectors within Malaysia. One of them is still the import substitution sector which was heavily promoted in the 1960s. The multinationals moved in to some extent, but so did domestic entrepreneurs, often through joint ventures with foreigners. We see a big increase in domestic firms' investments from the charts in Nigel Driffield's paper and the share of foreign equity going down. Where have these domestic firms invested? They are in import substitution sectors such as automobiles, which is still very heavily protected. In that sector Malaysia now has a serious problem. It is trying to unwind protection, but in doing so it is running into problems with its policy of supporting and discriminating in favour of Malay firms, which it does very heavily. It has problems in winding down tariff levels, since it is not the multinationals, but rather the indigenous firms, that will come under strong pressure from lower levels of border protection. So it has serious problems in contemplating further liberalisation of tariffs in terms of its earlier import substitution policies.

In order to keep growth going, therefore, rather than liberalising Malaysia has put in another level of market distortion on top of the tariff distortion. It started offering huge subsidies for the export-oriented sector, which is heavily dominated by multinational corporations. They are the ones who are pocketing the subsidies, and the subsidies are encouraging them to use Malaysia as one of their main export bases for the Asia region. As Nigel Driffield points out, in the electronics industry, the subsidisation of FDI has made Malaysia into the world's largest exporter of semiconductors.

Can this go on? To cut a long story short, where is Malaysia going now? It is already facing very stiff competition from other countries in the region. Singapore's position, for example, is very similar, very heavily dependent on investment subsidies in order to keep the export sector going. In the WTO, these countries are facing the threat that the main plank of their past industrial and export success could be threatened under WTO rules on investment – for example, restrictions on investment incentives, and on the use of performance requirements such as local content requirements and technology transfer requirements. With its resource allocation already distorted by import restrictions, by subsidies to the export sector, and by performance requirements, which as Nigel Driffield points out probably are ineffective. The question for Malaysia seems to be, can its current investment policy regime continue to produce results? What price will they be prepared to pay in higher subsidies to continue to attract multinationals to Malaysia to train their labour and generate their exports. What is the cost of continuing to offset the distortions that have been created by restrictive trade policies?

A second problem Malaysia would confront in a WTO investment agreement is its "Malays first policy" of Bhumiputra. Malaysia discriminates through its economic policies (e.g. investment approvals) for political purposes, to favour indigenous Malay entrepreneurs. This policy is quite obviously inconsistent with basic WTO principles of national treatement and most-favoured nation (MFN) policies.

Clearly, a case can be made that multinationals in Malaysia have generated enormous growth, considerable export revenues and foreign exchange. But the polices underpinning this success story have produced a very distorted industrial sector, which, at the moment, cannot stand serious liberalisation. I think Malaysia is in a very difficult situation at the moment and it is going to have to change not just its investment policy, but also its trade policies, to clear this up and that will involve quite a difficult transition.

DISCUSSION

Yasheng Huang provided some specific illustrations concerning the comments made by Richard Eglin. Figure 4.1 in Driffield's paper shows that the decline of the share of foreign equity in total equity dates to 1971. That was precisely when they formulated a new economic policy after the 1969 riots. When we say local business we should really differentiate between Malay controlled businesses and Chinese and Indian controlled businesses. The Bhumiputra policy was instituted to benefit the Malay controlled businesses at the expense of Chinese and Indian controlled businesses. And as a part of the new economic policy (NEP), businesses be they foreign owned or domestically owned, once they grew to a certain size, had to transfer a certain proportion of equity to the Malays at book value. And in the 1970s, when the Malays did not have the capital to buy these shares, the government set up SOEs, to buy these shares and hold them and then transfer these shares to the Malays. This decline in the foreign share of equity was mainly driven by this explicit policy to benefit the Malay controlled businesses, the Bhumiputra policy. Now they seem to be in serious trouble. Take the example of the Proton car which apparently is sold in the UK too. In the ASEAN trade negotiations, Malaysia is the only country that is holding off trade liberalisation by asking specifically for exemption from trade liberalisation for Proton cars for more than five years. This is because Proton is a Malay dominated business, and is massively inefficient. So essentially all the FDI incentives are designed to do two things. One is to upset the existing massive distortion in capital allocation. And the other is to attract foreign skills and know-how, precisely because the government has suppressed domestic know-how in the past. All the schools were required to discriminate against the Chinese. The best Chinese now leave the country to study in Australia. Fifteen per cent of Cabinet officials in Singapore – and this is a meritocratic government – are from Malaysia. So the best of the human capital, mainly Indian and Chinese left the country.

So essentially, when attempts are being made to promote growth, when there is this outflow, this drainage of domestic human capital, there is a need to import foreign capital more and more. You need to offer very favourable incentives to foreign firms. As Nigel Driffield pointed out, Malaysia has introduced massive distortions, delayed financial liberalisation and trade liberalisation and now China poses a threat in two ways. One is that China is seeking the same FDI as Malaysia and the other more subtle threat is, many of the Chinese owned companies in Malaysia want to leave the country, and invest in China, because the Malaysian business environment is poor. It is so bad for them that Robert Park, one of the biggest Chinese tycoons in

Malaysia, left altogether. He moved his operation to Hong Kong. He famously said that if you take away all the rights of a person and give back a few of these rights, you don't call them incentives. What is interesting is that the government imposed capital controls in 1998. Since then part of the control has been lifted for foreign investors but controls on national investors remain, in part because Mahathir is concerned about the drainage of Chinese companies in Malaysia to China. It is very difficult for Chinese companies in Malaysia to invest abroad, because they have to get approval. The approval system maximises political control and discretionary control of the government.

Frederik Sjöholm argued that both Malaysia and Singapore had managed their foreign investments quite well. They would not have achieved current growth rates and exports without FDI. It is also one of the reasons why they suffered from the Asian Crisis much less severely than other countries such as Indonesia, which were much more suspicious of foreign investments and to finance their current account they relied on bank loans which were much more volatile. But there are problems. Capital has moved not only to Singapore but more so to Vietnam and China. Why? This is because there has been a failure to upgrade investments. It is not necessarily absence of linkages and so forth to the domestic economy. Admittedly this is a problem. But take an economy such as Singapore which is dominated by foreign investments. Singapore has managed to upgrade operations of foreign firms within Singapore. This is not the case in Malaysia. It is still producing relatively low skill goods, mostly labour-intensive goods to the extent that they are importing labour from Indonesia, Thailand and the Philippines. When they tried to expel illegal immigrants recently the local firms protested; they couldn't survive without this immigrant labour. The labour-intensive industries have not been able to upgrade production. That is Malaysia's core problem. They have tried to increase R&D, but it doesn't seem to have worked. It has more to do with education levels. The irony is that Malaysia is one of the countries which has invested sizeable amounts (as a percentage of its GDP) in education, amongst the Asian countries. In fact, it was ahead of Singapore in according priority to education. But they have been going about it the wrong way. The Bhumiputra policy is one problem: 65 per cent of all university places are reserved for the Malays; the Chinese go to Singapore and other countries for their education. For whatever reason, be it cultural, the migrant people, Chinese tend to be the best students. Another problem is that Malaysia has been emphasising not engineering and science, but the social sciences. Probably Malaysia has to realign education investments and abolish affirmative action. But it is tough because of political problems.

Yasheng Huang intervened to say that it is very difficult to teach science and technology in Malay. They do not allow teaching in English. Frederik Sjöholm thought that if you teach science and engineering in Swedish, you can do so in Malay too!

David Sapsford posed three questions. First was there any relationship between the problems very clearly highlighted in Malaysia and those in Indonesia. Is Indonesia in the same situation? The second question relates to strategies the country has adopted of picking winners. What sort of methods of forecasting have been used and how effective are they? The last question is the idea that MNEs are training agencies. Is this seen in Malaysia as part of a longer term cycle whereby eventually they themselves take up the training role because there are some interesting things happening. For instance, commercial power companies have turned themselves into a university. It is actually giving its own training, so it is like the university of the national grid.

Nigel Driffield replied that if one sees the policy documents, it seems to be a policy of learning by watching. Whether that is actually sustainable or not was open to question. But that is the idea. As regards picking winners, they have been almost too selective. For instance, if it is not in semi-conductors a company is out of the loop as far as R&D subsidies are concerned. As regards the relationship between foreign firms and domestic firms and how much upskilling there is in the domestic sector, the answer is, not a lot. What is hoped particularly with the training is that somehow by giving somebody a particular set of technical skills, you can make them want to run their own business. But there does not seem to be an obvious link here. Just because some are trained to the level where they have a Ph.D. in semiconductor technology, it does not mean that they want to go and run their own business. They could very well get a very highly paid job working for Intel, either in Malaysia or Singapore, or in the US. But that does not make them decide to set up a firm and employ 100 indigenous people.

Peter Buckley said that he was in Kuala Lumpur, investigating what the Malaysian policy was for attracting foreign investment. Two things he found were interesting. One is that the Malays are very much worried about Chinese competition, both from Chinese firms leaving Malaysia as well as losing markets to China. Second, their response is exactly what Nigel Driffield suggested. It is more of the same. Just outside Kuala Lumpur, they are building this massive technology college and then cutting down half the rainforest, which is all multinational investments and the talk is about agglomeration economies. Malaysian policymakers are trying to rationalise all this. They have got a swift runner coming up behind them which is China is about to overtake them. The only thing they can think of doing is to run faster in the same small area that there is. There is no examination of an alternative development route outside. It is more intensification of the same strategy. Malays have got this mind set that they have to be the best in this narrower and narrower area and cannot seem to get out of it. This raises an issue that several papers have brought up. It is not just success, but how long can you be successful? Can you sustain it, which is very much the case with Ireland which is attracting substantial volumes of FDI. The Malaysians have got this view that it is going to run out and the success story is going to stop. And all they can do is more and more of the same and try a narrower and narrower approach to the problem.

John-ren Chen thought that there were two problems: misallocation of resources and the impact of FDI on income distribution. The distribution problem may be acute in China too though it hasn't got two distinct groups of population, the Chinese and the others, as in Malaysia. There may also be regional income distribution effects arising from inflows of FDI.

Annie Wei wanted to know the role of Chinese entrepreneurs in Malaysian economic development. What percentage of assets are owned by Chinese in Malaysia? What kind of complementary role with FDI do they play in Malaysia's development? Nigel Driffield replied that there was very little Chinese investment in the electronics sector. This issue of the role of the Chinese in Malaysia's development had to be investigated.

Mohammed Salisu drew attention to the fact that Nigeria too had suffered from positive discrimination policies of the sort practised by Malaysia. Such discriminatory policies may lead to inefficiencies, a sort of X-inefficiency. The northern part of Nigeria is relatively backward in terms of education and owns very few of the assets of the country. The political leaders who mostly come from the North have introduced a system of quotas for employment and provided other subsidies to the northerners. This dependence of the North on government subsidies and quotas had resulted in massive inefficiencies in the economy and kills entrepreneurship.

Frances Ruane elaborated upon the issue of linkages. The point Nigel Driffield made was that the indigenous sector was not developed in a manner to absorb whatever spillovers the foreign firms might be generating. The other has to do with R&D, a problem with multinationals in most developing countries. They put R&D together as a concept, but it is actually D, not R. Very often the governments satisfy themselves that the MNEs are doing something under R&D, but nothing much may be happening in the short term. The other point is that growth is high but mostly due to the foreign sector. The difficulty with this, as in the case of Ireland, is that when the foreign sector is driving growth people don't see a crisis. In the case of Malaysia it is more extremely of the enclave nature than in the Irish case; there is no reason to respond, there is no action. The growth rates look very good, but a crisis may be looming.

Nicholas Snowden thought that the papers on Mexico and Malaysia seemed to have interesting implications for empirical work on FDI. These sets of countries appear to have sought FDI in the first place for quite different reasons. It seems, at least in the beginning, Malaysia and Mexico were seeking foreign capital to bridge budding trade deficits. FDI was looked upon as source of capital. This may be the reason why there weren't much spillovers from FDI because it was sought for other purposes. The second point has to do with additionality. In the case of Malaysia it seems that whilst FDI was coming in, Chinese capital was going out. So in this case you have to net out the loss of capital that is the outflow of Chinese capital from Malaysia. This has to be taken account of in empirical studies investigating spillovers. The third point is about efficiency, particularly about social efficiency; there is an issue about social efficiency. One could say Malaysia has not had any race riots and this may be regarded as social efficiency. It just raises issues concerning liberalisation – how are you going to handle social issues if you are not able to intervene through factor and product markets. This is an important issue – we are bulldozing liberalisation through without asking questions of this sort.

Nigel Driffield replied that additionality appears to be discussed mostly by economists specialising in Regional Economics in the developed countries and not by development economists. Most of the work on this issue of crowding out is based on American and British data at the regional level. Work needs to be done on this issue in developing countries.

John Dunning stated that he had done a project on these sorts of issues for the department of trade and investment (DTI) in the UK. It seems to be an opportunity cost situation and that is correct. You must analyse the benefits and costs of FDI in terms of an alternative position.

5. Foreign Direct Investment in Mexico

David Griffiths and David Sapsford

5.1 INTRODUCTION

Mexico provides an interesting case study of the effects of inward foreign direct investment (FDI) because, like many other developing countries, it has gone from a highly protectionist regime focused on import-substituting industrialisation (ISI) to an open regime which actively attracts foreign investment. Following the onset of industrialisation a decade earlier, Mexico officially endorsed ISI policies during the 1940s as the government raised import tariffs, introduced import licenses, and imposed export controls in an attempt to encourage its domestic industry. These policies proved successful in developing a manufacturing base centred on Mexico City.[1]

Since the announcement of the North American Free Trade Agreement (NAFTA), which came into being in January 1994, considerable attention has been devoted to analysing the effects that the dismantling of trade and investment barriers would have on the US and Mexican economies (and the Canadian economy to a lesser extent). However, this belies the fact that Mexico effectively made the transition from a closed economy to an open economy during the 1980s after it announced in 1985 that it intended to join the General Agreement on Tariffs and Trade (GATT).[2] Hanson (1998) even suggests that given the geographical proximity of Mexico and the US, trade liberalisation by Mexico in 1985 constituted the beginning of integration, with NAFTA merely finalising the process a decade later.

The proximity of the world's most powerful nation is another reason why the Mexican economy provides such an interesting case study. Over the last two decades the US has consistently been the source of over half of Mexico's inward FDI (see Table 5.1). The attraction of FDI is that it is supposedly "a composite bundle of capital, technology, and know-how" (Balasubramanyam et al., 1996, p.6) that can be harnessed by the host economy to help narrow the 'ideas gap' (Romer, 1993) and hence increase domestic productivity. The degree to which FDI embodies technology and know-how will evidently vary from one investment to another. Given that the technological sophistication of the source country is likely to be one important determinant, the fact that the majority of Mexico's FDI comes from the US suggests that Mexico may be in an excellent position to benefit from FDI (and is therefore an ideal candidate in which to test for possible FDI spillovers).

Table 5.1 FDI Participation in Mexico, 1976-94

%

Period	US	Germany	Japan	UK	Switzerland	Spain	France
76-94	62.28	7.33	7.27	3.9	5.11	2.83	3.09
76-80	68.72	11.56	14.77	3.76	8.96	4.16	0.54
81-85	62.97	8.7	6.25	3.29	4.1	3.39	3.58
86-90	58.13	5.24	3.66	8.97	3.68	2.1	5.03
91-94	58.55	2.92	3.67	7.87	3.35	1.36	4.58

Source: Love and Lage-Hidalgo (2000).

This paper is organised as follows. Section 5.2 looks at the volume and structure of Mexican inward FDI. The determinants of this FDI are discussed in section 5.3. Section 5.4 reviews the extant literature on FDI spillovers. The results of a simple time series analysis of the growth effects of FDI in Mexico are presented in section 5.5 and section 5.6 concludes and offers some policy proposals.

5.2 VOLUME AND STRUCTURE

Mexico has long been a large recipient of FDI. During the 1980s it accounted for approximately 10 per cent of all FDI flows to developing countries and roughly a quarter of all flows to Latin America (Love and Lage-Hidalgo, 2000). Though many Mexicans once lamented that they were "so far from heaven and so close to the Unites States" (Blomstrom and Kokko, 1997, p.21), Mexico's proximity to the world's largest economy is perhaps its greatest advantage. Table 5.1 illustrates the primacy of the US in Mexican inward FDI.

Despite a modest decline in FDI participation in Mexico by the US between 1976 and 1994, the US remains by far the largest single investor. One of the principal advantages of this for Mexico is that the US economy is at the technological frontier and it may be expected that US FDI may be managerially and technologically well endowed. The principal advantage for researchers is that the US collects the most comprehensive data on the activities of its multinationals abroad, and hence provides detailed information pertaining to roughly 60 per cent of all FDI inflows into Mexico. Few other, if any, countries offer this wealth of data.

Figure 5.1 shows the stock and flows of FDI from the US to Mexico for the years 1966 to 2000. As flows in any individual year are heavily influenced by individual undertakings, they show a marked volatility in comparison with the stock data. For this reason, it is preferable to analyse the FDI trend by consideration of the stock as opposed to the flow. Whilst the figure shows a gradual increase in FDI stock from the outset, there appears to be a dramatic increase in FDI during the nineties.[3] In fact, Graham and Wada (2000) report that there is a trend break in 1989.

Figure 5.1 US FDI in Mexico, 1966-2000

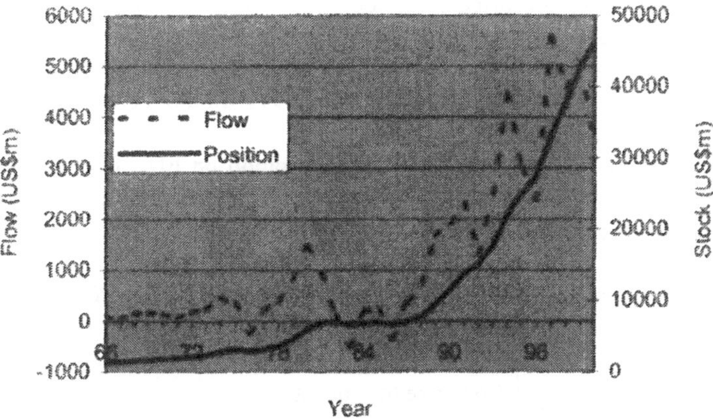

It is interesting that the timing of this trend break precedes the implementation of NAFTA by some five years. During the negotiations of NAFTA there was considerable concern expressed in the US and Canada that the abundant supply of cheap labour in Mexico would lead to sizeable negative effects on domestic wages and employment. What these concerns overlooked, however, was that trade and investment liberalisation in Mexico had begun in earnest ten years earlier; with corresponding adjustments in trade and investment volumes already having taken place.[4] Graham and Wada (2000) report that the earliest indications that NAFTA was in the 'pipeline' were from 'leaked' reports from the Mexican government in the spring of 1990, and so "the trend break cannot be attributed to NAFTA nor even to expectations that it would occur" (p.781).

Recognising that FDI typically involves long lead times between the decision of firms to invest and the actual investment taking place, Graham and Wada (2000) further discount the re-election of the incumbent Institutional Revolutionary Party (PRI) in 1988 and significant liberalisation of the Law on Foreign Investment (LFI) in 1989 as explanations of the trend break.

The true catalyst for the break in trend would seem to be the dramatic policy reorientation that Mexico was forced into in the mid-1980s due to its sovereign debt crisis. In 1995 Mexico announced its intention to join the General Agreement on Tariffs and Trade (GATT), began a series of bilateral negotiations to liberalise trade and investment with the US, and instituted unilateral policy reform. It is these significant changes in Mexico's policy environment that seem to have generated a marked increase of FDI from the US. Despite fears pertaining to the consequences of NAFTA, the major structural changes to the Mexican economy and their associated effects on trade and investment occurred some years prior. The main impact of NAFTA may actually have been to 'lock in' Mexico's policy liberalisation and to validate it on the international stage. An increase in the proportion of FDI originating from 'outside' countries after 1994 would certainly seem to validate this conclusion.

In a study of the impact of regional integration on FDI, Blomstrom and Kokko (1997) suggest that the effect of NAFTA is likely to characterise Mexico as being in quadrant 1 of Table 5.2.

Table 5.2 Factors Determining the Impact of Economic Integration

	Locational (positive to	Advantages negative →)
Environmental Change	1	2
(strong to weak ↓)	3	4

Source: Globerman and Schwindt (1996).

This area is reserved for those countries upon which the regional integration agreement (RIA) has a strong policy impact *and* which have positive locational advantages (such as low unit labour costs, sizeable domestic market etc.). It is expected that the potential for positive impacts from the formation of an RIA will be greatest for countries described by this scenario. Undoubtedly, low labour costs and proximity to the US market endow Mexico with strong locational advantages. However, our preceding discussion suggests that the environmental impact of NAFTA may not have been as strong as originally thought (or *feared*, in some cases), indicating that the impact of integration on Mexico may be more accurately categorised by quadrant 3.[5] In this region the impact of the RIA on inward FDI is still expected to be positive, but not as strong as it would be if the country was in quadrant 1.

Let us now turn towards the sectoral distribution of total world FDI in Mexico. Table 5.3 shows the breakdown for the last decade according to the Instituto Nacional de Estadistica. While the service sector received the majority of inward FDI in the early nineties, by the close of the century the industrial sector was by far the greatest recipient. The wholesale and retail trade sector has also enjoyed rapidly accelerating FDI during the decade, firmly establishing itself as the third most important sector. Extraction and Agriculture receive comparatively little FDI.

Table 5.3 Sectoral Composition of Mexican FDI

US$ million

Period	Total	Industrial	Services	Trade*	Extractive	Agriculture
1990	3722.4	1192.9	2203.1	171.4	93.9	61.1
1991	3565.0	963.6	2138.0	387.5	31	44.9
1992	3599.6	1100.8	1700.0	750.9	8.6	39.3
1993	4900.7	2320.5	1730.7	759.9	55.1	34.5
1994	10564.0	6114.6	3093.2	1250.5	95.1	10.6
1995	8201.8	4738.3	2367.4	1005.9	79.1	11.1
1996	7662.3	4682.1	2144.8	719.9	83.8	31.7
1997	11812.7	7233.0	2584.9	1853.7	130.2	10.9
1998	7612.0	4899.7	1774.3	866.9	42.4	28.7
1999	11964.5	8661.9	2176.2	926.3	122.9	77.2
2000	12451.6	7632.6	2886.4	1689.1	161.7	81.8

Note: * Wholesale & Retail Trade.

Source: Instituto Nacional de Estadistica.

In order to gain a more detailed insight into the industrial location of Mexican FDI it is once again necessary to examine data maintained by the US Department of Commerce. As before, this has the disadvantage that it accounts only for US FDI, but the advantage that the data are considerably more comprehensive and accurate than those available elsewhere.[6] Table 5.4 shows a detailed decomposition of US FDI flows into two-digit SIC Mexican manufacturing industries. It is evident that the three most important industries are Transport Equipment (SIC 37), Food (SIC 20), and Chemicals and Allied Products (SIC 28). Unfortunately, a number of the investment figures have been suppressed (D) to ensure that it is not possible to identify the activities of any individual firm. However, by subtracting the available data from the total for all manufacturing industries we can be certain that none of the suppressed figures is masking significant FDI flows.

Table 5.4 US FDI Flows in Mexican Manufacturing Industries, 1982-2000

US$ million

Year	Total	Food	Chemicals	Primary Metals	Industrial	Electronics	Transport	Other
1982	203	18	93	37	-3	37	-74	96
1983	-427	-58	-21	-42	-141	-56	-59	-51
1984	129	122	131	32	-279	85	48	-10
1985	200	33	55	6	-52	-18	87	89
1986	-351	-45	-52	-29	-111	-2	-83	-29
1987	264	-91	120	26	-79	48	5	236
1988	670	69	190	32	21	27	163	168
1989	1159	281	289	39	60	D	250	D
1990	1323	393	173	49	53	D	257	D
1991	1325	281	262	19	-9	-43	619	196
1992	720	28	152	D	D	-92	404	268
1993	1023	952	410	D	D	-95	-628	304
1994	2530	674	314	D	D	158	1028	281
1995	1785	360	289	D	D	-69	687	D
1996	1665	692	599	52	D	7	-211	D
1997	2499	1007	577	D	D	-14	144	D
1998	2472	713	107	D	D	D	1300	495
1999	2468	-23	729	80	D	D	774	656
2000	1710	507	483	D	D	D	726	D

Source: US Department of Commerce.

Finally, it is important to note that a significant proportion of FDI into Mexico has been in in-bond foreign assembly plants (maquiladoras) based overwhelmingly along the 3326 km US-Mexico border.[7] Although the maquiladora program has proved popular with foreign investors since its introduction in the 1960s, relaxation of restrictions in the early 1980s saw maquiladora employment increase from 150,867 in 1983 to 460,293 in 1990 as the share of maquiladora workers in national manufacturing employment grew from 4.9 per cent to 19 per cent (Feenstra and Hanson, 1997). Today there are some one million workers in nearly 4000 maquiladoras.

Gerber (2001) reports that maquila investment has accounted on average for 27 per cent of US FDI into Mexico for the period 1994 to 2000.[8] Furthermore, five cities located on the US-Mexico border share 50 per cent of the firms and 51 per cent of the workers in US origin maquilas. Feenstra and Hanson (1997) find that in the regions where FDI was most concentrated, growth in maquiladora investment can account for over half of the increase in the share of skilled labour in total wages that occurred during the late 1980s[9]. Given this, the authors claim that the "FDI boom…has resulted in a region-specific shock to labour demand" (p. 374).

Hanson (1996, 1998) draws similar conclusions investigating the spatial impact of FDI and Mexican-US integration. He argues that the massive US inward FDI concentrated in maquiladoras near the Mexican-US border has essentially created vertical production networks spanning the border. This has contributed to a significant contraction in employment in the Mexico City manufacturing belt, a rapid expansion of manufacturing employment in Northern Mexico, and an increase in wage inequality.

Interestingly, these studies also suggest that the impact of NAFTA on the US has been understated. Hanson (1996) examines data for US-Mexico border-city pairs (e.g. San Diego–Tijuana), concluding that export manufacturing in *maquiladoras* encourages growth in employment in US border cities.

Early evidence therefore seems to indicate that despite the benefits inward FDI can bring in terms of capital and productivity spillovers, it may also lead to rising inequality and regional deindustrialisation. The potential costs of such problems are well known and it is obvious that the spatial aspects of FDI and integration warrant further investigation.

In this section we have argued that Mexico's sweeping liberalisation and policy reform in the mid-eighties was the catalyst to a dramatic acceleration in inward FDI (with the implementation of NAFTA nearly a decade later serving to consolidate and validate these reforms). Given this, what factors explain the attraction of the Mexican economy to foreign investors, and what determines the industrial and geographical location of FDI in Mexico? These are the questions that we turn to next.

5.3 DETERMINANTS OF FDI IN MEXICO

The decision process prior to undertaking foreign investment will undoubtedly vary from one firm to another. However, there are many considerations (such as availability of factor inputs, domestic demand conditions, property rights protection etc.) that will be common to all firms. One theory that neatly encapsulates these diverse factors is the eclectic paradigm developed by Dunning (1988). This argues that FDI will be the appropriate mode of foreign market entry when multinationals find it most advantageous to exploit ownership and location advantages through internalisation rather than through exporting or licensing.

There are numerous recent empirical studies which seek to test the determinants of FDI.[10] Most of the issues under investigation can be categorised as location advantages, but there are also studies which seek to assess the impact of ownership advantages and strategic considerations on FDI. Despite the wealth of such studies, the number that specifically address Mexican FDI is unfortunately rather small. Two authors who seem intent on single-handedly remedying this are Love and Lage-Hidalgo. In one paper they test the ownership advantages of US multinationals as determinants of FDI flows into Mexico (1999a), while in other papers (1999b, 2000) they consider a derivative of the model employed by Buckley and Casson (1991) which takes the principal determinants of FDI to be the scale of demand in the host economy and relative factor costs in the capital exporting and importing countries.

In order to investigate the significance of ownership advantages the authors conduct an empirical analysis of sectoral data from the majority-owned foreign affiliates (MOFAs) of US MNEs.[11] The dependent variable is FDI flows, whilst the independent variables (which all apply specifically to the US MOFAs in Mexico) are R&D expenditures, capital expenditures, net tangible assets, employee compensation, and total Mexican sales. Their analysis reveals that all of the explanatory variables (with the exception of R&D expenditure) are positively related to FDI flows. They conclude that "direct investment into US MNEs' affiliates in Mexico is driven by benefits derived from embedded human knowledge and from technical knowledge embodied in plant and machinery" (p. 70).

To test their alternative model the authors employ data on US FDI flows to Mexico for the period 1967 to 1994. In this instance the independent variables are Mexican income per capita (as a proxy for the scale of domestic demand), the difference between US and Mexican hourly real wages, and an estimate of the difference between the cost of capital between the US and Mexico.[12] The model was able to explain two-thirds of the variation in FDI flows and strongly supported the belief that real wage differentials were an important locational determinant. Cost of capital differentials, on the other hand, were found to have a weak positive effect on FDI. The authors' suggested explanation for the unexpected sign on capital cost is that when the cost of capital increases in the home nation it encourages MNEs to raise capital from the host country which ultimately leads to increases in FDI. Mexican income per capita was also found to have a strong positive influence on FDI, which is interpreted as indicating that the domestic Mexican market is attractive to FDI in its own right (and not simply because it offers a plentiful supply of 'cheap labour').

One notable shortcoming of these studies (which is readily acknowledged by the authors) is their use of wage differentials instead of the more appropriate unit labour costs (ULCs) that take into account labour productivity as well as labour compensation. Fortunately, the recent provision of ULC measures for Mexico by the Key Indicators of the Labour Market (KILM) database enables this to be remedied.

Table 5.5 shows the regression results from an OLS regression with US FDI flows to Mexico and Canada for the period 1982 to 1996 as the dependent variable.[13] The independent variables include the GDP and population (POP_i) of the US (intended to capture the 'push' effects on FDI) and the GDP and populations (POP_j) of Mexico and Canada (capturing the 'pull' effects of domestic market demand). ULC_j is the unit labour cost in US$ in Mexico and Canada.[14] As the table shows, only the coefficients on GDP_j (host income) and ULC_j are statistically significant (at 6 per cent). The sign on these variables are as expected and indicate that, *ceteris paribus*, a larger host economy and lower unit labour costs encourage inward FDI. While this analysis is very crude and suffers from a very limited number of observations (a problem common to most studies on this topic), it appears to confirm the findings of other authors that labour costs and domestic demand are important determinants of the location of US FDI in Mexico.

In order to attempt a more comprehensive analysis of the determinants of Mexican inward FDI we constructed a data set of FDI flows disaggregated by two-digit SIC manufacturing industries. US flow data for the years 1987 to 2000 were taken from the Bureau of Economic Analysis (BEA) for the Food, Chemicals, Primary Metals, Industrial Machinery, Electronics and Transport industries. As disaggregated ULC data are not available for Mexico, we employed data on hourly compensation available from the US Bureau of Foreign Labour Statistics.

Table 5.5 FDI Flows and Unit Labour Costs in Mexico, 1982-96

	Coefficient	Standard Error	t-ratio	P-value
Constant	-49470.7	29950.4	-1.65	0.11
ULC_j	-11729.2	5966.19	-1.96	0.06
POP_j	0.00021	0.00013	1.57	0.12
POP_i	0.00019	0.00018	1.05	0.30
GDP_j	6.63E-08	3.37E-08	1.96	0.06
GDP_i	-4.65E-09	3.80E-09	-1.22	0.23

Notes: Dependent variable = FDI flows; Sample size = 30; Adjusted $R^2 = 0.61$

In addition to the compensation variable we included the GDP of the domestic US industry (IND_iY), and the GDP growth rates of the US (y_i) and Mexican (y_j) economies as explanatory variables.[15] We therefore estimated the following equation:

$$\ln FDI = \alpha + \beta_1 \, {}^{COMP_j}\!/_{COMPi} + \beta_2 \ln IND_i Y + \beta_3 y_i + \beta_4 y_j \qquad [5.1]$$

where i indicates the investing economy (in this case the US) and j represents the recipient (Mexico).

Unfortunately, due to data suppression by the BEA (to protect the identity of individual firms) and missing values for compensation in some years, our potential panel size of 68 observations was reduced to 31. Given this, it is somewhat unsurprising that we failed to achieve conclusive results, whether using a random effects model (REM) or a fixed effects model (FEM). The sole statistically significant coefficient was β_2, whose value ranged from 1.24 to 1.59 (significant at the 5 per cent level) depending on the model specification and sample used[16] (full results are available on request). This implies that, *ceteris paribus*, a given increase in the size of a manufacturing industry in the US will lead to a greater increase in FDI flows to Mexico.[17] Obviously though, the lack of data has prevented us from undertaking a sophisticated and comprehensive study and this conclusion should be taken with the caution that it deserves.

The simple empirical work we have undertaken, while not particularly inspiring, seems to offer some evidence to support the intuition that unit labour costs and growth of US manufacturing industries have been important in stimulating inflows of FDI to Mexico. An analysis of the attraction of factors such as tax breaks, special economic zones and agglomeration economies is beyond the scope of this review paper but would make a valuable contribution to the literature if a sufficiently comprehensive data set could be assembled.

5.4 SPILLOVER CHANNELS

The literature identifies four main channels through which spillovers from FDI are thought to occur: imitation, competition effects, human capital acquisition, and export spillovers. We briefly consider each in turn.

5.4.1 Imitation

The most convincing explanations in the theoretical literature on why multinationals invest abroad as opposed to licensing or exporting tend to assume that the firm has some sort of ownership advantage (such as patented technology) that it must internalise through direct investment to overcome market imperfections (such as poor intellectual property rights in the host country). As observed, the multinational will surely be disadvantaged in terms of local knowledge and so must have some proprietary advantage to counteract this. Either by imitation or demonstration, dispersion of this proprietary knowledge (whether it be technology, a product or process innovation, or simply managerial or organisation expertise) is believed to be one of the primary channels through which domestic firms can improve their productivity.

Immediately, it is obvious that a number of factors will be crucial in determining how successful domestic firms will be in gaining from this type of spillover. For instance, the level of technology or knowledge embodied in FDI can be expected to vary with the type of investment (e.g. initial capital or reinvested earnings), industry of investment (e.g. electronics or agriculture), and source country (e.g. US or Brazil). Furthermore, the host nation's ability to benefit from any spillovers likely depends on its technological sophistication, levels of human capital, cultural and social capital, and financial institutions and markets (factors which Abramovitz (1986) might refer to as determining a country's 'absorptive capacity'). Indeed, there is quite a debate in the literature as to whether the size of the 'technology gap' (that is, the difference in technological sophistication between the source and host countries) exerts a positive or negative influence on spillovers.[18] The argument that it is positive rests on the belief that the more 'backward' the host nation the greater the scope for it to make gains on the leading countries and hence the faster domestic productivity growth will be. However, if the gap is large it may prove too great for domestic firms to 'jump' and ultimately they may gain very little from FDI (and may actually be harmed by it if they are forced out of the market).

In a cross-section industry level study of Mexico for 1970, Kokko (1994) investigates the role of the 'technology gap'. He finds that "factors related to technology alone do not seem to inhibit spillovers, but that large productivity gaps and large foreign market shares together appear to make up significant obstacles" (p. 290). This finding may be of particular concern to Mexico because US investment in maquiladoras in Northern Mexico exhibits aspects of enclave behaviour.

5.4.2 Competition

A number of authors emphasise the role of competition effects in generating spillovers from FDI (Wang and Blomstrom, 1992; Glass and Saggi, 2001). Entry by a foreign firm will initially increase competition in the domestic industry which should force domestic firms to adopt new technologies or reduce X-inefficiency even if there are no gains in terms of imitation as discussed above.[19] This spillover mechanism is analogous to the standard gains associated with increased arm's-length trade and is often cited as potentially one of the most important benefits from FDI.[20] Of course, if foreign entry forces out some domestic firms that are unable to compete and hence ultimately leads to an increase in concentration and imperfection in the market, competition effects from FDI may actually harm the host economy.

5.4.3 Acquisition of Human Capital

Human capital has long been held to be a vital determinant of economic growth and has recently been incorporated into endogenous growth models to permit countries to enjoy increasing returns. Given this, the prospect that FDI is linked with training and on-the-job learning for domestic workers is particularly encouraging. Fosfuri et al. (2000) note that the fact that MNEs undertake substantial efforts in the education of local workers has been documented in many instances (e.g. ILO, 1981; Lindsey, 1986), and empirical research seems to indicate that MNEs offer more training to technical workers and managers than do local firms (Chen, 1983; Gerschenberg, 1987) (p. 206).

The possibility of spillovers is magnified when affiliate employees move to domestic firms or set up their own enterprises. Katz (1987) observes that managers of domestic firms in Latin America often started their careers and were trained in foreign affiliates. Aitken et al. (1996) investigate the possibility of human capital spillovers in Mexico, Venezuela, and the US by estimating the effect of foreign ownership on wages. They find for all three countries that FDI is associated with higher wages, but in Mexico and Venezuela higher wages were only found for foreign firms. This implies that

FDI does improve the human capital of domestic workers employed by foreign affiliates, but there is no evidence of human capital spillovers to workers of domestic firms.

5.4.4 Export Spillovers

There is a rich history of research on the export-led growth hypothesis. More recently, a number of papers have considered the prospect that involvement in exporting increases a firm's productivity.[21] Given that exports also secure foreign currency for the exporting nation, the prospect that FDI may enhance the ability of domestic firms to export has received significant attention. Multinationals have an obvious advantage over domestic firms when it comes to knowledge and experience of exporting. It is not difficult to imagine that some of this expertise may spill over from foreign affiliates to domestic firms, especially if the affiliate is itself engaged in export activity. Furthermore, if the affiliate is producing for export then it may encourage the formation of export infrastructure (such as transport, warehousing etc.) that can be utilised by domestic firms.

Aitken et al. (1997) employ cross-section firm level data for 1986 and 1989 to study the link between FDI and export spillovers in Mexico. They find that the probability that a domestic plant will export is positively correlated with proximity to multinational affiliates, but unrelated to general exporting activity. They conclude that "foreign-owned enterprises are a natural conduit for information about foreign markets and technology, and a natural channel through which domestic firms can distribute their goods. To the extent that foreign investors directly or indirectly provide information and distribution services, their activities enhance the export prospects of local firms" (p. 25).

5.4.5. Empirical Studies on Productivity Spillovers

As previously mentioned, Mexico has proved a popular area of study, although the most recent empirical studies have focused on other developing countries from Latin America and East Asia. Whilst overall evidence from empirical studies on FDI spillovers is mixed, there is a general consensus amongst the Mexican studies that FDI does lead to beneficial spillovers for domestic firms.

The earliest study of spillovers in Mexico was by Blomstrom and Persson (1983) who related the technical efficiency of Mexican manufacturing industries in 1970 to capital intensity, labour quality, scale of competition, degree of competition, and the presence of foreign affiliates. They found a positive relationship between technical efficiency and foreign presence, which they took as suggesting that 'spillover efficiency benefits' do occur from foreign plants to domestic plants. However, the study does not indicate through what channels these spillovers might take place.

Blomstrom (1986) attempts to remedy this failing by analysing the effects of FDI on the productive efficiency of the industrial structure in Mexico between 1970 and 1975. He does this by constructing an efficiency index, which is a measure of how far the average firm is from the industry frontier, and then running OLS regressions with a foreign share variable as one of the independent variables. In all of the regressions he finds a positive coefficient on the foreign share variable that he interprets as evidence that "MNCs have a positive independent influence on structure, so that industries dominated by foreign firms tend to be more efficient than others in the sense that the average firm is closer to the frontier" (p.105).

Then to investigate the possible channels through which the foreign firms may be contributing to structural efficiency, Blomstrom relates different aspects of structural change between 1970 and 1975 to changes in foreign presence during this same period. He finds that foreign entry is uncorrelated with both changes in the technological frontier and labour productivity in the least efficient plants, but that it is positively related to productivity changes in the industry average. This is interpreted as evidence that spillovers occur not through the transfer of technology but rather through competitive pressure. It may also indicate that FDI encourages the dualistic nature of developing country markets (i.e. foreign firms enter and improve the 'modern' sector of an industry, whilst the 'traditional' sector is unaffected and falls further behind).

Blomstrom and Wolff (1994) investigate the influence of multinationals on productivity convergence between Mexico and the US between 1970 and 1975. They report that "there is strong evidence that the presence of multinational firms acts as a catalyst to the productivity growth in Mexico and that foreign direct investment speeds up the convergence process between Mexico and the United States" (p. 275). Unfortunately, the study is unable to distinguish between the direct effect of FDI and possible indirect (spillover) effects and so it is possible that industry productivity in Mexico is improved simply by the entry of more productive MNE affiliates without any increase in domestic firm productivity.

It is important to note that all the spillover studies discussed above make use of cross-sectional industry-level data. Recently, Görg and Strobl (2001) have argued that use of cross section data may lead to biased results because of the problem of correctly identifying the causation between industry productivity and multinational affiliate entry. They recommend that panel data be used to circumvent this problem. Görg and Greenaway (2002) conduct an exhaustive survey of papers on productivity spillovers (covering a variety of developed, developing, and transition economies) and note that only "two studies using appropriate data and estimation techniques...report positive evidence for aggregate spillovers" (p. 7). The remaining sixteen find either negative or no statistically significant effects.

This would appear quite damning evidence against the positive spillovers found for Mexico. However, it must be realised that none of the studies which found negative or no effects was done for Mexico. As discussed previously, spillovers from FDI are likely to vary with the host economy under consideration. In fact, Kokko (1994) finds that "the technology imports of MNC affiliates seem to be larger in countries and industries where the educational level of the local labour force is higher, where local competition is tougher, and where the host country imposes fewer formal requirements on the affiliates' operations" (p. 280). This combined with the fact that the majority of Mexico's FDI comes from the US may be the actual explanation for why positive spillovers have been consistently found for Mexico, but no statistically significant effects were found for Morocco (Haddad and Harrison, 1993) or Uruguay (Kokko et al., 1996).

Many developing countries, including Mexico, actively compete to attract FDI in the belief that it can contribute not just to the quantity of capital, but also the *quality*. In some instances governments are so eager to attract foreign firms that they will even subsidise the investment.[22] Given this, it is disappointing that there is no consensus in empirical research confirming the existence of beneficial FDI spillovers.

5.5 DOES FDI ENHANCE GROWTH?

The majority of empirical studies investigating the host country effects of FDI focus on labour or output productivity in manufacturing as the variable requiring explanation. We take a different approach here and follow Balasubramanyam et al. (1996) and Carkovic and Levine (2002) in examining directly the growth rate of gross domestic product (GDP) in a model derived from a production function with FDI as an additional input alongside labour and physical capital. As alluded to previously, foreign investment is attractive to host countries specifically because it is believed to embody greater technology and human capital than domestic investment. Given this, it is appropriate that the stock of foreign investment and domestic investment should enter separately in the production function.

In the usual manner we can represent the production function as:

$$Y = g(L, K, F, t) \qquad [5.2]$$

where Y is real GDP, L is labour, K is domestic capital stock, F is foreign capital stock, and t is a time trend capturing technical progress.

Taking [5.2] to be linear in logs and differencing we arrive at the following expression for the growth rate of GDP:

$$y = \alpha + \beta_1 l + \beta_2 k + \beta_3 f \qquad [5.3]$$

where lower case letters denote growth rates and the beta coefficients therefore represent output elasticities.

With regard to measurement of the domestic and foreign capital stock we follow the precedent set by Balasubramanyam et al. (1996) and take the shares of domestic investment and foreign investment in GDP as adequate proxies for the growth rate of the domestic and foreign capital stocks respectively.[23]

Having so far adhered closely to the model and procedure employed in Balasubramanyam et al. (1996), we now depart in terms of the data to be analysed. Whereas Balasubramanyam et al. (1996) employed cross-section data on 46 countries averaged over the period 1970 to 1985, we utilise time series data pertaining to growth and FDI in Mexico from 1970 to 1999. In all instances the data are taken from the World Bank's World Development Indicators 2001.

Table 5.6 presents a selection of the most interesting results. Specification [1] is the regression specified above [5.3], estimated for the entire sample (details of the time trend are not reported). Of the independent variables, only the coefficient on I/Y (the proxy for the growth rate of the domestic capital stock) is statistically significant, with an output elasticity of 0.85 (significantly different from zero at the 1 per cent level).[24] This suggests that for Mexico for the period 1970 to 1999 FDI has not played a role in economic growth (the statistically insignificant coefficient on labour force growth indicates that labour also has been unimportant).

This finding is at odds with previous studies on Mexico cited earlier and also with Balasubramanyam et al. (1996) who report a statically significant, positive effect of FDI on growth (albeit for a cross-section of 46 economies). Fortunately, the work of Balasubramanyam et al. (1996) also hints at a convincing explanation for the finding of Specification [1]. Bhagwati (1978) hypothesised that the volume and efficacy of inward FDI will be dependent on the trade regime pursued by the host nation. Further, he suggested that FDI would be far more beneficial under an export promoting (EP) strategy than under a strategy of import substitution (IS).[25,26] By separating their sample into EP and IS countries, Balasubramanyam et al. (1996) find evidence to suggest that this is indeed the case. As Mexico has undergone a dramatic reorientation of its trade policy during our sample period, we are motivated to explore the possibility that this is masking a positive effect of FDI in our overall sample.

Our initial procedure for classifying our sample into an IS period and an EP period was to perform the CUSUM and CUSUMSQ tests of structural stability. However, even for a range of equation specifications, neither of these tests indicated a structural break. Given our failure to identify a natural break, we chose to divide the sample according to the date given by Sachs and Warner (1995) for the liberalisation of Mexico (1986). Specification [2] for the years 1970 to 1985 is therefore chosen to represent Mexico under an IS regime, and Specification [3] for the years 1980 to 1999 under an EP regime.

Table 5.6 Estimated Regression Equations

Specification	Intercept	FDI/Y	I/Y	l	FDI/Y_{t-2}	adj. R^2	F	Years
1	-16.45*	0.14	0.85***	1.01		0.20	3.46	70-99
	(1.95)	(0.14)	(2.90)	(0.59)			(3.26)	
2	-6.27	7.83	0.25	0.21		0.25	2.63	70-85
	(0.43)	(1.5)	(0.50)	(0.78)			(3.12)	
3	-7.51	-0.71	1.12***	-3.24		0.29	4.17	86-99
	(0.76)	(0.63)	(3.51)	(1.18)			(3.20)	
4	-15.77**		0.88***	0.66	-0.0017	0.22	3.66	70-99
	(2.50)		(2.99)	(0.52)	(0.67)		(3.26)	
5	-20.74		0.83	2.33	-0.0016	0.13	1.72	70-85
	(1.57)		(2.18)	(0.91)	(0.56)		(3.12)	
6	-32.02		0.60	6.05	3.45**	0.33	3.18	86-99
	(1.65)		(0.92)	(1.33)	(2.35)		(3.10)	

Notes: Dependent variable is the growth rate of real GDP. Estimation is by ordinary least squares (OLS). The time trend is not reported. Figures in parentheses are absolute t-ratios. *, **, and *** indicate significance at the 10%, 5%, and 1% levels, respectively.

The variable FDI/Y performs no better in the separate sub-samples. None of the coefficients are statistically significant in [2] and only I/Y is significant in [3] (though we may interpret the larger coefficient on I/Y in [3] as an indication that domestic investment provides a greater inducement to growth under an EP regime).

Another approach to investigating the possible impact of trade orientation was to include an interaction term between FDI/Y and a measure of openness as an additional explanatory variable.[27] If a liberal regime does indeed improve the efficacy of FDI then we should find a positive coefficient on the interaction term. However, the interaction term failed to enter significantly into any of the specifications tested and so the results are not reported here.

Finally, we experimented with varying lag lengths of both the foreign and domestic capital variables.[28] Given that there is often a substantial delay between the moment of entry of FDI and the point at which the foreign operation is 'up-and-running' or at least operating at expected efficiency (especially for initial investments), it does not seem unreasonable to expect that output growth may lag behind growth of the foreign capital stock.[29] While all lagged variables of domestic capital performed poorly, a two-period lag of foreign investment proved to be statistically significant in the EP sample [6]. What is more, the coefficient was economically highly significant, implying an output elasticity of FDI/Y of 3.45 for the period since liberalisation. This is far greater in magnitude than the coefficient achieved on I/Y under any of the specifications tried (both those reported and not reported), and suggests that (subject to a short lag) FDI has significantly contributed to output growth in Mexico since 1986.

Obviously the evidence supporting the beneficial growth effects of FDI in Mexico is not as strong as one might have expected. Without introducing lagged values of the variable, FDI/Y appears to exert no influence on growth. However, there is some evidence that, in the presence of an appropriate host environment (e.g. the increasingly liberal regime found in Mexico post-1986), FDI is a vital contributor to economic growth. This is encouraging news for Mexico, considering that it continues to attract increasing inflows of FDI and is consolidating its policies of liberalisation through the ongoing demands of NAFTA and negotiation of various bilateral treaties with countries such as the UK.

5.6 POLICY PROPOSALS

Many developing countries offer generous incentives to try to attract FDI in the belief that it offers a great social return. Given this, it is of great concern that the existence of positive spillovers, as supported by early cross-section studies, has been cast into doubt by recent empirical work. Many of these early studies focused on Mexico and we must investigate the cause of these empirical discrepancies. Though there is a suggestion (Görg and Strobl, 2001; Görg and Greenaway, 2002) that cross-section approaches lead to biased results, there are currently no panel data studies for Mexico. Until this is the case it is difficult to take a firm position either way. What should help support the view that there are spillovers in the case of Mexico, however, is the fact that around 60 per cent of Mexico's inward FDI comes from the world's most technologically advanced nation. Subject to some evidence that spillovers may be reduced if the technology gap is too large (Kokko, 1994, 1996), this suggests that the potential is there for Mexico to reap benefits from FDI.

How can Mexico ensure that it maximises the potential spillovers from FDI? As Caves (1999) observes, no systematic theory has emerged in the development literature to address this issue. This is a major failing that deserves investigation. Lacking sound micro-management policies on how to maximise spillovers, we are left to recommend broader macro objectives aimed at improving a country's 'absorptive capacity'. These include investment in human capital, physical and financial infrastructure development, and openness.

The advantage of 'investing' in 'absorptive capacity' is that it also attracts FDI. Indeed, in an ideal world there would be no competition for FDI (in terms of tax concessions etc.), rather multinationals would be left to choose investment locations based purely on efficiency and competitive advantage considerations. This would ensure the maximum social return for investment in a global sense and would limit MNEs' ability to privately capture the benefits of FDI. Despite this not being the case, and evidence that lower corporate tax rates do attract FDI (Hanson, 2001), we recommend that Mexico discontinue any attempts to 'artificially' attract FDI and instead focus on offering a favourable economic environment (e.g. high growth, educated labour force, good infrastructure etc.). By providing a 'distortion-free' environment Mexico would enjoy the greatest opportunity to benefit from FDI spillovers.[30]

Furthermore, given its geographical proximity to the US, Mexico need not fear loss of FDI flows. The formation of NAFTA has legitimised the liberalisation policies adopted by Mexico in the mid-eighties and appears to be attracting considerable non-member FDI intent on penetrating the US market. As the domestic Mexican market continues to grow and becomes more 'Americanised' it will attract more FDI in its own right.[31] Hopefully, this will allow it to move away from maquiladora-type operations to activities which add more value and provide greater opportunity for spillovers[32].

Ending on a note of caution, recent research suggests that FDI may result in undesirable spatial effects and inequality.[33] The costs of these are well documented and this issue deserves serious consideration. Although the Mexican government has implemented policies to try and attract FDI and maquiladora investment into the southern regions, economic factors (including transport costs and agglomeration economies) dictate that foreign investment will continue to be concentrated primarily along the US-Mexico border and near Mexico City. Future integration among the Southern Hemisphere economies may serve to revitalise the south of Mexico, but the effects of any such regional integration agreement (RIA) are hard to predict with much certainty.

Foreign direct investment, particularly with reference to developing economies, is a subject that will continue to attract a great deal of attention, and rightly so. Issues concerning the scope of FDI to confer spillover benefits on the host nation and how these benefits can best be realised are still far from resolved. The potential spatial effects of FDI also warrant further investigation. Regrettably, as is so often the case in economics, we are at the mercy of the available data.

NOTES

1. Between 1930 and 1970 the share of manufacturing in Mexican GDP grew from 12.9% to 23.3%, and Mexico City's share of manufacturing employment grew from 19.0% to 47.3% (Hanson, 1998).
2. In 1985 import licenses covered 92.2% of national production, the average tariff was 23.5%, and 85.0% of non-petroleum exports were covered by export controls. By 1987 export controls had been abolished, import licenses covered only 25.5% of national production, and the average tariff was down to 11.8% (Hanson, 1997).
3. Note that the apparent drop in stock in 1982 is due to a recalibration of the data by the US Department of Commerce and not an actual withdrawal of foreign investors (Graham and Wada, 2000).
4. Furthermore, despite the primacy of US activity in the Mexican economy, the relative size of Mexico somewhat precludes dramatic effects on the US and Canada.
5. Table 5.2 may more satisfactorily be depicted as a continuum in both environmental change and locational advantages, in which case we would argue that Mexico may be more properly located in the west of the diagram (as opposed to the northwest as suggested by Blomstrom and Kokko, 1997).
6. Concerning accuracy, it is interesting to note that the Instituto Nacional de Estadistica reports US inward FDI for 1999 as US$ 6635m, whereas the US Department of Commerce reports only US$ 5084m. This discrepancy is likely due to the fact that the Instituto records planned or announced FDI, but the Department of Commerce only records FDI that has actually taken place. This example serves to emphasise the importance of verifying investment data when and where possible, and offers an indication of the potential data problems that plague empirical studies.
7. Maquiladoras are subject to tax only on the value added of their activities. They import most of their intermediate imports from abroad and export virtually all of their output (until 1988 they were required by law to export 100% of their output). The vast majority of maquiladoras produce electronic equipment, clothing, plastics, furniture, electrical appliances, or auto parts.
8. In addition, US investment in maquiladoras was 87% of total world FDI in maquiladoras and around 80% of maquila output is shipped to the US.
9. US investment in ***maquiladoras*** is aimed at outsourcing low-skilled production tasks to take advantage of the lower unit labour costs in Mexico. However, these tasks which are viewed as low skilled to US firms are in fact relatively high skilled in terms of the skills and training of the Mexican workforce. In this manner, US FDI in Mexico can cause an increase in the relative demand for (relatively) skilled labour in both countries simultaneously.
10. For example, Lehmann (1999) investigates the role of country risk, Traxler and Woitech (2000) consider labour market regimes, Schoeman et al. (2000) analyse fiscal policy, List and

Co (2000) study environmental policy, Sung and Lapan (2000) assess exchange rate volatility.

11. MOFAs are those subsidiaries in which the US parent has a stake of 50% or more. As data for these firms are considerably more comprehensive than those for all affiliates (and given that the US Department of Commerce benchmark studies indicate that MOFAs typically represent approximately two thirds of overall US investment in Mexico) the authors opted to focus on these affiliates only.

12. The lagged stock of US FDI in Mexico is included as a fourth explanatory variable because "in any given period, actual and desired foreign capital stocks are unlikely to be equal as a result of adjustment costs and operating lags [so] flows of foreign direct investment will therefore be a lagged function of the difference between actual and desired capital stocks in previous periods." (p. 209/10)

13. Unfortunately, the availability of ULC data restricted our analysis to the years 1982-96.

14. While it is common practice in the literature to use a log-linear specification, a number of observations with negative FDI flows (indicating net disinvestment in that particular year) precluded this possibility.

15. IND_iY and y_i are intended to capture the 'push' effects on FDI and y_j the 'pull' effect. This is similar to the standard 'gravity model' which has proved empirically very successful at accounting for a whole range of factor flows.

16. In order to increase the number of observations available we also experimented with the inclusion of data for US FDI into Canada. However, this failed to meaningfully alter the results and β_2 remained the only significant coefficient.

17. Note that our regression specification assumes that all FDI in a given Mexican industry comes from US firms in that same industry. However, this may not be too unrealistic at the two-digit level.

18. See Findlay (1978) and Wang and Blomstrom (1992).

19. Although entry by a similar sized domestic firm would also increase competitive pressure, the fact that foreign affiliates are generally more efficient that domestic firms (Blomstrom and Wolff, 1994) leads us to expect that FDI will lead to greater and more beneficial competitive pressure than the equivalent domestic investment.

20. For example, the Cecchini Report on the benefits of completing the European Single Market identified competition effects as the primary source of gain (Görg and Greenaway, 2002).

21. See Bernard and Jensen (1999), Bernard and Wagner (1997), and Girma et al. (2002).

22. For instance, Head (1998) claims that the state government of Alabama paid the equivalent of $150,000 per employee to entice Mercedes to locate its new plant in the state.

23. In doing this Balasubramanyam et al. (1996) were themselves following "the precedent set in numerous previous studies by approximating the rate of growth of the capital stock by the share of investment in GDP" (p. 98). See, for example, Mankiw et al. (1992).

24. An alternative interpretation of the coefficient is that a one per cent increase in the growth rate of the domestic capital stock will engender a 0.85% increase in output growth, *ceterus paribus*.

25. The reasoning for this being that an EP strategy offers a distortion-free environment, whereas an IS strategy offers artificial and transitory incentives. So FDI will locate in an EP environment based purely on efficiency considerations, but tax and other such incentives in an IS environment may encourage FDI to locate in sub-optimal locations.

26. Bhagwati (1978) also hypothesised that the volume of FDI would be greater under an EP regime. Balasubramanyam and Salisu (1991) offer evidence supporting this contention.

27. The openness variable was defined as (imports+exports/GDP).

28. Note, we also experimented with the inclusion of year dummies for 1982, 1983, 1984, 1994, and 1995 (to try and account for periods of crisis in Mexico during our sample period) and with a variable measuring export growth (acknowledging the vast literature on the export-led growth hypothesis). The inclusion of these did not change the results on our variables of interest (although the dummies 1982, 1983, and 1994 were negative and statistically significant and the export variable entered significantly and positively in some specifications). Results available on request.

29. Anecdotal evidence in Hanson (2001) of investments by General Motors and Ford in Brazil would seem to support this assumption.

30. Furthermore, there is evidence (Love and Lage-Hidalgo, 1999a) that Mexico and Canada do not compete for US investment (i.e. increased US investment in Canada will not lead to decreased investment in Mexico).

31. Using Hofstede's four dimensions of national culture (power distance, uncertainty avoidance, individuality, and masculinity) Kogut and Singh (1998) estimate the 'cultural distance' between the US and Mexico as 3.13 (compared with 0.08 for the UK, 0.11 for Canada, 1.63 for India, and 3.60 for China).

32. Despite a pervasive view in the popular press that maquiladoras are little more than 'sweatshops' employing young female labour (Feenstra and Hanson, 1997), Silver (2002) reports that each maquiladora job indirectly supports 3.5 more jobs at suppliers, transport companies and other service providers.

33. Given that the top 20% of earners account for 55% of the income in Mexico (CIA World Factbook, 2001), inequality is already a serious issue that needs no exacerbation.

References

Abramovitz, M. (1986), 'Catching Up, Forging Ahead, and Falling Behind', *Journal of Economic History*, 46, 385-406.

Aitken, B., G. Hanson and A. Harrison (1997), 'Spillovers, Foreign Investment and Export Behaviour', *Journal of International Economics*, 43, 103-132.

Aitken, H., A. Harrison and R. Lipsey (1996), 'Wages and Foreign Ownership: A Comparative Study of Mexico, Venezuela and the United States', *Journal of International Economics*, 40, 345-371.

Balasubramanyam, V.N. and M. Salisu (1991), 'EP, IS and Direct Foreign Investment in LDCs', in *International Trade and Global Development* (eds. Koekkoek, A. and L.B.M. Mennes), London, Routledge.

Balasubramanyam, V.N., M. Salisu, and D. Sapsford (1996), 'Foreign Direct Investment and Growth in EP and IS Countries', *Economic Journal*, 106(434), 92-105.

Bernard, A.B. and J.B. Jensen (1999), 'Exceptional Exporter Performance: Cause, Effect, or Both?' *Journal of International Economics*, 47, 1-25.

Bernard, A.B. and Joachim Wagner (1997), 'Exports and Success in German Manufacturing', *Weltwirtschaftliches Archiv*, 133, 134-157.

Bhagwati, J. N. (1978), *Anatomy and Consequences of Exchange Control Regimes*, Balinger Publishing, New York.

Blomstrom, M. (1986), 'Foreign Investment and Productive Efficiency: The Case of Mexico', *Journal of Industrial Economics*, 35, 97-110.

Blomstrom, M. and A. Kokko (1997), 'Regional Integration and Foreign Direct Investment', NBER Working Paper 6019.

Blomstrom, M. and A. Kokko (1998), 'Multinational Corporations and Spillovers', *Journal of Economic Surveys*, 12, 247-277.

Blomstrom, M. and H. Persson (1983), 'Foreign Investment and Spillover Efficiency in an Underdeveloped Economy: Evidence from Mexican Manufacturing Industry', *World Development*, 11, 493-501.

Blomstrom, M. and N. Wolff (1994), 'Multinational Corporations and Productivity Convergence in Mexico', in Baumol, W., R. Nelson, and N. Wolff (eds.), *Convergence of Productivity: Cross National Studies and Historical Evidence*, Oxford, Oxford University Press.

Buckley P.J. and M. Casson (1991), *The Future of the Multinational Enterprise*, MacMillan, London.

Carkovic, M. and R. Levine (2002), 'Does Foreign Direct Investment Accelerate Economic Growth?' University of Minnesota Working Paper.

Caves, R. (1999), 'Spillovers from Multinationals in Developing Countries: the Mechanisms at Work', *University of Michigan*, Working Paper 247.

Chen E.K.Y. (1983), *Multinational Corporations, Technology and Employment*, London: Macmillan.

Dunning, J. H. (1988), *Explaining international production*, Unwin Hyman/ Harper Collins, London.

Feenstra, R. and G. Hanson (1997), 'Foreign Direct Investment and Relative Wages: Evidence from Mexico's Maquiladoras', *Journal of International Economics*, 42, 371-393.

Findlay, R. (1978), 'Relative Backwardness, Direct Foreign Investment, and the Transfer of Technology', *Quarterly Journal of Economics*, 92, 1-16.

Fosfuri, A., M. Motta, and T. Ronde (2000), 'Foreign Direct Investments and Spillovers Through Workers' Mobility', Economics Working Papers 258, Universitat Pompeu Fabra.

Gerber, J. (2001), 'The Structure of US Outward Foreign Direct Investment in Mexico's Export Processing Industry', paper prepared for *International Conference Latin American Studies*, July.

Gerschenberg, I. (1987), 'The Training and Spread of Managerial Know-How. A Comparative Analysis of Multinationals and Other Firms in Kenya', *World Development*, 15, 931-939.

Girma, S., D. Greenaway and R. Kneller (2002), 'Does Exporting Lead to Better Performance? A Microeconometric Analysis of Matched Firms', GEP Research Paper 02/09, University of Nottingham.

Glass, A. and K. Saggi (2001), 'Innovation Incentives and Wage Effects of International Outsourcing', *European Economic Review*, 45, 67-86.

Globerman, S. and R. Schwindt (1996), 'International Trade Agreements and Foreign Direct Investment in the Agri-Industrial Sector', report prepared for *Agriculture and Agri-Food Canada*, mimeo, May.

Görg , H. and D. Greenaway (2002), 'Much Ado About Nothing? Do Domestic Firms Really Benefit from Foreign Direct Investment?' Leverhulme Centre for Research on Globalisation and Economic Policy.

Görg, H. and E. Strobl (2001), 'Multinational Companies and Productivity Spillovers: A Meta-Analysis with a Test for Publication Bias', *Economic Journal*, 111(475), F723-F739.

Graham, E. and E. Wada (2000), 'Domestic Reform, Trade and Investment, Financial Crisis, and Foreign Direct Investment into Mexico', *The World Economy*, 23(6), 777-797.

Grosse, R. and D. Thomas (2001), 'Country-of-Origin Determinants of Foreign Direct Investment in an Emerging Market: the Case of Mexico', *Journal of International Management*, 7, 59-79.

Hanson, G. (1996), 'US-Mexico Integration and Regional Economies: Evidence from Border-City Pairs', NBER Working Paper 5425.

Hanson, G. (1997), 'Increasing Returns, Trade, and the Regional Structure of Wages', *Economic Journal*, 107, 113-133.

Hanson, G. (1998), 'North American Economic Integration and Industry Location', NBER Working Paper 6587.

Hanson, G. (2001), 'Should Countries Promote Foreign Direct Investment', G-24 Discussion Paper Series No. 9.

Harrison, Anne E. and M. Haddad (1993), 'Are there Positive Spillovers from Direct Foreign Investment? Evidence from Panel Data for Morocco', *Journal of Development Economics*, 42, 51-74

Head, Keith (1998), 'Comment on Doms and Jensen', In Robert Baldwin, Robert Lipsey, and J. David Richardson (eds.), *Geography and Ownership as Bases for Economic Accounting*, The University of Chicago Press, Chicago.

Helpman, E. and P. Krugman (1985), *Market Structures and Foreign Trade*, MIT Press, Cambridge.

International Labour Organization (1981), *Multinationals Training Practices and Development*, Geneva.

Katz, Jorge M. (1987), *Technology Creation in Latin American Manufacturing Industries*, New York: St. Martin's Press.

Kogut, B. and H. Singh (1998), 'The Effects of National Culture on the Choice of Entry Mode', *Journal of International Business Studies*, 19, 411-432.

Kokko, A. (1994), 'Technology, Market Characteristics, and Spillovers', *Journal of Development Economics*, 43, 279-293.

Kokko, A., R. Tasini and M. Zejan (1996), 'Local Technological Capability and Productivity Spillovers from FDI in the Uruguayan Manufacturing Sector', *Journal of Development Studies*, 32, 602-611.

Lehmann, A. (1999), 'Country Risks and the Investment Activity of U.S. Multinationals in Developing Countries', IMF Working Paper 99/13, Washington, DC: International Monetary Fund.

Lindsey, C.W. (1986), 'Transfer of Technology to the ASEAN Region by US Transnational Corporations', *ASEAN Economic Bulletin*, 3, 225-247.

List, J.A. and C.Y. Co (2000), 'The Effects of Environmental Regulations on Foreign Direct Investment', *Journal of Environmental Economics and Management*, 40, 1-20.

Love, J. and F. Lage-Hidalgo (1999a), 'Is There Competition for US Direct Investment? A Perspective on NAFTA', *The World Economy*, 22, 207-221.

Love, J. and F. Lage-Hidalgo (1999b), 'The Ownership Advantage in Latin American FDI: A Sectoral Study of US Direct Investment in Mexico', *Journal of Development Studies*, 35, 76-95.

Love, J. and F. Lage-Hidalgo (2000), 'Analysing the Determinants of US Direct Investment in Mexico', *Applied Economics Letters*, 32, 1259-1267.

Kokko, A. (1996), 'Productivity Spillovers from Competition Between Local Firms and Foreign Affiliates', *Journal of International Development*, 8, 517-530.

Mankiw, G., D. Romer and D. Weil (1992), 'A Contribution to the Empirics of Economic Growth', *Quarterly Journal of Economics*, 107, 407-437.

Romer, P. (1993), 'Idea Gaps and Object Gaps in Economic Development', *Journal of Monetary Economics*, 32, 543-73.

Sachs, J. and A. Warner (1995), 'Economic Reform and the Process of Global Integration', *Brookings Papers on Economic Activity*, 1, 1-118.

Schoeman, N.J., Z.C. Robinson and T.J. de-Wet (2000), 'Foreign Direct Investment Flows and Fiscal Discipline in South Africa', *South African Journal of Economic and Management Sciences*, 3(2), 235-44.

Silver, S. (2002), *Financial Times*, February 11.

Sung, H. and Lapan, H. (2000), 'Strategic Foreign Direct Investment and Exchange Rate Uncertainty', *International Economic Review*, 41, 411-423.

Traxler, F. and Woitech, B. (2000), 'Transnational Investment and National Labour Market Regimes : A Case of 'Regime Shopping'?' *European Journal of Industrial Relations*, 6, 141-160.

Wang, J.Y. and Blomstrom, M. (1992), 'Foreign Investment and Technology Transfer: A Simple Model', *European Economic Review*, 36, 137-155.

COMMENTS

Frederik Sjöholm

David Griffiths and David Sapsford have written a very useful paper on an important topic. The paper is informative, interesting, and reveals with clarity the nature of FDI inflows to Mexico and its economic impact. Mexico is of special interest for studies on inflows of FDI for a number of reasons. Most importantly, Mexico has undergone a deeper trade liberalisation and integration with the world economy than perhaps any other country since the mid-1980s. It is of course of great interest to examine how this change in economic policy has affected the volume and nature of inward FDI. In addition, Mexico's position next to the US, and its membership of NAFTA in 1994, is likely to have an impact on FDI. If Mexico found it difficult to attract FDI, this would certainly cast large doubts on the potential for economic development through inflows of FDI, a development approach that has become increasingly popular throughout the world in recent decades.

The authors find FDI inflows to have been very high since the 1980s, with a gradual move away from the service industry and with an increased focus on manufacturing. The main boom in FDI inflows came before Mexico's membership of NAFTA, but increased further after 1994. Not surprisingly, FDI from the US dominates. However, it seems that FDI from other countries has become increasingly important and the US share has actually decreased over time. Unfortunately, the authors only provide figures until 1994 which prevents a more detailed analysis of why the US share has declined. One plausible reason is that other countries are increasingly selling to the US market from Mexican plants.

The authors continue with an analysis of the determinants of US FDI to Mexico. Ownership advantages, in the form of superior technology, together with Mexican location advantages, seem to explain the bulk of FDI. It should be noted that the result that both low wages and high incomes in Mexico are important determinants is slightly contradictory.

The authors discuss, at some length, the presence of spillovers from foreign owned firms to domestically owned ones. In recent years, there is a focus on spillovers from FDI and one sometimes gets the impression that if and only if such spillovers exist, governments should encourage inflows of FDI. This is in my view not correct and I would like to stress that FDI might benefit a host country through several mechanisms other than spillovers, such as increased tax revenues, employment and exports.

Spillovers of different types seem to be present in Mexico; domestic firms in sectors or regions with a large number of foreign firms tend to have high levels of productivity and high exports. Together with the finding that foreign firms have been important in generating employment and exports, it seems obvious that FDI has had a positive impact on Mexico's economic growth. It is, therefore, surprising that the authors do not find such an effect in their econometric analysis, although they suggest that FDI might have increased growth during the period of outward economic policy. I am inclined to believe that the lack of evidence of a positive growth effect from inward FDI is caused by various econometric difficulties. For instance, time-series analysis with 30 observations or fewer, are likely to produce statistically insignificant coefficients, and the estimates are also likely to suffer from causality problems. Moreover, whereas the economic literature has identified a number of variables to be important for economic growth, the authors restrict their analysis to employment, private-, and foreign investments. Perhaps the most severe problem is that this analysis is likely to understate the effect of FDI since it does not capture the effect of FDI on employment or on local firms' investments. For instance, the authors mention in the paper that FDI has been of importance in generating employment. This increased employment will positively affect economic growth but the effect is not captured in the econometric estimation since employment is controlled for. Accordingly, they suggest that FDI has been important in increasing competitive pressures in Mexico, which might spur investments by domestic firms and thereby increase economic growth.

The issue of FDI and regional development is of considerable interest considering the regional tensions that sometimes plague Mexico. FDI tends to increase economic concentration. Foreign firms establish themselves in Mexico for two reasons: to gain access to the domestic market and/or to access favourable production sites. FDI driven by market considerations is likely to locate as close to the centre of the market as possible. In other words, FDI focused on supplying the Mexican market with goods or services will minimize transport costs by being close to areas with large (and wealthy) populations. In the case of Mexico this will be around Mexico City. The second reason for FDI, localization centred on production advantages, is less obvious. It is likely, however, that foreign firms will try to minimise transport costs by locating close to the US border. As a consequence, FDI will tend to locate in the north of Mexico. This is what has happened in the last 20 years, which has hurt the traditionally poor part of Mexico – the south. The economic divide between the north and the south has therefore increased during the outward economic orientation of Mexico. In addition, the oil producing southern provinces of Campeche and Tabasco have seen their relative GDP also lowered because of declining oil prices. In the wealthier north, trade liberalisation and inflows of FDI have diminished the previous domination by Mexico City through a shift of manufacturing to the provinces bordering the US. The reason is, of course, that Mexico City is not an ideal entry or exit point for international trade.

To sum up, FDI inflows to Mexico have been substantial and they have been spurred by a liberalisation of the trade and FDI regime in the 1980s as well as from integration with its wealthier northern neighbours through NAFTA. It seems that the inflow of FDI has benefited Mexico in terms of employment growth, increased exports, and technological spillovers to domestically owned firms. Economic liberalisation can be pursued by other countries. This, in fact, has been the case in recent years. The outcome might not necessarily be as positive as in the case of Mexico. The reason is Mexico's fortunate location close the US. For Mexico, the future development challenge is to make further use of the location advantage and try to encourage an upgrading of production away from simple assembling to production with an advanced knowledge and technology content. This is an issue for future studies to examine, studies which will benefit from this well written paper on FDI inflows to Mexico.

DISCUSSION

John Dunning noted that the World Investment Report does publish data on stocks and flows of FDI in Mexico dating back to 1984. In the context of the growing significance of non-US sources of FDI in Mexico, the gateway to the US that Mexico has provided for European and Japanese investors, especially for the efficiency seeking type of FDI, is important. Indeed, firms from the developing world may also have entered Mexico to export to the US. This could be incorporated into the statistical analysis of determinants of FDI in Mexico.

Balasubramanyam elaborating Dunning's point noted that the rules of origin of components imposed on non-US investors may have induced Japanese and other non-US firms to source components within Mexico and enhanced growth effects of FDI. This may be well worth discussing, for a tariff on imports from non-US sources may lead to increased FDI into Mexico and may have a larger impact on growth than US investments because of the rules of origin relating to components. FDI into Mexico had begun to increase before it became a member of NAFTA. This was so in the EU also, intra-regional FDI increased with the announcement of the intention to form a Single European Market.

Yasheng Huang drew attention to the fact that in the US when the intention to formulate NAFTA was announced there were doubts whether it would succeed because of political factors. One may recall that during the late eighties worldwide flows of FDI increased, and Mexico may have shared in the increased flows. The specific Mexico factor, i.e. NAFTA, might have come into play only after 1994. It is also possible that after NAFTA domestic investments in Mexico increased because of improved access to credit and therefore the ratio of FDI to domestic investment might not have changed. Both domestic and foreign investments might have increased after NAFTA. Another factor is that Mexico undertook capital market reforms and stabilisation policies; this might have attracted more FDI. Some of this was portfolio investment but classified as FDI because it exceeded the 10 per cent threshold of equity owned by specific firms, which is then registered as FDI.

John Dunning agreed that FDI flows during the early 1990s increased but this was mostly due to M&As between firms of developed countries, the developing countries did not experience all that much of an increase in FDI flows. It is interesting that in 2001 FDI fell dramatically because there was a dramatic fall in M&A activity. And the share of FDI going to developing countries increased, and some countries such as China have maintained this growth in inflows of FDI.

Nicholas Snowden was of the view that it is possible that increased flows of FDI and portfolio capital into Mexico may have led to an appreciation of the real exchange rate and hence a decline in exports. In fact, during the late eighties and early nineties the real exchange rate did appreciate and one would expect capital inflows to have a suppressing effect on overall exports. It is a part of the capital transfer mechanism.

Balasubramanyam was of the view that as much of American investments in Mexico is in the export processing zones (EPZs) and such investments, which are mostly in assembly operations, may have very few spillover effects. And with the formation of NAFTA capital from America had moved to Mexican labour. Does this have relatively higher welfare effects than when Mexican labour goes to capital in America and repatriates funds back home? This observation led to a discussion on illegal and legal immigration and the size of repatriated earnings by Mexicans.

Peter Buckley remarked that the comment that EPZs had low spillover effects was an assertion and there was evidence to show that in China low-tech foreign investments from Hong Kong and Taiwan had substantial spillover effects. Was there any evidence of such spillovers from FDI in Mexican EPZs?

David Griffiths observed that there was some evidence that FDI in EPZs did lead to multiple job creation through backward linkages but he was not aware of evidence on spillovers.

Yasheng Huang expressed the view that there was not much evidence of spillovers from FDI in EPZs in China. In any case if such investments are providing only a low level of technology, why rely on FDI for such technologies? Why not resort to licensing agreements and other forms of contractual arrangements? Huang also argued that both domestic exporters and foreign exporters usually tend to invest in the same geographical location or region. Such cluster formation may result in technology spillovers. Here geography is important, more important than the hypothesis which says that if a domestic firm is located nearby a foreign firm, spillovers are likely to be high.

David Sapsford replying to the issues raised by the discussant and others thanked Frederik Sjöholm for his comments. He agreed with most of Sjöholm's comments. He accepted the statistical data limitations in the paper, but had used the most comprehensive data available – one of the strengths and one of the weaknesses of these types of studies. The special relationship between Mexico and US makes this case study interesting. Also we can look at what has happened to FDI from other sources. The drop in US flows appears to have been compensated for by other sources.

David Sapsford elaborated on two of the issues raised in the discussion. One of them is the general regional issue. On the Mexico–US relationship his view was that it is not about Mexico as a whole but it is about those areas that lie along the US border. One of the results reported in the paper, a surprising one, is the weakness of the growth effects of FDI on the Mexican economy. One possible reason for the general weakness of the growth effects is that we are looking at the issue much too broadly, the extent of spillover effects from the border areas to the rest of Mexico may be limited. It is, however, possible, if one looked at regional growth in relevant areas of Mexico growth might be heavily influenced by FDI. What we are picking up is a lack of spillovers within the Mexican economy from regions where FDI is located to other regions. This may be due to factor market imperfections and infrastructural problems. The regional dimension is something to be looked at in some detail.

The second issue is related to the competitive effects in the domestic economy which are underestimated. How do you quantify competitive conditions in the relevant economy? We can't proxy it by concentration ratios as in the case of developed economies; such data are not available for developing countries. Sapsford acknowledged the econometric problems, especially the small size of the sample.

FDI and inequality issues are important. We need to look into this in detail taking the geographer's perspective rather than a pure economist's perspective.

Sapsford reaffirmed the findings relating to spillover effects. Spillovers are not automatic; effective spillovers need certain preconditions such as infrastructure facilities and absorptive capacity and the technology gap between domestic and foreign firms shouldn't be too large.

6. Foreign Direct Investment in Ireland

Frances Ruane[1]

6.1 INTRODUCTION

Using any of the standard indicators, such as net output, exports, and employment, Ireland's economic performance during the 1990s was exceptional in EU and even world terms. This performance, following so rapidly during a period when Ireland's economic prospects were viewed as being very grim,[2] inevitably generated considerable interest among policy makers across a range of countries[3] and a growing economics literature.[4] Furthermore, in the context of preparing Ireland's National Development Plan 2000-2006, further substantial analyses have been produced, both for and by the government (see, in particular, the National Development Plan (2000) and the key analysis underlying it by the Economic and Social Research Institute (Fitz Gerald et al., 1999). Leaving aside the more official publications, the academic literature has sought to explain what has happened and how it could have happened so quickly and what would happen if the economy were to slow down as it is now beginning to do. In terms of *what has happened*, some authors have been quite sceptical, seeing the aggregate figures as representing more of a mirage than a miracle (e.g., Murphy, 1998; O'Sullivan, 2000). Others have suggested that what has happened has merely been a "catch up" – in other words that the 1990s simply made up for the disastrous 1980s when Ireland should have achieved greater convergence towards European living standards (see Gray, 1997; Braunerhjelm et al., 2000). Figure 6.1, which shows five-yearly growth rates for Ireland and the EU over a thirty-year period, can be interpreted as supporting this view. It shows that the average growth rate over the 30 years, while significantly higher than the EU average for the period, is markedly higher in the past decade. Others see the data as indicating that considerable structural change has actually occurred and concentrate on attempting to understand *how it could have happened so quickly*, by attempting to identify the causes of the sudden and rapid growth (e.g., Barry, 1999; MacSharry and White, 2000; Duffy et al., 2001). In this context, they focus on the recent growth in employment and the inter-sectoral reallocation of labour out of agriculture and into industry and market services, as shown in Figure 6.2, and the intra-manufacturing reallocation, out of traditional manufacturing and into high-technology sectors, as shown in Figure 6.3. An interesting attempt (Gray, 1997) to have some of the world's leading economists explain the phenomenal growth rates served to confirm that local economists and policy makers in Ireland seemed to have identified the key issues correctly as (a) improved domestic macro policies based on national social partnership (government/employers/unions) agreements and supported by EU structural and cohesion funds, (b) trends towards globalisation which reduced the effective costs of Ireland's geographic peripherality and improved its terms of trade,[5] (c) European integration which, supported by Irish industrial policies, enhanced the attractiveness of Ireland as a base for foreign direct investment (FDI) in both traded goods and services,[6] and (d) an improved labour force, reflecting the benefits of investments in the education and training systems over three decades.[7] All commentators would agree that these factors interacted positively in generating growth and bringing about structural adjustment in the economy.

In this paper, I will examine the role of FDI in Ireland's growth process. While I emphasise the more recent decade both because of the dramatic changes which have taken place and because of better data coverage, I will outline the industrial policy context in which FDI has grown, both in terms of the objectives of that policy and how the policy regarding the promotion of FDI has been pursued in practice. I will concentrate on the manufacturing sector (which exceptionally in Ireland has been growing at a substantial rate in recent times, primarily because of FDI), as data on services and consequently research on services is much more limited.[8] I will examine the issues under discussion regarding FDI in Ireland at present, in a changed EU environment and how policies are evolving in this context. The paper concludes with a discussion of which, if any, parts of Ireland's strategy are relevant to other countries.

6.2 IRELAND'S TRADITIONAL INDUSTRIAL POLICY OBJECTIVES

Perhaps of all EU countries, the Republic of Ireland has been the most pro-active in fostering economic development using industrial-policy type tools in an increasingly free-trade environment, and the promotion of FDI has played a central role in this process for over four decades. Since the late 1950s, Ireland's economic development strategy has focused on employment creation and has been characterised by actively promoting:

Figure 6.1 Comparison of Irish and EU Growth Rates, 1970-2000

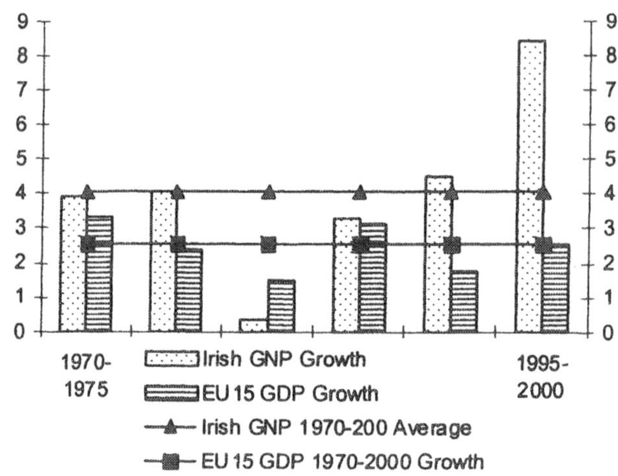

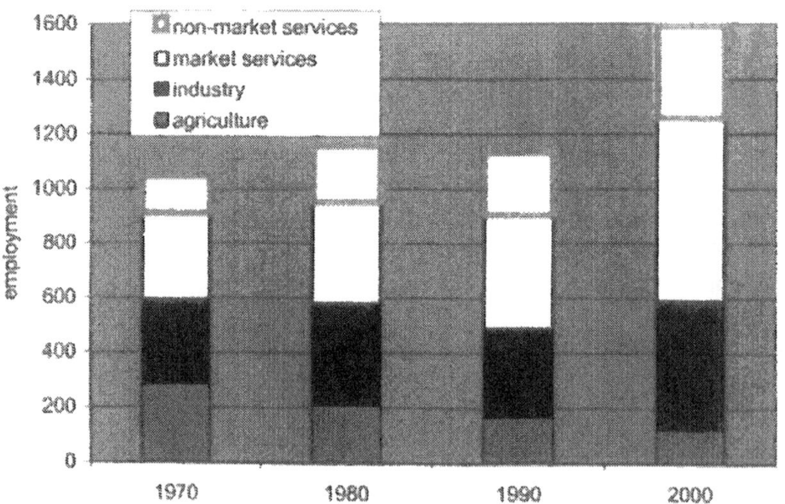

Figure 6.3 Sectoral Employment Shares in Manufacturing (Absolute Figures)

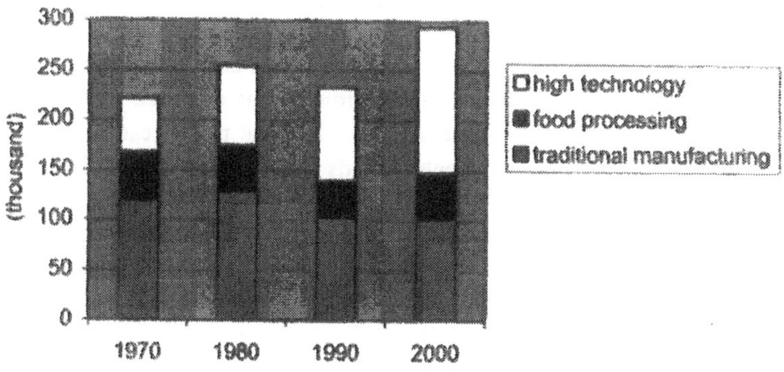

- the development of a modern export-led-growth manufacturing sector (and latterly internationally traded services) through financial and fiscal supports,
- new greenfield investments by foreign companies in the manufacturing and internationally traded service sectors, producing output specifically for export markets,
- the establishment of upstream linkages between foreign and indigenous companies,[9]
- the deliberate creation of industrial clusters by foreign and indigenous companies in certain sub-sectors of manufacturing and internationally traded services, and
- a pattern of economic development that would bring private sector investment to the less-developed (Western) areas of the country.[10]

Effectively Ireland's industrial development strategy was driven by the need to create employment, in order to reduce historically high rates of unemployment and net out-migration.[11] This focus on employment has been key to the consensus across all parties (political groups, trade unions, employers groups, public servants) that inward FDI should be actively promoted and encouraged. Thus the strategy has centred on using industrial incentives to promote export-led growth, driven by FDI firms (in manufacturing, and more recently, internationally traded services) locating a production base in Ireland from which to serve the European market. Throughout the period industrial development policy has been highly centralised[12] but with a regional dimension – in effect, with industrial dispersal being promoted where it is consistent with the financial viability of the enterprise. Thus industrial development and regional development have been interconnected through the location of mobile projects in less developed regions, with regional infrastructural investments being linked to the developing economic base in the different areas of the country.[13] Since FDI is seen as being inter-regionally mobile compared with indigenous investment, it was regarded as having particular potential in achieving regional balance.

This strategy of promoting market-led activities and following, rather than leading, with major infrastructural investments has operated since the early 1960s in an evolving, consistent manner. Over the past decade EU regional policy resources have supplemented funds both for regional infrastructures (roads, bridges, ports) and for regional industrial incentives, at a time when the fiscal resources of the national government were highly constrained. Until recently EU policy has impacted on the detail rather than the substance of the evolving strategy, primarily because of Ireland's designation, until 2000, as an Objective 1/Article 92(3)(a) region; this allowed Ireland considerable leeway in granting aid to industry. Nonetheless, the impact of the Commission on Irish industrial policy has been considerable through the formal process of planning and on the preferential support that it has given to the use of particular incentives.[14] As Ireland began to reach full employment in the late 1990s and as it became re-designated as an *Objective 1 region in transition*, industrial development policy, with regard to both FDI and indigenous companies, began to change. We return to this below.

6.3 INDUSTRIAL POLICY APPROACH: 1970-2000

While projects in all manufacturing and internationally tradable service sectors were in principle eligible for financial support under Ireland's industrial development policy,[15] the level of support given varied widely, according to project characteristics, sector and location. Over the past two decades, the approach has become increasingly proactive and selective. Since it was expected that FDI would lead the process of modernisation in the Irish manufacturing sector, investments were sought in new sectors with global growth potential and where FDI opportunities were strong.[16] In the early 1970s the electronics and pharmaceutical sectors were identified as providing the most promising opportunities for foreign investment projects for Ireland.[17] Furthermore, the US was identified as the most likely market source for such projects and Ireland was aggressively promoted as an export base for US companies within the EU.[18] Already in 1991 the share of total employment in FDI manufacturing companies accounted for by US-owned enterprises was almost 45 per cent and this share rose to over 61 per cent by 1999, over which period employment in US-owned companies increased by over 90 per cent. As the policy developed, the deliberate creation of industrial clusters (in effect, the generation of agglomeration economies) especially in electronics and pharmaceuticals became increasingly important,[19] with strong links among the FDI companies and with outsourcing linkages to domestic firms in these sectors.[20] A specific proximate operational target of policy with regards to extra-EU FDI companies was to have the Irish operation become the sole or key production/distribution centre within the EU, ideally involving headquarter, marketing and R&D functions.[21]

The process of project selection evolved naturally from the identification of key sectors. Within these high growth sectors, agency personnel initiated contacts with the companies for whom investment in Ireland could be a credible strategy, and sought to persuade them to visit Ireland in the context of a specific project proposal.[22] The discretionary financial support system (see below) led inevitably to a bargaining process between state-agency executives and potential investors,[23] subject to maximum limits; when the absolute amount of support was large, Cabinet approval was required. Information on the amount of financial support given to companies is eventually in the public domain, so that transparency is assured about the final out-turn of the negotiations but not about the process of arriving at it. In practice, however, the tradition of publishing the amounts given annually to individual companies disappeared during the 1980s because it was seen as revealing too much information to competitive countries seeking FDI.

With increasing pro-activity and selectivity, the role of government institutions in the process has become increasingly significant. (The institutional structures have changed several times in the past decade; at present IDA Ireland deals with foreign-owned industry and Enterprise Ireland deals with indigenous industry, while a third agency, *Forfás*, is responsible for developing the policy framework in which these other agencies promote FDI and indigenous industry in a complementary manner.) In the case of indigenous companies, institutional supports have increasingly taken the form of assisting the establishment of SMEs and building the capability of larger medium-sized firms through the provision of information, supporting of networks, etc. Associated with this is often the provision of 'soft' financial supports, as well as, increasingly, support for linkages into foreign sub-supply chains.[24] In the case of foreign firms, the institutional approach has been to facilitate the establishment of the company in Ireland, by minimising bureaucratic costs, providing information, contacts with sub-suppliers, etc.[25] As a consequence of the financial support system (see below), there is an on-going relationship between the foreign-owned companies and IDA Ireland, which agency personnel use to promote the development of clusters and agglomerations. This is effected by having potential investors visit plants already operating in the same sector in Ireland. Incumbent plants facilitate these visits (often by their competitors in global product markets) as they expect to benefit from further agglomeration. IDA Ireland operates informal mechanisms to ensure that a newly established plant does not poach labour excessively from any existing plant, thereby avoiding inter-firm tensions as the agglomeration develops. In addition, to foster linkages, information on sub-supply is provided to both foreign-owned and indigenous firms, and potential for sub-supply linkages contributes to favourable treatment for financial supports. Since the late 1990s, the linkage programme has developed to take account of global outsourcing trends – we return to this development below.

6.4 INDUSTRIAL POLICY INSTRUMENTS: 1970-2000

The pro-active development strategy adopted in Ireland involves a combination of fiscal incentives and financial incentives.

6.4.1 Fiscal Incentives

As far as FDI manufacturing companies locating in Ireland are concerned, the main industrial incentive is a highly favourable regime of corporate taxation. Starting in the mid-1950s, all companies establishing in Ireland were entitled to a full tax holiday for up to 15 years on profits associated with export sales.[26] Because of its export bias, this incentive was deemed incompatible with the Treaty of Rome and in 1980, it was replaced with a preferential tax rate of 10 per cent on all corporate profits in manufacturing, independently of whether the output was an export or an import-substitute (i.e., was trade-neutral).[27] While this incentive did not legally constitute a state aid in terms of EU competition policy,[28] its continued operation was subject to agreement between the Irish government and the European Commission, which, in the early 1990s, indicated that the pro-trade bias inherent in the two-tier tax rate was no longer acceptable.[29] The essence of a new agreement in the late 1990s was that a standard rate of tax of 12.5 per cent would come into operation for *all* corporate income from 2003, with the 10 per cent rate "grand-parented" up to 2010 for all companies already in operation.[30] The corporate tax rate on the non-traded sector has been reduced annually since the mid 1990s and reached 16 per cent in the 2002 budget, in preparation for the reduction to 12.5 per cent in 2003. The low corporate tax rate is widely recognised as the crucial instrument in attracting mobile FDI projects to Ireland[31] and remains so despite the general reductions in rates of corporate tax in the EU in recent years. In the context of European tax harmonisation, the low tax rate in Ireland, while not a state aid, is under continued discussion and scrutiny within Europe, with high-tax countries protesting to the Commission about its impact on their ability to attract FDI projects. The Irish response has been that (a) tax policy is a national and not an EU issue, and (b) while the differences between nominal tax rates in Ireland and elsewhere in the EU is low, the differences between the effective rates is much less as Ireland has much wider corporate tax rates (fewer tax allowances) than found in other EU countries. In recent times several of these countries (UK and Germany) have significantly reduced their corporate tax rates, so that differences continue to decline.

6.4.2 Financial Incentives

The financial incentives to support investment have traditionally been in the form of cash grants, which are non-repayable as long as companies meet the initial targets agreed by them and the state agencies. In the 1960s and early 1970s these operated as *automatic* investment grants, paid as a fixed percentage of the cost of the new plant and machinery, and available to higher maxima in the *designated areas,* reflecting regional policy objectives. Over the past two decades, the system has operated in a more *discretionary* manner.[32] First, the range of financial aids has widened to meet the specific needs identified by the project promoters; the policy package available to foreign firms (and domestic firms) has included, along with investment grants, training grants, subsidised rents, low-interest loans, technology-transfer supports, and R&D grants.[33] Second, the scale of actual grants given has varied widely, based on fairly precise evaluation criteria. A formal process of project evaluation is used,[34] and the allowable maxima are set in terms of "grant per sustainable job equivalent" as well as "grant per unit investment". This dual approach, reflecting the historic emphasis on job generation in Irish industrial policy, is seen as addressing previous concerns by economists that the grants were capital biased, which was not appropriate given the concern with employment.[35] Although the grant is paid ostensibly towards capital, the grant has to be repaid should the associated job targets not be met in the agreed time-frame, thereby ensuring that the grant per job maximum figure is not violated. For this reason, the agencies continuously monitor all supported investments, with annual surveys (on employment, output, export behaviour, expenditure, etc.) and regular plant visits.

The increasingly discretionary, project-centred approach adopted by Irish policy makers has resulted in a policy culture that focuses on the requirements/demands of the companies, and underpins the establishment of separate agencies in the 1990s to handle foreign and domestic industry. Perhaps because of its company-centred approach, Irish policy has, relative to that in other countries, emphasised the importance of both minimising the bureaucratic costs associated with establishing a business in Ireland and establishing policy certainty for incoming and indigenous investors. Policy certainty has been achieved primarily through policy continuity.[36] Fiscal certainty has been achieved by providing the investing firms with a long and certain time horizon, with tax incentives fully grand-parented,[37] while financial uncertainty has been minimised by the payment of the cash grant up-front, with repayment required only if the company fails to meet its agreed employment objectives.[38]

6.5 HAVE IRISH POLICY OBJECTIVES BEEN MET?

We now look at the impact of Ireland's FDI policy in terms of the objectives set out in Section 6.2.

6.5.1 Export-Led-Growth in the Irish Manufacturing Sector (and Latterly Internationally Traded Services)

Ireland has succeeded in developing a rapidly growing export-based manufacturing sector. As noted above, Figure 6.3 shows how the sectoral composition of employment within manufacturing has changed since 1960 towards high-tech sectors and away from food processing and traditional manufacturing. Table 6.1 shows internationally comparable data for the ratio of merchandise trade to GDP for Ireland and other EU countries over the period 1970-2000. Ireland's ratio at 67 per cent in 2000 is the highest in the EU, with the exception of possibly Belgium/Luxembourg. This reflects the high degree of openness in the economy. The export-output ratio in manufacturing is high and continues to grow. In 1999, 17 per cent of the manufacturing output of indigenous companies was exported, compared with 78 per cent for FDI companies.[39]

Table 6.2 shows the changed profile of exports since 1960, with reduced dependence on the traditional export market, namely the UK, which took 75 per cent of Irish export in 1960, and increased emphasis on markets outside the EU area, which in 1999 took 35 per cent of Ireland's exports.

6.5.2 New Greenfield Investment by Foreign Companies in Export-Oriented Manufacturing and Internationally Traded Sectors

The success in winning FDI companies is reflected in several ways. Table 6.3 shows comparative capital outflow and inflow data (relative to GDP) for several countries, and the scale of flows in Ireland, which are dominated by inflows over the past three decades, is striking.

Table 6.4 provides a perspective in terms of the scale of US FDI in manufacturing which went to Ireland during 1998 – in the context where Ireland has less than one per cent of the EU GDP, this figure is quite remarkable.

Table 6.1 Ratio of Average Merchandise Exports and Imports to GDP, 1970-2000

%

Country	1970	1980	1990	1998	2000
France	13.0	18.9	18.9	20.7	23.0
Germany	17.4	23.5	25.1	23.7	28.0
Italy	13.1	19.9	16.1	19.8	22.1
Netherlands	42.8	50.4	45.5	50.9	55.7
Belgium-Luxembourg	45.5	56.9	60.9	66.2[a]	-
United Kingdom	16.7	21.0	21.0	21.6	21.8
Ireland	33.8	48.7	48.8	67.5	67.8
Denmark	24.0	26.6	25.3	26.7	28.7
Sweden	20.5	25.6	24.3	34.1	35.1
Austria	21.6	26.7	28.3	30.9	35.1
Norway	24.5	28.0	26.5	26.0	27.9
United States	4.2	8.9	8.2	9.9	10.3
Japan	9.4	12.8	8.8	8.8	9.0
Australia	12.5	13.8	13.8	16.5	17.3

Notes: [a] This figure for Belgium-Luxembourg refers to 1997 due to unavailability of data.

Sources: Merchandise export and import figures from International Monetary Fund (2001). GDP figures up to and including 1998 are from the website related to Lane and Milesi-Ferretti (2001). GDP figures for 2000 are from the OECD website.

Table 6.2 Market Restructuring 1960-99: Destination of All Exports

%

	UK	Rest of Europe	US	Other	Total
1960	75	6	8	11	100
1970	62	11	13	14	100
1980	43	32	5	20	100
1990	34	41	8	17	100
1999	22	43	15	20	100

Source: Forfás.

In terms of the manufacturing sector domestically, the importance of FDI is evident in terms of the growth of the sector overall and in its changing sectoral composition.[40] In 1999, the latest year for which data are available, foreign companies accounted for 85 per cent of net output in the

Table 6.3 Ratio of Average Inflows and Outflows of FDI in Merchandise Goods to GDP per Period, 1970–2000

%

Country	1970-74	1975-79	1980-84	1985-89	1990-94	1995-2000	1970-2000
France	0.7	0.8	0.9	1.8	3.5	6.3	2.3
Germany	1.2[a]	0.8	0.7	1.3	1.3	5.0	1.7[b]
Italy	0.6	0.4	0.6	0.7	0.9	1.4	0.8
Netherlands	5.2	3.7	4.3	5.6	7.5	18.3	7.4
Belgium-Luxembourg	2.2	2.1	1.5	4.4	7.4	22.8	6.7
United Kingdom	3.2	3.4	3.0	6.0	4.1	12.0	5.3
Ireland[c]	0.7	2.0	1.1	0.3	2.8	8.1	2.5
Denmark	0.9	0.3	0.4	1.3	3.0	10.8	2.8
Sweden	0.8	0.7	1.4	4.1	4.5	14.3	4.3
Austria	1.8	0.4	0.5	0.7	1.4	3.4	1.2
Norway	1.1	1.4	1.0	2.0	1.7	5.6	2.1
United States	0.7	1.0	0.9	1.6	1.6	3.2	1.5
Japan	0.3	0.3	0.4	1.0	0.8	0.6	0.6
Australia	2.0	1.2	1.6	4.2	2.5	3.5	2.5

Notes: [a] Refers to 1971-74. [b] Refers to 1971-2000. [c] Inflow and outflow data for Ireland from 1998 onwards have been amended to take account of changes in the methodology and coverage.

Sources: Inflow and outflow data and GDP data up to and including 1998 are from the website related to Lane and Milesi-Ferretti (2001). Data for 1999 and 2000 for inflows and outflows come from the IMF (2001) and data for GDP come from the OECD website.

Table 6.4 Ireland's Share of US FDI Outflows, 1998

	% of FDI to Europe	% of FDI to World
Manufacturing	7.0	4.4
Chemicals	15.4	9.1
Electronics	39.2	15.3

Source: Forfás from US Department of Commerce.

manufacturing sector and 49 per cent of total manufacturing employment; the corresponding figures for 1991 are 70 and 44 per cent respectively. See Table 6.5. While FDI companies are represented in all sectors, it is clear that they dominate all of the high-tech sectors both in terms of net output and

Table 6.5 Significance of Foreign Firms in the Irish Manufacturing Sector, 1999

	Total Net Output		Total Employment		Exports as % of output	
Sector	Sectors as % of total	Foreign as % of sector	Sectors as % of total	Foreign as % of sector	Irish-owned firms	Foreign-owned firms
Food, Drink & Tobacco	10.9	66	10.3	26	21	49
Textiles & Clothing	0.6	50	3.6	35	32	88
Wood & Wood Products	0.2	34	0.9	19	7	43
Paper & Paper Products	0.3	32	0.7	19	15	47
Publishing & Printing	11.2	86	5.5	34	6	65
Pharmaceuticals	7.5	92	5.5	82	22	80
Chemicals	39.5	98	9.6	80	47	95
Rubber & Plastics	0.5	46	3.5	40	16	75
Other Non-metallic Minerals	0.3	17	1.3	15	11	56
Basic & Fabricated Metals	0.7	37	3.1	24	12	80
Machinery & Equipment	1.2	60	5.4	46	18	77
Office Machinery & Computers	11.7	98	14.4	88	44	78
Electrical Machinery	1.9	80	8.3	70	23	84
Radio, Television & Communications	7.9	97	9.7	89	56	91
Medical, Precision & Optical	4.3	91	11.6	85	54	91
Motor Vehicles & Transport	0.7	71	4.2	54	16	90
n.e.c.	0.7	40	2.4	27	17	79
Total	100	85	100	49	17	78

Source: CSO data from the Census of Industrial Production, 1999.

Table 6.6 The FDI Sector: Growth of Employment, Net Output and Firm Numbers, 1991-99

	Employment			Net Output (£m)			Number of Firms		
Sectors	1991	1999	1991-99	1991	1999	1991-99	1991	1999	1991-99
Food, Drink & Tobacco	12,683	12,580	-1%	1,369	2,685	96%	77	76	-1%
Textiles & Clothing	9,733	4,379	-55%	162	139	-14%	79	32	-59%
Wood & Wood Products	480	1,094	128%	18	50	172%	7	8	14%
Paper & Paper Products	1,113	888	-20%	33	69	108%	15	12	-20%
Publishing & Printing	2,223	6,670	200%	431	2,776	545%	22	33	50%
Pharmaceuticals	3,085	6,742	119%	241	1,860	673%	34	40	18%
Chemicals	8,261	11,720	42%	1,485	9,763	558%	100	116	16%
Rubber & Plastics	4,360	4,267	-2%	126	134	7%	58	49	-16%
Other Non-metallic Minerals	1,848	1,545	-16%	60	85	42%	22	18	-18%
Basic & Fabricated Metals	3,637	3,809	5%	129	172	33%	59	47	-20%
Machinery & Equipment	7,001	6,616	-5%	247	291	18%	66	57	-14%
Office Machinery & Computers	6,767	17,602	160%	902	2,899	221%	35	36	3%
Electrical Machinery	7,811	10,138	30%	216	466	116%	57	58	2%
Radio, Television & Communications	4,128	11,855	187%	186	1,944	947%	27	31	15%
Medical, Precision & Optical	8,554	14,114	65%	429	1,064	148%	69	67	-3%
Motor Vehicles & Transport	1,590	5,146	224%	34	169	397%	18	20	11%
n.e.c.	3,595	2,966	-17%	149	167	12%	33	28	-15%
Total	86,869	122,131	41%	6,217	24,735	298%	744	688	-8%

Source: CSO data from the Census of Production, 1991, 1999. Growth in Net Output is in terms of 1985 prices.

employment. The share of total net output generated by foreign-owned companies varies sectorally (from 17 per cent in Other Non-metallic Minerals to over 98 per cent in Chemicals and Office Machinery and Computers (two of the main targeted ***high-tech*** sectors)), reflecting differences in the degree of international mobility of investments across sectors and the selective approach to policy implementation. The sectoral composition of FDI overall is highly concentrated in high-tech sectors; over 55 per cent of jobs in foreign companies are in high-tech sectors whereas the corresponding percentage for indigenous jobs is less than 10 per cent.[41] Both employment and output figures confirm the importance of the ***high-tech*** sectors, with three out of every four jobs in the Chemical and Electronics related sectors accruing to foreign-owned companies.[42] Not surprisingly, the export ratio of FDI companies in Ireland is very high, given that the economy has been promoted as an export base within the EU. On a comparative basis, FDI companies have export ratios that are more than 4.5 times the average of Irish owned companies. In all but five sectors the export ratio is above 90 per cent and in only one sector (Non-metallic Minerals) is the ratio below 70 per cent.

Turning to Table 6.6 we see that over the 1990s net output grew by almost 300 per cent in real terms, while the corresponding increase in employment was just 41 per cent.[43] This difference reflects the expansion of sectors with very high labour productivity, such as Office Machinery and Computers and Pharmaceuticals. Employment in foreign firms in the promoted electronics sectors doubled over the period 1991 to 1999, following a relatively modest increase (11 per cent) in this sector in the previous decade; this reflected a restructuring of the electronics sector in Ireland in this period with significant gross job gains and losses. Employment in FDI companies in the Chemicals (including Pharmaceuticals) sector increased by 75 per cent in the same period. In both sectors export ratios are exceptionally high – with Chemicals and Electronics FDI companies exporting 98 and 94 per cent of their outputs respectively. A feature of the past decade is that employment in indigenous firms has increased – in the previous two decades employment fell in Irish owned firms giving rise to the issue of whether foreign firms were crowding out indigenous firms through increased competition in the Irish factor markets.[44]

The employment stock data hide a considerable amount of job creation and destruction, as discussed by Strobl *et al.* (1998) and Walsh and Whelan (1999). Even in the high-tech sectors targeted by industrial policy, foreign firms have experienced very high rates of job gains and losses over the last two decades. This suggests that, if the Irish economy is to continue to pursue a policy of fostering growth through expansions of high-tech companies, continuing policy activity may be required if it is to retain its present scale of FDI activity. The present recession shows evidence of this as data from IDA

Ireland for 2001 indicate that job gains continue at a high level but that job losses (especially in Electronics) have surged with the global downturn. As a result, net job creation was negligible in 2001, and 2002 saw the first year of net job loss in manufacturing since the late 1980s.

6.5.3 Establishment of Up-stream Linkages between Foreign and Indigenous Companies

The potential for local linkages has increasingly been used as an argument for fostering foreign direct investment in economies seeking to develop quickly.[45] Ireland has directly pursued this strategy for over thirty years, and with particular emphasis on the electronics sector during the 1990s. The policy up to the late 1990s was considered to have been quite successful, with a three-fold increase in local sourcing of raw materials by foreign companies between 1988 and 1998. In the late 1990s, Forfás reported that approximately 20 per cent of total raw materials were sourced in Ireland, compared with 15 per cent in 1988.[46] However, as pointed out by Görg and Ruane (1999), it is not possible to identify from the data whether these linkages are between downstream FDI firms and upstream indigenous firms; given the scale of multinational presence in many sectors in Ireland, it is to be expected that at least some of the linkages are between upstream and downstream MNCs.[47] The present policy is to maintain and to increase this share where possible, recognising that the scale of backward linkages by foreign companies is much less in employment terms than those of indigenous companies.[48] There is also growing recognition that in an increasingly integrated international economy, global rather than local outsourcing is likely to undermine some of the outsourcing arrangements which have developed over the 1990s and this is being increasingly reflected in the development of programmes designed to encourage (a) smaller indigenous firms to form strategic alliances with international partners and (b) larger indigenous firms to position themselves to become global rather than local sub-suppliers to FDI companies based in Ireland.[49]

6.5.4 Creation of Industrial Clusters in Certain Sub-sectors of Manufacturing and Internationally Traded Services

As already noted, the sub-sectors identified for development were in electronics and pharmaceuticals. Since the late 1980s and early 1990s this targeting has begun to yield very significant benefits especially with US companies in the electronics and health care sectors.[50] The clusters are both horizontal and vertical, the latter elements relating to the policy of promoting outsourcing linkages. Thus in electronics the aim of developing activities across the full range of production from upstream (e.g., semi-conductors, PCBA) to downstream (computers, consumer electronics, software production) has been achieved very successfully,[51] and in recent years, significant numbers of indigenous firms have entered those sub-sectors where local linkages are possible.[52] As part of the post-2000 EU restrictions on state aids, significant resources have been earmarked to support strategic R&D in Ireland by third level institutions. These investments are focused on Biotechnology[53] and Informatics and Communications Technologies (ICT)[54] and a specific part of their remit is to support the emerging clusters of FDI companies over the next decade by enhancing relevant human capital.[55] These developments are widely supported, reflecting the fact that the sectors involved are, in historical terms, relatively new to Ireland and thus facilitating the acceptance of their having received favourable promotion by all the major players in the policy process.

6.5.5 A Pattern of Development that Brings Investment to the Less Developed Areas of the Country

Reviewing the 1990s, this is probably the least achieved policy objective, primarily because with high levels of unemployment nationally for most of the decade, it did not get priority. Arguably the gap in incentive support between the more developed areas – now referred to as the South and East (SE) region – and the less developed areas – now referred to as the Border, Midlands and West (BMW) region – did not capture the relative disadvantages of location. Data for the period 1991-99 show that net output in FDI manufacturing companies grew at more than three times the rate in the developed SE region compared with the less developed BMW region, while employment grew at almost twice the rate. The failure to achieve a better regional distribution of economic activities is seen as a cost to the single region designation, as manufacturing industry in Ireland appears to have become more geographically concentrated over the past decade. Ironically, this may in part be due to the successful development of strong clusters in electronics in the more developed areas of the country – in effect success in achieving one policy objective (clustering) was at the expense of the second (regional dispersal). In terms of the distribution of manufacturing jobs across regions, the role of FDI historically has been very important, with some of the largest concentrations of employment in peripheral regions being in FDI companies that in 1999 accounted for 49 per cent of manufacturing jobs in the BMW region.[56]

The confinement of full Objective 1 status to the BMW region has raised the importance of regional aids to project location in Ireland. The present strategy is to seek FDI projects that can locate successfully outside Dublin.[57]

These are inevitably projects for which the economic benefits of clustering are few, and internal transportation costs are lowest.[58]

6.6 POLICY EVALUATION

In evaluating Ireland's recent economic success in winning FDI projects increasingly over the past 15 years, it is important to note its modest success in winning such projects prior to Ireland's entry into the EEC in 1973. This suggests that Ireland, as an individual small economy on the periphery of Europe, had very little to offer to FDI projects directly and that its success in attracting them has much to do with the growth and integration of the European market. Undoubtedly Ireland's entry into the EU gave the economy a new role as an English-speaking, politically stable, export base within the EU market, making it especially attractive to US companies. While the 1970s could be seen as a successful decade in terms of FDI investment, the 1980s saw a strong downturn, followed by an exceptional upturn in the 1990s. Indeed, it is striking, and maybe ironic, that this recent FDI growth has taken place at a time when the *relative* impact of Ireland's incentives has been eroded both by domestic reductions in incentives and by the increasing use of regional incentives elsewhere in the EU.[59] Since there were no major changes in the industrial policy regime, and such changes as have occurred have reduced Ireland's relative attractiveness, one has to look elsewhere for the source of the surge in FDI in the 1990s.

There are several external factors, which enhanced the effectiveness of Ireland FDI strategy during the 1990s:

- the spectacular world-wide growth of the high-tech sector (which Ireland has promoted since the 1970s), well above what might have been expected;
- the fall in global telecommunication and transport costs, which reduced the real costs of peripherality *per se*;
- the exceptional boom in the US economy, which effectively translated into a boom in the Irish economy, and
- the provision of substantial EU funds to support regional investments and incentives at a time when the Irish economy could not have provided these resources without undermining its corrective macro policies.[60]

All four have combined to support the development of Ireland as an ideal production base for Non-EU, and especially, US companies engaged in producing "weightless products" primarily for the EU market. Figure 6.4 shows in very simple terms how the composition of manufacturing employment has changed over the 1990s, with the bulk of employment growth in the Non-EU MNCs, and virtually no growth in EU MNCs during the same period, while local companies (LCs) grew by 15 per cent. The export patterns of the different groups are shown in Figure 6.5. For all groups exports increased over the 1990s, but in the case of Non-EU MNCs the share of output exported outside the EU grew most rapidly, in line with expectations in an environment where manufacturing is becoming increasingly globalised.

Figure 6.4 Distribution of Employment in Manufacturing, by Ownership, 1991-98

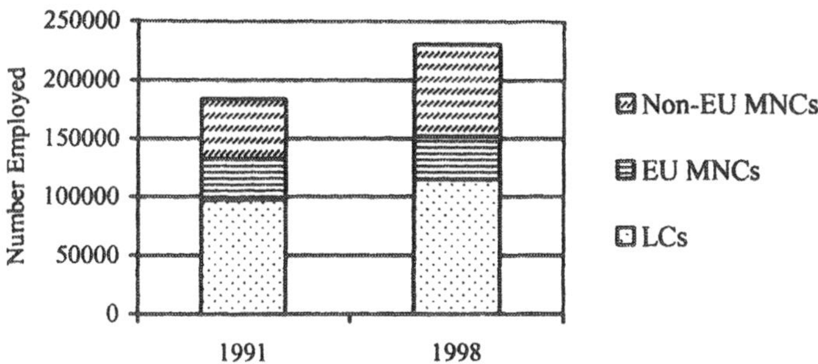

Source: Ruane and Sutherland (2002) based on CSO Census of Manufacturing.

Figure 6.5 Distribution of Irish Manufacturing Exports by Ownership and Destination, 1991-98

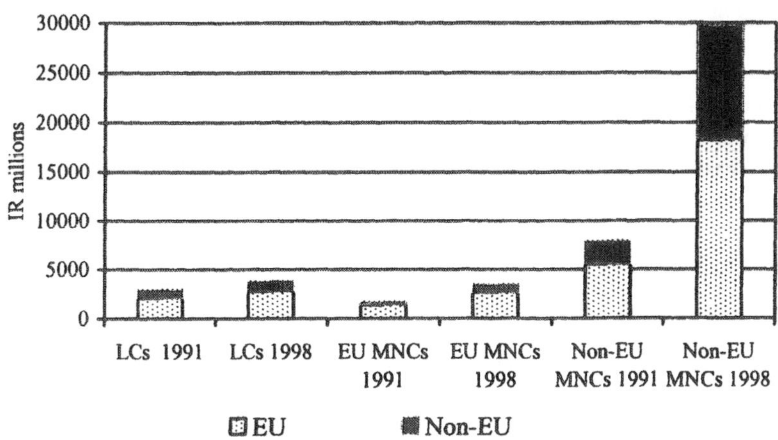

Note: Deflated where appropriate, 1985=100.

Source: Ruane and Sutherland (2002) based on CSO Census of Manufacturing.

Three direct policy factors seem to have worked exceptionally well:

- the strategy of deliberately creating horizontal and vertical agglomerations, a strategy which lay outside the realm of what economists generally would have recommended;
- the timely extension of incentives to cover internationally traded services, an extension which would not have been favoured generally by economists, and
- the generation by Ireland over several decades of a pro-FDI reputation based on a proactive, efficient and consistent industrial policy, an effect which would not have been valued highly by most economists.

In terms of general economic policy factors, factors which were seen as crucial to creating an environment attractive to FDI, were:

- the establishment of appropriate macro policies and a restrained wage-setting environment (which recognised the country's labour market problems) in the late 1980s,
- the introduction of competition policy and deregulation (which is increasing cost competitiveness) in the early 1990s, and
- the rapidly improving physical and human capital infrastructure (as a result of major investment in telecommunications and education in the 1970s, 1980s and 1990s).

While no individual policy could explain Ireland's recent success in winning FDI, what seems to have happened was that various policies worked in a reinforcing manner, starting in the late 1980s. And, as pointed out by Krugman (1997), Ireland was also lucky. To use the US vernacular, its strategy of wooing Intel and Microsoft has *paid off in spades*, providing the basis for the consolidation and growth of the electronics sector. In the absence of these two investments the performance of the Irish economy over the past decade might be less spectacular and more akin to that of Portugal and Spain, which have also experienced convergence within the EU but at a more modest rate.[61]

6.7 FUTURE POLICY OBJECTIVES

The dramatic increase in employment in the late 1990s, has, for the first time since the 1950s, raised real questions for policy makers about the long-standing focus on employment as a policy goal for industrial policy in general and for promoting FDI as a strategy in particular.[62] If employment is no longer the target, what should the target be? Should the target reflect economic welfare more generally, say by focusing on per capita income? What about labour productivity or total factor productivity? Is there an inadequate emphasis on developing indigenous industry? Should Ireland move to more proximate targets, relevant to industrial development, e.g., increasing the scale of BERD (Business Expenditure on Research and Development) in Irish industry, expanding the scale of product innovation (as measured, for examples, in terms of patents),[63] and extending the degree of export diversification. In addition, Ireland's success in attracting FDI over the past decade has raised questions such as: has it generated too much dependency? Is it wise that 49 per cent and 85 per cent of employment and net output respectively in manufacturing are in FDI firms? Are the present levels of sectoral and nationality concentration in FDI investment appropriate, or are we simply ahead of many of our European neighbours in terms of being truly globalised?[64] Is it a source of concern that many of the young indigenous companies that are being established in the high-tech sectors are likely to be "taken over" by global companies in the same fields? Has the linkage policy increased the overall dependence of the indigenous sector on FDI firms – and are these relationships increasingly vulnerable to global outsourcing?

6.8 FUTURE POLICIES

If new targets can be agreed, what policies should be pursued to achieve these? Are the traditional state aids completely redundant for FDI companies even in Objective 1 regions, given the preferential 12.5 per cent corporate tax rate? Is there any merit to having some bargaining aid, if this is compatible with EU policy? Might the absence of such aid reduce agency-FDI company contacts, damaging the networks currently in place to aid the process of attracting and assimilating successfully FDI plants?

As the economy increasingly hits capacity constraints, should policy shift away completely from project-based incentives towards improving the domestic infrastructure, in terms of both physical and human capital, in order to make Ireland a competitive environment for FDI?[65] Would this risk losing an element of the strategy that has arguably been important over the past decade, namely, the close link between policy agencies and individual enterprises? If, as the National Development Plan seems to suggest, there should be more expenditure on both public and private R&D, is there a need to ensure, through policy intervention, that the mechanisms in place will result in the anticipated growth in innovations and continuing modernisation of the industrial sector? While, as Fitz Gerald et al. (1999) point out, the labour force is becoming increasingly skilled (through the increased rate of participation in education), is there still a need for government involvement in actively supporting training and skills generation in the industrial sector, given the traditionally low investment pattern of companies in upgrading the skills of their workforces?

The widespread use of state aids has been limited since January 2000 for most of the country and for the Eastern region in particular. While state aids continue to be allowed, they no longer have EU regional policy funding and their maxima are set to a net grant equivalent of at most 20 per cent (compared with 45 per cent previously) for FDI and 30 per cent for SMEs. In the Western region, Objective 1 status continues to apply, but the net grant equivalent maxima have fallen to 40 per cent for FDI and expansion of large indigenous companies and 55 per cent for SMEs. Since the current levels of grants lie well within these new maxima, the impact of the changes in terms of financial support have not been very large in practice. In the case of FDI, the greater impact of the change may be reflected in a shift towards horizontal aid rather than regional aid, especially in the context of the stated emphasis on R&D expenditure.

6.9 RELEVANCE OF IRISH EXPERIENCE

To what extent, if any, is Ireland's apparent success in winning FDI relevant to other environments? I would argue that much of the rapid success of the recent decade has been a feature of the very special circumstances in the world economy and we must wait and see how well these will be sustained during the next decade. Already with the slowdown in the world economy, the impact on Ireland is beginning to show.[66] Furthermore, some very specific factors that have worked in Ireland's favour cannot be ignored, such as close links with the US, English as the first language, changes in technology that reduced the cost of regional peripherality. However, there are some features of what Ireland has done that I think are relevant to other countries:

- Maintaining policy consistency is important – winning FDI is not done on the basis of policies that change mid-stream, irrespective of how attractive these policies are. This means that policy consensus is essential across all the key actors involved in determining the policy environment;
- Pursuing openness rather than protectionism, both in terms of trade policy and in terms of seeking replacement projects rather than seeking to shore up existing projects where these become unprofitable;
- Focusing on the international (perhaps regional) rather than the national market, in an increasingly globalized era (even if the scale of increase will slow down) leads to greater likelihood of having more sustained FDI. This points to winning FDI which has an export focus from the beginning and is not simply there to gain domestic market share;

- Establishing firms where the country has a comparative advantage and working as far a possible with that – or at least avoiding developments which run against comparative advantage;
- Ensuring the incentives are appropriate and at least partially performance-based – this is the key advantage of low corporate tax rates, in that they only benefit profitable projects;
- Generating an overall environment for FDI which is positive – there is little sense in trying to attract FDI if national attitudes are hostile and the institutional framework is full of red tape; and
- Providing an economic environment (taxes, prices, infrastructure) that is workable – to provide financial aid at a project level to compensate for broadly deficient infrastructure simply does not make sense.

Finally, if sectoral selectivity is being pursued, ensure that this is market driven, broad based in terms of companies, and that there is a project-evaluation system in place. While Ireland may have looked as if it picked winners, in reality it followed the market – by the time Intel and Microsoft came to Ireland, they were global companies – in effect we invited winners! In this context it is always important to recall that the environment is dynamic – not all projects will survive and thrive, and the scale of assistance they are given should not presume that they will.

NOTES

1. This paper draws on joint work done with Holger Görg, Allan Kearns, Julie Sutherland and Ali Ugur. I am grateful to Ali Ugur and Julie Sutherland for assistance in preparing the paper and to the Central Statistics Office in Dublin for access to data used in the paper.
2. It was suggested in 1982 that Ireland could become "North Dakota of Europe". Guiomard (1995) provides a critical analysis of the limitations of the policy process operating in Ireland in the early 1990s in terms of its ability to embrace change and deal with the challenges of that time.
3. Delegates have visited Ireland very extensively from CEE countries and from the smaller LDCs in an attempt to ascertain what the secret of Ireland's success has been.
4. The reader is recommended to look particularly at Barry (1999) for a wide-ranging analysis of the issues, and to Clinch et al. (2002) for a discussion of Irish growth prospects in the light of the recent downturn in the global economy. Other relevant references include Sweeney (1998), Gray (1997), O'Hearn (1998) and O'Sullivan (2000).
5. See Görg and Ruane (2000).
6. See Ruane and Görg (1996), Barry and Bradley (1997) and O'Sullivan (2000).
7. See Fitz Gerald et al. (1999).
8. This is not to understate the increasing importance of FDI in internationally traded services.
9. In adopting this approach, the policy makers had implicitly recognised the type of indigenous/foreign relationship anticipated by and formalised in Markusen and Venables (1999).

10. The development strategy was introduced gradually at the end of the 1950s when the Irish-owned manufacturing sector was orientated towards the domestic market (heavily protected by tariffs and quotas) and the only significant foreign-owned projects were pre-independence investments. The pro-FDI strategy, which followed on a period when foreign direct investment (FDI) was heavily controlled, arose from widespread recognition of the real failure of the protectionist strategy, which lasted from the early 1930s to the mid-1960s. Key to the strategy adopted around 1960 was that the economy should move to free trade and that foreign investment should play a key role in this process, being entitled to the same treatment as indigenous industry.

11. Ireland suffered population decline for over 100 years and one of the most acute periods of emigration was during the 1950s.

12. Historically there have been two exceptions to this centralisation. The Midwest region has had much greater regional autonomy (with its own development agency) as has the Gaeltacht (Irish speaking) area. However, in terms of the issue of regional incentives, their approaches have essentially followed that used throughout Ireland by the centralised agencies. In very recent times, there has been some further regional decentralisation under the EU structural funds programmes, with certain very limited funds being made available to local enterprise boards to support local initiatives.

13. In essence industrial policy has been the driver of regional development with infrastructure following rather than preceding industrial location decisions. Examples include the location of regional institutes of technology (formerly regional technical colleges) to build up human capital in the regions and the development of Cork harbour in tandem with the location of a cluster of pharmaceutical and chemical firms in the 1970s.

14. For example, over the 1970s Ireland provided a lot of support for industrial development in the form of advance factories. This was not approved of by the European Commission and hence disappeared as an incentive during the 1990s.

15. Activities in other sectors (agriculture, tourism, minerals, utilities) are not eligible for support under this policy.

16. By the mid 1970s it was seen as preferable to seek new FDI projects to replace unprofitable indigenous projects in stagnant sectors rather than attempting to shore up these projects. Similar policies used in the 1960s (to assist Irish firms so that they could compete with the imports following the removal of tariffs) were very unsuccessful, merely delaying rather than avoiding job losses and firm closures.

17. These were sectors exhibiting high growth rates and for which transportation costs were relatively low – arguably the ideal projects for a peripheral, island location in Europe (see Görg and Ruane, 2000a, for a further discussion).

18. Görg and Ruane (1999) show that Ireland received a disproportionate scale of global and EU investment by US companies in these sectors during the 1990s.

19. The success of this strategy is noted in Krugman (1997).

20. Görg and Ruane (2001) find that foreign electronics firms are increasingly sourcing material inputs in Ireland. However, because of data limitations, they cannot identify the extent to which these purchases are from other FDI companies (probably because of the large share of foreign companies in the sector) or from indigenous companies.

21. This is seen as important from the point of view of achieving high-income jobs and of encouraging a deepening of the companies' commitment to Ireland.

22. Implicit in the approach adopted to looking at potential foreign investment was the type of framework subsequently developed by Dunning (1988), who suggests that foreign investment depends on (i) special firm characteristics which enable companies to produce profitably abroad, (ii) an incentive to internalise this advantage, and (iii) location characteristics in the host countries.

23. While foreign project investors argued for more support on the basis of the attractiveness of alternative international investment locations (usually in the EU), Irish state-agency executives offered support by reference to the attractiveness of the project to Ireland and the levels of support given to other projects.

24. We return to this issue below.

25. In effect IDA Ireland provides a "one-stop-shop" for foreign companies, whereby all aspects of establishing in Ireland are handled in the agency. Legislation in August 1999 provides additional powers to the relevant ministry to ensure that planning delays as minimised for strategic projects seeking to locate in Ireland.

26. The standard rate of corporate tax during the 1960s and 1970s was 50 per cent. During the 1980s, this tax rate was reduced to 45 per cent.

27. Given the small size of the Irish market and Ireland's membership of the European Economic Community (EEC), the switch to a trade-neutral incentive away from a pro-exporting incentive had little effect on the behaviour of foreign firms in particular, with exporting remaining the driving force behind their investments in Ireland. Its removal facilitated the development of clusters based on production linkages between FDI companies resident in Ireland, in that it no longer penalised them in terms of higher tax rates for selling on the local compared with the international market.

28. Thus it is not factored into any of the calculations of state aids in determining whether assistance to companies (foreign or domestic) in Ireland falls within the allowed maxima. The Commission treats the International Financial Services Centre in Dublin and the Shannon Airport Free Trade zone as exceptions to this rule without the agreement of the Irish government.

29. While the 10 per cent tax rate met the EU criterion of neutrality in not favouring exports over import substitutes, it failed to meet the criterion of overall tax neutrality, i.e., as between traded and non-traded goods and services.

30. The agreement also allowed for a limited number of new projects to be established annually until 2003 at the ten per cent tax rate.

31. IDA Ireland personnel suggest that tax incentives are particularly popular with US firms. A Deloitte Touche Tohmatsu survey (Deloitte Touche, 1996) found that almost 60 per cent of foreign companies interviewed found the 10 per cent rate to have been very influential in their location choice. Similar results were also found by Hannigan (1998).

32. The grants are implemented at the discretion of the relevant state development agencies.

33. See Yuill et al. (1997) pp 299-318.

34. In practice, the supports offered are based on an *explicit* form of cost-benefit analysis, which takes account of factors such as employment potential (in terms of both job numbers and skill mix), location of the projects within Ireland, the profits tax potential and the strategic potential of a particular project to Ireland's development process. Thus a key investment project, such as Intel, might expect to receive a higher rate of grant than a routine project in the electronics sector. See Honohan (1998).

35. See, for example, Ruane and John (1984).

36. The continuity in policy has been possible primarily because there is exceptionally widespread consensus in Ireland on the strategy of promoting FDI and on the use of the financial and fiscal incentives in that process. All of the major political parties, and the unions and employers groups have supported the FDI strategy over the past 40 years. Thus changes in government have had not a serious impact on the policy environment faced by FDI companies located in Ireland.

37. Thus, for example, firms locating in Ireland in the 1960s were given a fifteen year tax holiday and those locating in the 1980s were assured that the corporate tax system which they would face would be unchanged until 2000; in 1990 this was extended to 2010. Furthermore,

policies have always been 'grand-parented', i.e., once granted, an individual firm always holds its tax status.

38. The government's money is secured by linking the payment to fixed assets lest the project fail. Recent examples of major grant repayments arose with the relocation of a Seagate plant to Hungary and part of Fruit of the Loom to Morocco.

39. The export ratios are significantly higher when companies below 15 employees are excluded. In the case of FDI companies the export ratio rises to over 90 per cent while for indigenous companies it exceeds 30 per cent.

40. Unfortunately we do not have corresponding data available for internationally traded services.

41. Ruane and Ugur (2002) show that the correlation between employment growth across sectors between foreign and Irish firms is only 25 per cent.

42. The foreign share of net output by sector exceeds the foreign share of employment in all but one sector. These differences could be due to (i) differences in sub-sectoral activities, (ii) differences in factor intensities in the same sectoral activity, resulting in foreign firms being less labour-intensive than indigenous firms, or (iii) transfer pricing. Because of the latter, employment shares rather than net output shares are a preferred indicator.

43. The corresponding increase in employment in indigenous firms in the same period was 15 per cent; combined with the performance of the FDI companies, this resulted in an increase in manufacturing employment overall of 26 per cent.

44. Since foreign sales were predominately on export markets, there was no issue of crowding out in the domestic product markets. There has been some concern in the literature that indigenous firms may have been crowded out by multinational companies (Barry and Hannan, 1995). The contrary argument is that, even if some crowding out has taken place, MNCs have assisted a necessary structural change in the Irish manufacturing sector, away from traditional sectors to ***high-tech*** sectors (Ruane and Görg, 1997).

45. See UNCTAD, ***World Investment Report 2001: Promoting Linkages***.

46. These data relate to non-food manufacturing, since the bulk of its raw material comes from the agricultural sector.

47. Görg and Ruane (1999) conclude, on the basis of a firm level econometric study of the electronics sector that individual foreign firms increase their linkages over time, generating additional sales for and employment in indigenous firms. Görg and Strobl (2002) present econometric evidence that supports the conclusion that foreign firms in Ireland have had a positive effect on the entry of indigenous firms through this linkage mechanism.

48. See O'Malley (1998).

49. Ruane (2001) outlines the evolution of Ireland's linkage policy which is focussed increasingly on helping FDI companies to find sub-suppliers in Europe generally and not just in Ireland, and in helping indigenous companies to find and on occasions fund global sub-suppliers where they recognise that they will not be able produce inputs competitively as Irish wage rates increase in real terms.

50. For example, many of the high profile investors that located in Ireland in the late 1980s and early 1990s, such as Intel, Hewlett Packard, Dell, Compaq and Microsoft, had been targeted by IDA Ireland over many preceding years, with regular presentations made as to why they should locate in Ireland and what assistance they would receive, etc. It would appear that there is a lead-time of at least five years between the first presentation of a case to the senior management in these companies and the eventual decision to locate a plant in Ireland.

51. Görg and Ruane (1999) estimate the spread of employment in the electronics sub-sectors of multinationals for 1995. They find the following: Semiconductors (17%), Peripherals & Media (13%) PCBA (4%) Instrumentation (4%), Consumer electronics (6%), Computers (12%), Components (7%), Telecommunications (9%), Software production (14%), Software

developments (14%) and Services (5%). This contrasts with the regional development strategies in other regions of the world which have developed horizontal clusters only (e.g., Kyushu in Japan which has semiconductor firms only).

52. Görg and Ruane (1999) find evidence of new indigenous firm start-ups in all sub-sectors apart from semiconductors.

53. In Biotechnology, large-scale research campuses have recently been planned in Ireland by Wyeth and General Electric.

54. IBM is one of a number of ICT companies which have established major research facilities in Ireland in recent years.

55. The government established a new agency in 2002, Science Foundation Ireland, to promote strategic research in Irish universities and colleges and research links between them and major companies (primarily MNCs) which were willing to establish major research centres in Ireland.

56. While the proportion of manufacturing jobs that are in FDI companies is virtually the same in the SE region, the high and growing levels in the BMW regions have given rise to some concerns about excessive local dependency if investments which are exceptionally large run into difficulty, because of the high dependency of the BMW regions on employment in manufacturing.

57. Project viability is seen as crucial; Killen and Ruane (1998) find evidence that the success rates of MNCs in the Western periphery are no lower than in the Eastern core.

58. In this context, the location of international call-centres has recently been promoted by IDA Ireland.

59. These point to the fact that while incentives may have been necessary to Ireland's success in winning FDI projects, they have not been sufficient.

60. Undoubtedly the small size of the Irish economy has been a contributory factor, as the impact of a given volume of US investment can be expected to have had a greater impact than it would have had on a larger European economy.

61. See European Commission (1997a, b) and Braunerhjelm et al. (2000).

62. This increase has occurred simultaneously with a reduction in unemployment and evidence of increasing immigration by non-nationals.

63. See O'Sullivan (2000).

64. Three quarters of all FDI is in the Electronics and Chemical sectors and over one quarter of all jobs in Irish manufacturing are now in US owned companies. (In recent years US companies have accounted for over eighty per cent of all new jobs created by multinationals.)

65. This is evident in recent policy debates that focus on the importance of the environment facing industry (e.g., the impact of high income taxation on wage demands, the need to provide more skilled labour for domestic industry, the need to improve the road network, etc.) See Forfás (2000).

66. While the impact on FDI firms in Ireland has been relatively modest to date, there is growing recognition that, given the structure of the Irish economy, when the US high-tech sector sneezes, the Irish high-tech sector is at risk of pneumonia.

References

Barry, Frank (ed.) (1999), *Understanding Ireland's Economic Growth*, London: Macmillan Press.

Barry, Frank and John Bradley (1997), 'FDI and Trade: The Irish Host-Country Experience', *Economic Journal*, 107, 1798-1811.

Barry, Frank and Aoife Hannan (1995) 'Multinationals and Indigenous Employment: An 'Irish Disease'?' *Economic and Social Review*, 27(1), 21-32.

Braunerhjelm, Pontus, Riccardo Faini, Victor Norman, Frances Ruane and Paul Seabright (2000) *Integration and the Regions of Europe: How the Right Policies can Prevent Polarisation*, Centre of Economic Policy Research, London.

Clinch, Peter, Frank Convery, and Brendan Walsh (2002), *After the Celtic Tiger: Challenges Ahead*, Dublin: The O'Brien Press.

Deloitte, Touche (1996), *European Investment Decisions: The Impact of Tax Legislation on Investment in the European Union*. Deloitte Touche, Dublin.

Duffy, David, John Fitz Gerald, Hore Jonathan, Ide Kearney and Conall MacCoille (2001), *ESRI Medium Term Review, 2001-2007*, Economic and Social Research Institute, Dublin.

Dunning, John H. (1988), *Explaining International Production*, Unwin Hyman, London.

European Commission (1997a), 'The Cases of Greece, Spain, Ireland and Portugal', *Single market Review, Sub-series VI: Aggregate and Regional Impact, Volume 2*. Brussels: European Commission

European Commission (1997b), 'Regional Growth and Convergence', *Single Market Review, Sub-series VI: Aggregate and Regional Impact, Volume 1*. Brussels: European Commission.

Fitz Gerald, John, Ide Kearney, Edgar Morgenroth and Diarmaid Smyth (eds.) (1999), *National Investment Priorities for the Period 2000-2006* Dublin: Economic and Social Research Institute.

Forfás (2000), *Enterprise 2000: A New Strategy for the Promotion of Enterprise in Ireland in the 21st Century*. Dublin: Forfás.

Görg, Holger and Ruane, Frances (1999), 'US Investment in EU Member Countries: The Internal Market and Sectoral Specialization', *Journal of Common Market Studies*, 37(2), 333-348

Görg, Holger and Frances Ruane (2000), 'European Integration and Peripherality: Lessons from the Irish Experience', *World Economy*, 23(3), 405-421.

Görg, Holger and Frances Ruane (2001), 'Multinational Companies and Linkages: Panel-Data Evidence for the Irish Electronics Sector', *International Journal of the Economics of Business*, 8(1), 1-18.

Görg, Holger and Eric Strobl (2002), 'Multinational Companies and Indigenous Development: An Empirical Analysis', *European Economic Review*, 46(7), 1305-1322.

Gray, Alan W. (ed.) (1997), *International Perspectives on the Irish Economy*. Dublin: Indecon.

Guiomard, Cathal (1995), *The Irish Disease and How to Cure It*, Dublin: Oak Tree Press.

Hannigan, Kevin (1998), 'The Business Climate for Multinational Corporations in Ireland', *Irish Banking Review*, 2-13.

Honohan, Patrick (1998), *Key Issues of Cost-Benefit Methodology for Irish Industrial Policy*, Dublin: Oak Tree Press.

International Monetary Fund (IMF) (2001), *International Financial Statistics CD-ROM*, International Monetary Fund, Washington D.C..

Lane, Philip R. and Gian Maria Milesi-Ferretti (2001), 'The External Wealth of Nations: Measures of Foreign Assets and Liabilities for Industrial and Developing Countries', *Journal of International Economics*, 55(2), 263-294.

Killen, Lynn and Frances Ruane (1998), 'The Regional Dimension of Industrial Policy and Performance in the Republic of Ireland' Trinity Economic Papers, Policy Paper No. 98/3. Trinity College, Dublin.

Krugman, Paul R. (1997), 'Good News from Ireland: A Geographical Perspective', in Gray, Alan W. (ed.), *International Perspectives on the Irish Economy*. Dublin: Indecon. 38-53.

MacSharry, Ray and Padraic White (2000), *The Making of the Celtic Tiger: The Inside Story of Ireland's Boom Economy*, Dublin: Mercier Press

Markusen, James R. and Anthony J. Venables (1999), 'Foreign Direct Investment as a Catalyst for Industrial Development'. *European Economic Review*. 43, 335-356.

Murphy, Antoin (1998), *The Celtic Tiger - The Great Misnomer: Economic Growth and the Multi-nationals in Ireland in the 1990's*. Dublin: MMI Stockbrokers.

National Development Plan (2000), Government of Ireland publication

O'Hearn, D. (1998), *Inside the Celtic Tiger: the Irish Economy and the Asian Model*. London: Pluto Press

O'Malley, Eoin (1998), 'The Revival of Irish Indigenous Industry 1987-1997'. In: Baker, Terry; Duffy, David and Shortall, Fergal (eds.), *Quarterly Economic Commentary, April 1998*. Dublin: Economic and Social Research Institute.

O'Sullivan, M. (2000), 'The Sustainability of Industrial Development in Ireland', *Regional Studies*, 34 (3), 277-290.

Ruane, Frances (2001), 'Reflections on Linkage Policy in Irish Manufacturing – Policy Chasing a Moving Target?' Paper delivered at UN-ECE Conference, Geneva, December 2001.

Ruane, Frances and Holger Görg (1996), 'Aspects of Foreign Direct Investment in Irish Manufacturing since 1973: Policy and Performance'. *Journal of the Statistical and Social Inquiry Society of Ireland*, 27(4), 37-85.

Ruane, Frances and Holger Görg (1997), 'The Impact of Foreign Direct Investment on Sectoral Adjustment in the Irish Economy', *National Institute Economic Review*. No. 160. 76-86.

Ruane, F.P. and A. Andrew John, (1984), 'Government Intervention and the Cost of Capital to Irish Manufacturing Industry', Economic and Social Review, 16(1), 31-50.

Ruane, Frances and Julie Sutherland (2002), 'Globalization, Europeanization and Trade in the 1990s: Export Responses of Foreign and Indigenous Manufacturing Companies' in Henryk Kierzkowski (ed) *Europe and Globalization* London: Palgrave.

Ruane, Frances and Ali Ugur (2002), 'Labour Productivity and Employment in Irish Manufacturing Industry', *TCD Mimeo*

Stewart, J.C. (1976), 'Linkages and Foreign Direct Investment'. *Regional Studies*. 10 (2), 245-258.

Strobl, Eric A., Patrick P. Walsh, and Frank Barry (1998), 'Aggregate Job Creation, Job Destruction and Job Turnover in the Irish Manufacturing Sector'. *Economic and Social Review*. 29(1), 55-71.

Sweeney, Paul (1998), *The Celtic Tiger: Ireland's Economic Miracle Explained*, Dublin: Oak Tree Press.

Walsh, Paul and Ciara Whelan (1999), 'The Importance of Structural Change in Industry for Growth', Paper delivered to *the Statistical and Social Inquiry Society of Ireland*, November 25th.

Yuill, Douglas, John Bachtler and Fiona Wishlade (eds.) (1997), *European Regional Incentives 1997-98*, 17th edition, Bower Saur, Glasgow.

COMMENTS

Peter Buckley

This paper is a model of clarity. The first question it asks is has Ireland done well over the last thirty years? Should we care? Ireland is after all a relatively small country compared to China and India and Africa. The reason we have to be interested in Ireland is because it has thirty years experience of attracting FDI. We have a fantastic case study of a country which deliberately set out to attract FDI as a centrepiece of its economic policy. There is a good deal of information on FDI in the Irish Republic and even in the seventies when I was working on FDI in Ireland the country had better information on FDI than most other countries.

Has Ireland done well? The answer is Yes. If you look at employment, exports, growth rates, penetration of European markets, over a thirty-year period we can't dispute the fact that Ireland has done well.

What is the contribution of inward FDI to growth and development in Ireland? And the second related question is what is the contribution of industrial policies to attracting FDI and what is the contribution of industrial policies to the success of Ireland? These are cognate types of questions in the Irish case. Industrial policies have been directed at bringing in FDI. There is also the question of doing something about the domestic economy – the Irish owned part of the economy. But in Ireland the two are interlinked; that is one key aspect of the success. It is a long run story, and there is a great deal of consistency in policy. Ireland throughout has had an outward looking policy over the thirty years we are concerned with, although in the sixties it had an import substitution (IS) and building up the local economy oriented policies.

What have been the successes and developments over this long period? The first massive change is the growth of exports and what the long run position also shows is that there is a remarkable change in the destination of exports. Irish exports have changed in favour of European as opposed to British markets. It is often said that Ireland is an export platform for American companies into the European Union. It is almost impossible to overestimate the impact of the EU on Ireland. Integration of Ireland into the EU is absolutely central to its success and the acceptance of the rest of the EU of Ireland's policies is also absolutely crucial to the success of Ireland. Ireland with occasional lapses has been more pro Europe than other countries.

Ireland has adopted a strategy of attracting greenfield ventures; there was a system of providing factories into which companies could move in at the beginning. But as we know, a major route for FDI is mergers and acquisitions. The question then is whether Ireland is attracting FDI in a relatively small area. Ireland's success is in greenfield ventures which are export-oriented. This narrows down Ireland's sphere of activity. In a way this makes Ireland's success even more remarkable. It has managed to continuously reinvent itself as a platform even with all these dynamic changes going on within sectors.

Dermot McAleese and Michael Counahan wrote a paper about stickers and snatchers. There will always be snatchers in Ireland. This is a concern – they come in and snatch the incentives and go off. But in fact, Ireland has had a large number of stickers. Lots of companies that were there in the eighties are still there and have proved to be stickers. This is a tribute to the success and intelligence of Irish policies. The IDA Ireland is the first institution to regard FDI as a process and not a once and for all decision and to pay particular attention to that process. In the seventies and the eighties there may have been one or two fly by night operations and they have now been weeded out. Now with all its expertise and knowledge the IDA Ireland can spot these snatchers.

Now for policies – most people talk about linkages, clusters, regional development. All these have been genuinely sought after by Irish policy. Frances did bring about possible conflicts between these objectives. Can you build clusters and agglomerations which happen to be in the richest areas – east coast of Dublin – and still get companies to go to less developed areas? This is a problem. Maybe policy should emphasise one of the objectives and downplay the others and then switch about. If you look at the long run Irish policy, this has actually happened.

What is the reason for the success for Irish policies? There is CORCE. That is what it is all about. CORCE is my acronym for elements of success. C is for consistency of policy over a long period. Foreign investors abhor uncertainty. Ireland has always stood ready to help. If you have problems with risks we will try and ameliorate them. O stands for openness – there is a clear outward orientation in Irish policies. R stands for regional. Ireland has gone for the key regional market – the EU. Within that it has achieved diversification of markets from the UK to the rest of the EU. Ireland has been successful in playing the regional card – European centre with a global framework. C is for comparative advantage. I don't know how proactive is Ireland in this context; I think it has been reactive. MNEs have dictated what the comparative advantage of Ireland is rather than Ireland deciding on what to specialise in. Now the question is, is Ireland sitting back and waiting for things to happen or is it actually identifying key sectors? Certainly Ireland has identified certain key sectors but Ireland has not been rigid. It has taken a project based approach. If a project looks good we will go with it. I would like to know what projects are ruled out.

Now about incentives. Incentives are not just about handouts, they are about policy certainty, information, active care and not just cash handouts. Most managers of MNEs attach little importance to cash they receive from the host countries and the final E stands for Environment. Here again there are a lot of things – institutional environment, lack of red tape, the economic environment, and the immediate one-stop shop of the IDA Ireland. This is a formidable list of factors behind Ireland's success. But this is a list which is incredibly difficult to replicate though it may look obvious. It is difficult to replicate the locational factor of the EU, politically very difficult to replicate the sort of powers the IDA Ireland wields.

Can Ireland continue to be successful? Will the supply of greenfield ventures continue? Will manufacturing continue to provide the goodies? The IDA Ireland is unique and it has been effective in picking winners.

There are some points I would like to pick up in conclusion. First, relates to targeting the diaspora-people with Irish contacts. The second is the dynamics of FDI – how long can Ireland hang on to its advantages and weather competition from other host countries to FDI? The third point relates to macro conditions – there are worries about inflationary pressures which may be a problem. The growth dynamics may not have fully worked itself out in Ireland, as according to the investment cycle, Ireland at some point should be investing abroad. This is yet to take place.

This is a story of transformation. In the past I spent a lot of time looking at emigration from Ireland and costs per job. The story has changed dramatically since then. We could ask has Ireland overpaid for the benefits; what is the cost per job created by the MNEs?

The final issue which needs attention is totally outside the Irish case. This has to do with the changing strategies of MNEs around the globe, long run problems for Ireland are posed by these strategies of MNEs, not by its own policies. The global restructuring of the value chain of MNEs may pose a problem to Ireland.

DISCUSSION

Nigel Driffield wanted to know if there was a change in Ireland's status relating to EU structural funds and would it make a difference to Ireland's growth prospects. He also wanted to know if there were any studies on crowding out of domestic firms by foreign owned firms.

Several participants commented on the role of the IDA in attracting FDI to Ireland. Yasheng Huang wondered if the consensus in favour of FDI in general in the country was created by IDA. Countries such as Ireland, Singapore and Costa Rica need the IDA type of agencies to attract FDI. In the case of countries such as India and China it may be more important to get the politics, infrastructure and macro determinants right rather than focus on specific bureaucratic devices to attract FDI.

Peter Buckley asked about the kind of internal debates which had taken place in the IDA. To his knowledge Singapore was the only country which had achieved the sort of success in attracting FDI Ireland had achieved.

Sanjaya Lall wanted to know how the IDA identified prospective investors, how did they target them, how did they cultivate them and gear domestic policy to meet their needs? Somehow the investment agency appears to become the planning agency. What is the political economy of the operations of the IDA? He also expressed the view that even large countries such as India and China need to promote their economies to foreign firms, especially so if the country wishes to attract FDI into high-tech sectors. And if markets are imperfect promotion is necessary.

Nicholas Snowden observed that Ireland was overexposed to FDI in certain sectors, especially the high-tech sectors. MNEs do bring in technology and know-how but they also make and repatriate profits. He wondered whether over the long haul Ireland was actually exporting capital in the sense that it was offering substantial inducements to foreign firms which earned substantial profits and repatriated them.

Reply by Frances Ruane

The questions and comments made by Peter Buckley and the participants raise several interesting issues. I shall address these by grouping them together under different headings.

Why Ireland is an interesting case study

As Peter Buckley has pointed out, the size of the economy of Ireland is miniscule relative to those of China and India. Many of the issues that arise for these large countries do not apply to Ireland. One reason why Ireland is so interesting, as Peter suggested, is that it has actively pursued FDI for over forty years – and, as such, provides lessons for other countries. Consistency of policy, which Peter and others have mentioned, has been particularly important. Changes in policy have been gradual and all changes are grand-parented, i.e., companies were not affected by changes in policies which occurred subsequent to their establishing in Ireland. This has meant that there were no nasty surprises for companies investing, and this in turn built confidence in Ireland as a safe place to invest. In contrast to many countries where the actions of government increase investor risk, in Ireland they reduce it.

A particular feature about Ireland, which is different from that in many countries, is that it began the process of moving towards openness and trade *before* it brought in FDI. In other words, the anticipated trade environment for FDI locating in Ireland was always a free trade rather than a protectionist environment. When Ireland had highly protected markets (and an import substitution policy) in the 1940s and 1950s, it legally banned FDI from entering into these protected markets. In effect, the promotion of FDI coincided with the opening up of the economy to trade.

At that time, the indigenous manufacturing sector was incredibly stagnant with low productivity and little interest in exporting. The government recognised that if it did reduce protection and open up markets to freer trade, there would be a massive reduction in jobs, as domestic firms would not be able to compete with imports and would not have the capacity to start exporting. The strategy adopted was to promote Ireland as an export platform for FDI – these foreign companies were incentivised through the tax and financial aid systems to export and not compete on the domestic market with indigenous companies. It was fully recognised that there would be a shake up of domestic industry; but that if the adjustment could be gradual, a major unemployment problem (which in the Irish case would inevitably mean an emigration problem) would be avoided.

In its approach to opening up to FDI, Ireland contrasts strongly with the transition economies in Eastern Europe. In the first place, FDI into Ireland was all greenfield, whereas in Eastern Europe, much of the FDI involved taking over existing plants. Second, FDI in transition countries was promoted through grant of privileged access to markets that still enjoyed trade protection, whereas in Ireland the promotion took the form of export supports in the face of world prices.

The political economy of consensus on the FDI strategy

The political economy underpinning Ireland's FDI strategy is also an issue of considerable interest. People outside Ireland are always intrigued by how it has managed to have such a consistent and rational strategy over such a long time. The origins of the strategy are important. When the IDA was set up in the early 1950s, it was established as a regional body whose intention was to promote investment by German and French manufacturing companies into the less developed areas of the country. As such, it began life as a promoter of regional policy rather than industrial policy, and thus was uncontentious, especially as there was no tradition of manufacturing investment in these areas and hence no expected displacement. During the mid-1950s, a decision was made to introduce a tax holiday for the profits of additional exports of all manufacturing industry – ostensibly to encourage existing Irish firms to export. Again, this was uncontentious and would have had the support of employers and unions in the sector. However, this tax holiday immediately created an incentive for FDI to use Ireland as an export platform, since all exports would be additional and thus the new FDI companies would qualify for full relief from tax on profits. But again, the inflow was not seen as generating displacement and hence did not undermine the consensus. When, in the late 1950s, the legal ban on FDI was removed, the stage was set for the development of Ireland's FDI-led industrial strategy.

In political terms, there were two reasons for cross-party support for all of these policies. First, when the key policies (the tax holiday, the industrial grants and the IDA supports) were introduced, the Irish economy was in very poor shape with no growth and emigration rates running at historic highs. Thus, the prospect of inward flows of capital was seen as eminently preferable to outward flows of labour – and hence the very positive attitude to FDI in Ireland at that time. During this crisis period for the country, there was a change of government, and every party (in desperation) supported these policies. There was no critical debate on them – the politicians were in favour, the unions were in favour, the employers were in favour and even the media were in favour. In fact, the only area of dissent to be found was in the Irish Department of Finance, which objected strenuously (but with no effect) to the introduction of the tax holiday on export profits.

The initial positive consensus in favour of FDI has been strongly supported by the actions of the IDA. The fact that the agency has consistently talked about employment as the measure of the impact of FDI has helped build the consensus. The organisation never boasted about how much FDI it has got in terms of £, $ or € - but rather focused on how much employment was being generated. That is undoubtedly one of the reasons why the consensus has survived and Ireland's attitude to FDI remains very positive.

That consensus in turn translated into generous budgets for the IDA as long as unemployment remained high. Only in very recent times, when unemployment rates have fallen to historic lows, has the issue of funds for the IDA been seriously questioned – and that raises the issue of what we now expect from FDI.

Benefits of FDI

Peter Buckley and John Dunning raised the issue of what benefits have accrued from FDI. Clearly FDI has generated huge employment and now accounts for close to 50 per cent of employment in the manufacturing sector. The question now is whether there are spillover effects or other positive effects of FDI.

There is mixed evidence from research that I have done with various graduate students in this area of spillover effects. Productivity spillovers emerge only when the scale of foreign employment is used as the explanatory variable; they do not seem to arise when one uses the standard measure of employment share. There are export spillovers associated with the growth of FDI in individual sectors, and perhaps unsurprisingly, there is no link found with the export behaviour of foreign companies. There is some evidence of R&D spillovers, especially where indigenous companies are engaged in R&D that allows them to absorb the technological superiority of FDI companies. There is also evidence of important linkages, especially in sectors (mostly in electronics) where they have been promoted by the IDA and Enterprise Ireland. More recently IDA and Enterprise Ireland have moved their focus from domestic to regional (i.e., EU-wide) linkages, this being the obvious approach with the growth in globalisation. This change is indicative of the way in which policy in Ireland has responded gradually to changed circumstances. As the policy makers see it, there is no point in forcing domestic linkages that will not make the investment profitable when there are regional linkages which will ensure its financial prosperity. This is very much part of the approach to regionalisation which Peter Buckley mentioned in his comments.

Peter also asked whether there were any studies on crowding out of domestically owned firms by foreign firms. Given that the policy emphasised export-oriented FDI, operating in an economy with an open capital market, an effective surplus of labour and an unlimited supply of land, there is, unsurprisingly, not much evidence of crowding out. Frank Barry has examined this issue in a macro context over the 1980s and early 1990s. However, the crowding out issue has come up recently in a more micro context in terms of the labour market, as FDI firms are able to offer better pay and career opportunities than smaller Irish firms. Consequently, it is argued that an expansion in their number could not be seen as detrimental to indigenous firms when the unemployment rates are low.

Peter also asked if FDI companies were stickers, rather than snatchers, as they were in the 1980s. The evidence seems to suggest that they are still stickers. With the current international downturn, it transpired that most of the MNEs who were downsizing in Ireland were downsizing equally at home.

This presumably reflects the fact that many are US companies for which Ireland is the key European base and not merely a cheap cost centre.

Implementation of policy

Ireland has always adopted a project-based approach to FDI within a framework where foreign industries were to be treated on a par with domestic industries in terms of grants and incentives. (This of course helped the consensus building discussed above.) But similarity of treatment does not yield similarity of results. A foreign company setting up a branch plant in Ireland would probably be profitable within a year or two of commencing production and hence would gain immediately from the tax relief, whereas a newly established domestic company would be expected to take a longer time to become profitable. Hence benefits from low corporate tax rates and tax holidays would be greater for foreign than for domestic firms.

As Sanjaya Lall has suggested, the process of attracting FDI has been well developed by the IDA, which certainly has been a world leader in identifying and cultivating potential investors. This is a topic on which I have written elsewhere. The flexibility of the grant packages has meant that it was relatively easy to gear government aid to the specific needs of firms; the clout of the IDA enabled it to influence policy changes in a whole range of areas relevant to prospective FDI companies in Ireland. For example, in years gone by, IDA negotiated with the government (in the interests of FDI companies planning to invest in Ireland) to expand the supply of certain skills through the expansion of university places. In more recent times, IDA acted with Microsoft and Intel to speed up the process of telecoms deregulation in Ireland, taking on vested interests when the political process would not do so. In the case of the former intervention, it may be questioned whether this raised the cost of FDI projects excessively; in the case of the latter intervention, this would not have been an issue.

Future Prospects

The change in Ireland's status regarding EU structural funds, an issue raised by Nigel Driffield, is not expected to have a marked impact on Ireland's growth prospects, as the extent of EU capital funding in our current development plan is only 4 per cent. However, the benefits of the structural funds in the early 1990s, when Ireland was in an unfavourable fiscal climate, were considerable and are recognised as such.

One risk which arises from Ireland's success in winning FDI into the high-tech sector during the 1990s is that manufacturing industry is now highly concentrated in those sectors. The recent downturn in those sectors, starting with the bursting of the dot.com bubble did give rise to concern. The approach being taken is to recognise that Ireland can no longer compete in certain high-tech sectors such as assembling components and that no attempt should be made to try to retain plants in those areas.

Undoubtedly there will be increased competition for FDI in Europe in the coming decade. If countries compete excessively for FDI, they will lose collectively and companies will gain. In other words, if all countries follow the Irish model of lowering taxes to promote FDI, they cannot expect the success that Ireland has achieved. In any event, the tax policy alone was not the sole driver of success. I agree with the view expressed by many of the respondents today that Ireland, like Singapore and Costa Rica, which have no national markets to attract FDI, needs an IDA type of agency. For larger countries, the role of development-type agencies is much smaller, but it still exists if there are features of the economy that need to be marketed and information flows that are imperfect. The reason one finds such agencies in operation even in developed countries and in the individual states of the US is that there is a reward to countries from helping companies to overcome the costs of entry.

There are mixed views in Ireland regarding the extent to which the IDA is still needed and on whether it has paid too much for what it has achieved. Some take the approach that "the job is done" while others take the view that industrial promotion, as Sanjaya Lall and others note, is still the order of the day. Even though grant giving is now negligible, the informational and promotional roles remain, as do services that ease the costs of establishment. The emphasis at the moment is very much on promoting investment that plans to undertake R&D functions in Ireland – both because there is more flexibility in aiding such projects and also because these are seen as crucial to Ireland moving up the value chain.

The absence of any xenophobia in Ireland with regard to FDI, and the positive attitude to foreign employers over forty years are seen as ways of reducing emigration. As high unemployment rates fall, it may be the case that attitudes to FDI will be less positive and more in line with other western European countries. History shows that while Ireland has been consistent in its policy framework, attitudes do change. For example, as several respondents have noted, Ireland was very positive about the EU in the early years and yet in more recent times, referendums on the EU have produced rather uncertain outcomes.

Another issue which was raised is whether Ireland is now an FDI exporter as well as importer. In the last ten years, Irish companies have engaged in FDI in other, mostly European, countries. Such developments are inevitable given (a) the small size of the Irish market, and (b) the proximity of low cost locations in Eastern Europe which can produce inputs that can no longer be produced profitably in Ireland. Government policy here is understated, but there is positive encouragement for companies to undertake such FDI – the commitment to openness goes both directions. There is however one asymmetry – much of the FDI is in the form of mergers and acquisitions in contrast with inward FDI which is mostly in greenfield investments. That said, of late there is some M&A inward investment, as foreign companies have bought up newly established indigenous software companies. This has raised some interesting issues for policy in terms of supporting new projects with state equity rather than state grants, so that the benefits of success are transferred back to the agencies.

Reference

McAleese, Dermot and Michael Counahan (1979), ''Stickers' or 'Snatchers'? Employment in Multinational Corporations during the Recession', *Oxford Bulletin of Economics and Statistics*, 4, 345-358.

7. Foreign Direct Investment in Sub-Saharan Africa

Mohammed Adaya Salisu[1]

7.1 INTRODUCTION

Africa lags behind other developing regions on most indicators of growth and development. Judged by conventional indicators such as per capita income levels, life expectancy, literacy rates, and absolute levels of poverty, the development record of African countries, with rare exceptions, is disappointing. This relatively poor economic performance of Africa over the years is the subject of widespread debate with a welter of explanations and policy proposals. Africa's trade performance and policies and its ability to attract and effectively utilise foreign direct investment (FDI) in the growth process have figured centrally in these debates. A recurring theme in these debates is Africa's inappropriate trade and domestic policies, which is estimated to have cost the region around $11 billion a year (*South Magazine*).

In recent years several Sub-Saharan African (SSA) countries have initiated economic and political reforms designed to improve the environment for private sector participation in general and FDI in particular. The success of these reforms in promoting growth and development depends on the ability of these countries to attract equity-based as opposed to debt-based external capital. FDI constitutes the most significant component of external equity-based capital for African countries for several reasons. Very few of the African countries are able to attract portfolio capital mostly because they lack developed stock markets; nineteen SSA stock markets had a total capitalisation of less than $1 billion in the year 2001. FDI is also important for African countries because it can share the risks of fluctuations in export markets, a characteristic of Africa's exports. Also FDI is the major source of managerial know-how and technology, which the SSA countries badly need.

The principal objective of this paper is to analyse the determinants, efficacy and policies towards FDI in SSA. Section 7.2 discusses the extent and nature of FDI in SSA. Section 7.3 reviews the theoretical and empirical literature on factors influencing the volume of FDI in Africa. Section 7.4 analyses the impact of inward FDI on the economies of SSA. Section 7.5 provides a case study of Nigeria, which exemplifies several problems associated with attracting and efficiently using FDI in Africa. Section 7.6 concludes.

7.2 EXTENT AND NATURE OF FDI IN SUB-SAHARAN AFRICA

FDI in Sub-Saharan Africa is unevenly distributed across the continent. The bulk of FDI is concentrated in natural resource endowed countries such as Angola, Botswana, Nigeria and South Africa.[2] The absolute size of FDI in Africa is meagre in comparison with that in other continents. In 2002, for instance, the stock of FDI in SSA as a whole (including South Africa), at $123 billion, accounted for less than 5 per cent of the $2.5 trillion stock of FDI in the developing countries. Although this figure contrasts sharply with that for Asia and Latin America (Table 7.1), it represents a substantial increase over the 1980 stock of $28 billion. This growth in the stock of FDI can be attributed largely to a series of macroeconomic reforms and liberalisation of trade and investment policies pursued by many African countries since the 1980s.

Table 7.1 Inward Stock of FDI, 1980-2002

	1980	1985	1990	1995	2000	2001	2002
World							
(US$ billion)	699	978	1954	3002	6147	6607	7123
Developed Countries (DCs)							
(US$ billion)	392	571	1400	2041	3988	4277	4595
(%)	56.0	58.4	71.6	68.0	64.9	64.7	64.5
Developing Countries (LDCs)							
(US$ billion)	307	407	554	961	2159	2330	2528
(%)	44.0	41.6	28.4	32.0	35.1	35.3	35.5
Geographical Distribution of FDI Stock in LDCs:							
Africa (%)	10.5	8.3	9.2	8.1	6.7	6.8	6.8
Sub Sahara Africa (%)	9.1	6.3	6.1	5.3	4.9	4.9	4.8
South Africa (%)	5.4	2.2	1.6	1.6	2.2	2.2	2.0
L/America & Car.(%)	16.4	19.7	21.1	21.0	28.2	30.3	30.2
Asia (%)	72.4	71.7	68.8	66.4	58.9	56.1	55.5
Other (%)	0.7	0.3	0.9	4.5	6.2	6.8	7.5

Source: World Investment Report (various issues).

FDI in SSA increased from less than $3 billion in 1991 to nearly $13 billion in 2001 before declining drastically to around $8 billion in 2002 (Table 7.2). The exceptionally high FDI inflows in 2001 can be attributed to the large number of mergers and acquisitions (M&As) that took place in that year. In fact, "if the large cross-border M&A deals in Morocco and South Africa in 2001 are excluded from FDI figures for that year, FDI inflows in 2002 actually increased by [only] 8%" (UNCTAD, 2003). Despite the large inflows in 2001 the gap in FDI flows between Africa and other developing regions appears to have increased since the mid-1990s (see Figure 7.1).

In sum, FDI flows to Africa have increased perceptibly in recent years. Even so, Africa currently accounts for less than 1 per cent of world FDI inflows (Figure 7.2). Thus, despite improvements in Africa's economic policy environment during the 1990s, FDI flows to Africa continue to be relatively low.

Table 7.2 FDI in Selected Sub-Saharan African Countries, 1991-2002

% of total inflows	1991-96	1999	2000	2001	2002
Angola	11.6	28.5	16.4	16.1	17.6
Nigeria	42.2	11.6	17.3	8.3	17.2
South Africa	15.0	17.3	16.6	51.1	10.1
Mozambique	1.3	4.4	2.6	1.9	5.4
Equatorial Guinea	2.2	2.9	2.0	7.1	4.3
Uganda	2.2	2.6	4.7	1.7	3.7
Congo	2.9	6.0	3.1	0.6	3.3
Tanzania	2.1	6.0	8.6	2.5	3.2
Côte d'Ivoire	5.3	4.4	4.4	0.3	3.0
Zambia	3.6	1.9	2.3	0.5	2.6
Namibia	3.7	1.3	2.9	2.1	2.4
Cameroon	0.3	0.5	0.6	0.5	1.1
Seychelles	0.8	0.7	1.0	0.4	0.8
Ghana	3.5	3.1	2.1	0.7	0.7
Kenya	0.4	0.5	2.4	0.4	0.7
Botswana	-0.9	0.4	1.0	0.2	0.5
Mauritius	0.7	0.6	5.2	0.2	0.4
Rest of SSA	3.1	7.3	6.8	5.2	12.6
Total SSA	100	100	100	100	100
(US$ million)	2992	8663	5364	13295	7452

Source: Calculated from data obtained from UNCTAD (2003).

Figure 7.1 FDI Inflows in Developing Countries 1988-2002

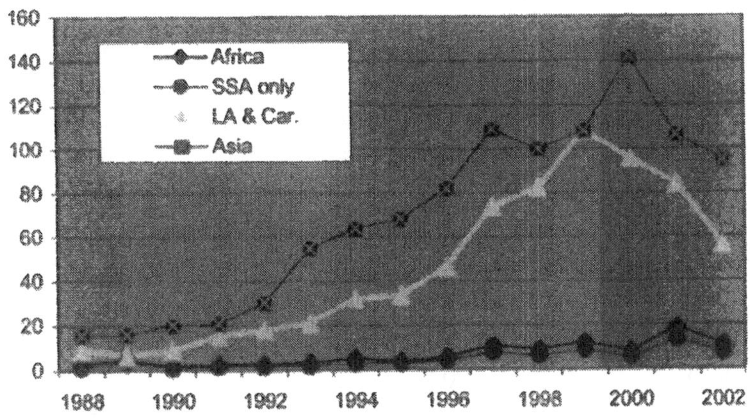

Source: UNCTAD, World Investment Reports, various years.

Figure 7.2 Geographical Distribution of FDI Inflows: 1970-2000

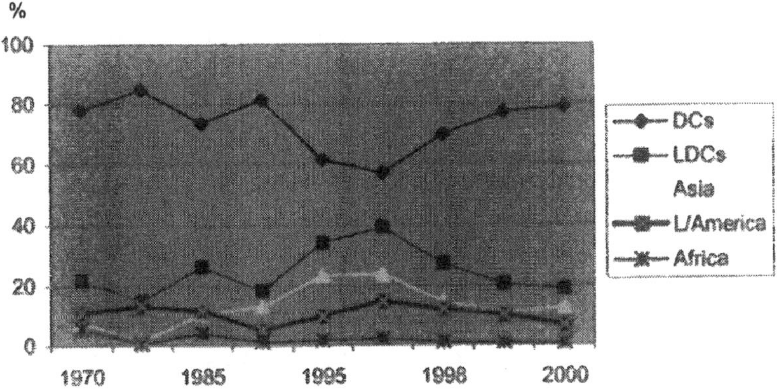

Source: UNCTAD, World Investment Reports, various years.

In spite of the less than impressive overall picture of FDI in Africa, some countries have attracted relatively high volumes of FDI in recent years. Most of these countries are mineral-based economies, such as Nigeria, Angola, and South Africa. These three countries together accounted for more than 75 per cent of FDI flows to Africa in 2001 (see Table 7.2). As stated earlier, the exceptionally high proportion of FDI in South Africa (51.1% or US$ 6.8 billion) in 2001 was largely the result of an unbundling of cross-share holdings (UNCTAD, 2002). The bulk of FDI in Africa in general is concentrated in the oil exporting countries. In recent years, however, some non-mineral resource based countries in the region have attracted a sizeable amount of FDI. These include Uganda, Tanzania, Côte d'Ivoire, Mauritius, Namibia, and Seychelles (Table 7.2). It is hoped that the recent African initiative (New Partnership for Africa's Development – NEPAD), which emphasises stronger national efforts to promote FDI, along with ongoing trade and investment initiatives by the triad (i.e. EU, US and Japan) is likely to boost FDI flows to Africa.

Table 7.3 FDI as a percentage of GDP (1980-2002)

%

	1980	1990	2000	2001	2002
Angola	1.8	10.0	90.0	106.9	98.3
Nigeria	3.7	28.3	49.1	51.5	42.4
South Africa	20.5	8.1	37.1	44.0	48.7
Mozambique	0.4	1.7	29.1	37.4	44.8
Equatorial Guinea	7.0	19.2	90.0	115.0	92.8
Uganda	0.7	0.1	21.3	26.1	30.0
Congo	18.5	20.6	58.8	65.9	69.5
Tanzania	0.9	2.2	19.6	22.6	25.0
Côte d'Ivoire	5.2	9.0	36.4	32.1	31.3
Zambia	9.1	30.8	72.6	66.5	70.0
Namibia	86.4	80.9	36.7	25.2	34.1
Cameroon	4.9	9.4	14.3	15.7	15.7
Ghana	5.2	5.4	29.4	29.3	26.4
Kenya	5.3	7.8	9.5	9.2	9.3
Botswana	61.8	34.8	37.2	28.5	38.6
Mauritius	2.3	6.4	15.6	15.9	15.6
Africa	8.2	10.8	25.9	28.5	30.6
Asia	17.9	17.9	32.1	32.7	33.3
Latin America & Caribbean	6.5	10.4	30.6	36.2	44.7

Source: UNCTAD (2003).

Measured as a proportion of GDP or gross domestic fixed capital (GDFC), the volume of FDI in Africa compares favourably with that in other developing regions. This does not, however, suggest that the volume of FDI that the African countries attract is adequate to facilitate and promote the rates of growth required to increase employment and alleviate poverty. If anything, the high proportion of FDI to GDP suggests that the growth rates of GDP in SSA countries are low. Moreover, the proportion of FDI to GDP that is much above the average of the continent as a whole at 30.6 per cent is mostly in oil and minerals endowed and oil and mineral exporting countries such as Angola (98.3%), Equatorial Guinea (92.8%), Nigeria (42.4%), and Congo (69.5%). These figures contrast sharply with those for non-mineral based countries such as Uganda (30.0%), Ghana (26.4%), Kenya (9.3%), and Madagascar (9.9%) (Table 7.3).

The high ratio of FDI to GDP in most African countries since the early 1990s should, however, be treated with caution due to exchange rate translation problems largely due to the massive devaluations of official exchange rates. For example, Nigeria's GDP estimated in Naira and converted into dollars at the market exchange rate understates the true value of the country's GDP, hence the estimated ratio of FDI to GDP at market exchange rate overstates the relative volume of FDI Nigeria receives. This explains why the FDI to GDP ratio in Nigeria was less than 4 per cent in the 1980s, when the Naira was strong, but in excess of 40 per cent in 2000 and 2002 when the local currency was very weak! The appropriate indicator should be FDI as a percentage of GDP at the purchasing power parity (PPP) exchange rate as opposed to the official exchange rate. In PPP terms, FDI in Sub-Saharan African countries accounts for less than 5 per cent of GDP, on average, as opposed to around 30 per cent of GDP at the market exchange rate.

Table 7.4 Sources of African FDI – Cumulative Outflows from Developed Countries (1981-2000)

US$ million

	1981-1985	1986-1990	1991-1995	1996-2000
Total flows	5864	5599	6657	24681
Canada	0.5	0.7	2.2	2.5
France	21.1	17.9	31.0	17.7
Germany	8.6	5.9	6.0	10.0
Italy	7.8	3.9	3.2	2.7
Japan	6.0	20.4	3.0	1.4
Netherlands	1.6	2.7	4.5	3.3
UK	15.0	39.2	35.7	13.2
US	31.8	7.2	4.2	37.5
Other	7.6	2.1	10.2	11.7

Source: Calculated from data obtained from UNCTAD (2002).

Around 90 per cent of the stock of FDI in Africa during the 1990s was accounted for by the triad (US, Japan, and EU, particularly the UK, France and Germany). During the latter half of the 1990s, the US accounted for the largest share of cumulative FDI in Africa (37%), followed by France (18%) and the UK (13%) (Table 7.4). It is noteworthy that the UK, which had been the largest investor in Africa since the mid-1980s, with a share of nearly 40 per cent, lost ground to the US and France. Much of US FDI in Africa is in the petroleum sector – a focus that is likely to continue in view of the promise of extensive oil reserves in the Gulf of Guinea. Most of Germany's stock of industrial FDI in Africa is located in South Africa. Much of the German FDI is concentrated in the non-extractive sectors. Available data on stocks of FDI from Japan suggest that much of it is in South Africa. One distinguishing feature of Japanese FDI though is its heavy commitment to Liberia, mainly in the transport sector.

The available data for the UK are revealing. Despite its variability, a number of parallels arise with the US FDI stock in Africa. First, although a considerable amount of money was devoted to primary resource extraction in the late 1990s, much of FDI is in minerals rather than the petroleum sector. Second, the bulk of the UK's FDI stock in Africa was concentrated in one country (South Africa). With the exception of South Africa, manufacturing-related flows have been both modest and declining in most countries. Again as in the US case, FDI in the services sector appears to be increasing.

7.3 DETERMINANTS OF FDI

As stated earlier, there is an upward trend in FDI flows to several African countries and not all of the FDI in Africa is in minerals and oil. An increasing proportion of FDI flows from the UK, Germany and Japan in recent years is in manufacturing and services. Even so, the volume of FDI Africa receives as a proportion of total flows to developing countries as a whole is low. The observed relatively high proportion of FDI to GDP in several countries suggests that domestic savings and investment rates are low and most African countries are heavily dependent on external sources of finance. The issue then is what are the factors which influence the location decision of foreign firms and how do the African countries measure up against the principal determinants of FDI identified in the literature?

The principal determinants, though they are interrelated, can be grouped into three categories: those related to the objectives of prospective investors, those related to the FDI policy framework of host countries and those related to the economic and business environment in the host countries. The objectives of investors include desire to capture expanding markets signified by the size and growth rates of the economies of host countries; natural resource seeking objectives signified by investments in oil, minerals and agricultural raw materials and efficiency seeking investments centred on the search for relatively low cost but productive labour.

The presence of a set of stable and transparent policies towards foreign firms is also a principal detemiant of FDI. In so far as trade policy is related to FDI it too will influence the decision of foreign firms to invest in particular locales. It is by now the received wisdom that open trade policies or, to be specific, neutral trade regimes which do not favour either the domestic market-oriented activities or export-oriented activities attract relatively large volumes of FDI than policies which favour one or the other sector through tariffs and subsidies (Bhagwati, 1978; Balasubramanyam et al., 1996, 1999). Here, the emphasis is on the presence of a distortion free economic environment open to market forces unencumbered by artificial incentives for investment such as tariffs and subsidies.

Another set of factors includes not only a transparent policy framework but also a bureaucracy free of bribery and corruption and one which makes for speed of decision making. In fact, lack of transparency of policies engenders and facilitates corrupt practices and bribery. In addition, investors seek political and macroeconomic stability in the host countries.

How do the African countries fare judged against these determinants of FDI? The relatively large volumes of FDI in Nigeria, Angola, Namibia and Botswana are of the resource seeking variety. FDI appears to have been attracted to Nigeria and Namibia despite political instability in these countries. Perhaps the stability that matters for foreign investors is not the stability of regimes, be they dictatorships or democracies, but the stability of policies, especially assurances against expropriation, which the successive governments in these countries appear to have provided, principally because they are reluctant to kill the goose that lays the golden egg. The joint venture arrangement between the Nigerian government (through the Nigerian National Petroleum Corporation – NNPC) and oil companies such as Shell, ExxonMobil, and BP provides adequate guarantees against expropriation.

There are though countries which are not endowed with an abundance of natural resources but have succeeded in attracting relatively large volumes of FDI. Apart from the well-known examples in East Asia such as Singapore and Hong Kong, this set includes the African countries – Mozambique, Uganda, Mauritius, Mali and Ghana. Here, there are a variety of explanations. Two of the factors listed above – macroeconomic stability and a distortion free factor and product market regime – are especially significant in this context.

Low inflation rates and stable exchange rates are important determinants of FDI for more reasons than one. First they attest to the stability and the underlying strength of the economy. Second, they provide a degree of certainty relating to the future course of the economy and impart confidence in the ability of firms to repatriate profits and dividends. Weak economies with high levels of domestic borrowing and debt, measured by the ratio of budget deficits to GDP and total volume of borrowing to GDP, are often compelled to institute exchange controls on the capital account of the balance of payments. Third, more often than not a stable macroeconomic environment also implies a stable political environment. Political and economic stability are usually intertwined (Balasubramanyam and Salisu, 1991).

Mozambique's success with attracting FDI illustrates the importance of macroeconomic stability. Inflation, which averaged about 75 per cent per annum in the eighties, was sharply reduced to single digits during the nineties. Budget deficits were contained and Mozambique also carried out a fairly sweeping programme of privatisation; well over 900 state enterprises have been privatised including the entire banking sector and a number of manufacturing firms. The success of these measures is reflected in the growth rate of GDP which was around 5.7 per cent per annum during the nineties compared with negligible rates during the sixties and the seventies. Admittedly the relatively high growth rate during the nineties reflects the fact that the base year rate was close to zero. This is also reflected in the high level of absolute poverty and low per capita income. Even so, Mozambique's performance is impressive compared with the desolate state it was in during the eighties. Its success in attracting relatively high volumes of FDI is largely due to the macroeconomic stability it has achieved and its reform of the tariff structure with the average rate of tariff at a low of 14 per cent in recent years. The experience of Mali, which too has begun to attract increased volumes of FDI, is similar to that of Mozambique (Morisset, 2000).

A distortion free environment is another prerequisite for attracting increased volumes of FDI. A predictable consequence of such distortions is the misallocation of resources and investments away from sectors and activities in which the country possesses a competitive advantage. Such distortions also have an impact on the volume of FDI host countries are able to attract. For long it was believed that restrictions on imports in the form of tariffs and quotas would induce increased flows of FDI. This belief is based on the proposition that trade and capital flows are substitutes and a restriction on trade would induce firms to invest in the protected markets (Mundell, 1957). Recent research, however, suggests that trade and FDI are complements and need not necessarily be substitutes (Greenaway and Milner, 1988). Trade and FDI do go together. Openness to trade would attract export-oriented FDI, and the freedom to import components and parts would attract FDI oriented towards domestic markets. In Dunning's schema of different forms of FDI, openness to trade would attract efficiency seeking FDI. It is thus that countries with a distortion free market environment, free of policy induced incentives and restrictions, tend to attract relatively larger volumes of FDI than distortion ridden economies.

This proposition finds support in the case of African countries too. An econometric study of FDI in 29 African countries for 1990-97 by Morisset (2000) concludes that both openness to trade (defined as the ratio of trade to GDP) and the growth rate of their GDP promote a foreign business investment climate. The regression results of the study suggest that openness is a significant determinant of FDI inflows.

The importance of trade and macroeconomic reforms in attracting FDI is illustrated by Uganda's experience. Since the mid-nineties Uganda's real GDP has grown at around 6 per cent per annum on average. Growth has attracted FDI mainly into the manufacturing sector. Inflows of FDI which averaged around $65 million during the years 1991-96 increased more than fourfold and stood at $275 million in 2002. FDI accounts for around 24 per cent of the gross fixed capital formation in the economy. Uganda's success in attracting FDI and promoting growth is to be attributed to fiscal discipline, trade policy reforms and the institution of a favourable climate for FDI. Since 1995 Uganda has eliminated all quantitative restrictions on trade except for restrictions in place for moral, health, security and environmental reasons. Tariffs are now the main trade policy instrument. The simple average rate of Uganda's applied most-favoured nation (MFN) tariff rate is 9 per cent. However, withholding tax and commission on import licensed move it up to 15 per cent. The tariff structure has been simplified through the reduction of the number of bands from five to three (zero, 7% and 15%). The only export tax that is levied on exports in excess of 15 per cent is on exports of coffee collected by the Uganda Coffee Development Authority[3].

Tariffs in general have come down in African countries from around 30 per cent to 16 per cent in 1990. But there are other barriers to trade such as discriminatory policies on imported products. Other impediments to trade include red tape and complicated procedures relating to traded goods.

Corruption and poor governance appear to be a much more significant deterrent to FDI in Africa than elsewhere. Other constraining factors include weak infrastructure, crime and insecurity, macroeconomic instability, political instability and FDI regulations (Asiedu, 2003). It would, therefore, be in order to explore the extent and causes of corruption in Africa in some detail. Many African countries top the world corruption league tables. Nigeria, in particular, has earned the accolade of being the world's most corrupt country in successive league tables for the last five years.

Corruption, when combined with administrative weakness, can both undermine policy reform and repel FDI, as recent empirical literature suggests. It is therefore not surprising that corruption ranks high on the list of obstacles to FDI in Africa identified by firms surveyed by four independent international bodies.[4] The results of these surveys identify corruption as the main impediment to FDI in SSA. What are the causes of corruption in

Africa? Is it a culture-bound phenomenon? Has economics, as a discipline, anything to offer in explaining it? Although corruption is often simply defined as the misallocation of public resources to private ends, it can be broadly described as "an arrangement that involves an exchange between two parties (the demander and the supplier), which has an influence on the allocation of resources either immediately or in the future; and involves the use or abuse of public or collective responsibility for private ends" (Macrae, 1982, p. 678).

It is often argued that bureaucratic interference in the market mechanism is one of the principal causes of corruption. What sorts of interventions raise the demand price of corruption by bureaucrats and under what circumstances will the MNEs increase their supply price of corruption? Are the demand and supply forces much more different in Africa and other developing countries than in developed countries? Equally interesting questions arise in the context of the impact of corruption on economic efficiency. Some amount of corruption, it is said, is necessary for the smooth functioning of governance; it oils the wheels of commerce and administration. But is there a theoretical optimum for such corruption?

The literature on rent-seeking and directly unproductive profit-seeking economic (DUPE) activities provides some insight into the questions raised above. Policy-induced sources of corruption arise when pervasive regulations exist and government officials have discretion in applying them. Private parties may be willing to pay bribes to government officials in order to obtain some of the rents generated by the regulations. As Tanzi (1994) argues, the problem becomes worse when regulations lack simplicity and transparency.

The following are some of the government-induced sources of corruption that have been identified in the literature (see Mauro, 1995, 1997): trade restrictions, government subsidies, multiple exchange rate practices and foreign exchange allocations, as well as low wages in the civil service relative to private sector wages. Although the bulk of the theoretical literature on rent-seeking behaviour has generally concentrated on quantitative restrictions on international trade, it can be extended to cover other forms of government restrictions on economic activity. Whilst such rent-seeking may sometimes be legal, in many instances it takes illegal forms such as bribery, corruption, smuggling and other 'hidden' activities. Multiple exchange rate practices and foreign exchange allocations (whose importance may be proxied by parallel exchange market premia (Levine and Renelt, 1992) also lead to corruption. In developing countries, in particular, where state-owned commercial banks ration foreign exchange at the discretion of bank managers, the supply price of bribes could be substantial.

Endowments of natural resources, such as crude oil, provide a major source of economic rents since they can be sold at a price that far exceeds their cost of extraction. Sachs and Warner (1995) argue that resource-rich economies are more likely to be subject to extreme rent-seeking behaviour than are resource-poor economies. It is argued that natural resources generate rents which lead to rapacious rent-seeking and increased corruption which adversely affects long-run growth. (Sala-i-Martin and Subramanian, 2003). In Nigeria, for example, oil wealth is seen to be one of the main causes of the pervasive rent-seeking activities and corruption. The use of oil revenues to finance large-scale public expenditure programmes introduced large-scale political corruption in Nigeria.

Sociological and/or cultural factors such as customs and tradition, and ethnicity also constitute potential sources of corruption. In Africa, although the tradition of gift-giving and paying tributes to leaders often lead to what Brownsberger (1983) describes as "polite corruption", the extent of such corruption is relatively small. Much of the corruption in Africa is underlined by the ethics of dependency relations, ethnic loyalties and attitudinal tendencies, such as greed or love of ostentation. Poverty, political instability and other societal forces also induce public servants to be corrupt. This is especially so when officials know that opportunities for rent-seeking may cease following a coup d'état or a defeat at the polls or when their kinsmen place extended demands on them or they feel compelled to maintain a high visible standard of living (Colins, 1965; Nye, 1961). Similarly, where accumulated wealth for the legal support of their activities or families is lacking, there is pressure on public officials and organisations to use public resources for personal or sectional ends via embezzlement, the taking of bribes, or distributing jobs and contracts to one's family and friends.

These sociological and cultural causes of corruption are likely to continue for a long time in Africa, unless credible legal enforcement measures are put in place. The forces which deter corruption are often weak as some, if not most, of the law enforcement agencies are themselves corrupt. In addition, where politicians and civil servants are highly corrupt, professional organisations may be incapable of sanctioning their members. In other words there are no agencies which can restrain corruption.

The third set of FDI determinants relates to a healthy business environment. Indeed, macroeconomic stability and a distortion free economic environment presupposes transparency of policies and an efficient administration with a minimum of red tape and bureaucratic hurdles in the functioning of the FDI regime. Another much discussed determinant of FDI is the various sorts of incentive schemes including tax concessions, tax holidays and subsidies provided by host countries to foreign firms. It is doubtful if these incentives weigh heavily in the investment decision process of foreign firms. The evidence on the issue is not conclusive (Guisinger, 1986). A survey of 30 multinational companies covering 74 investment projects in automobiles, computers, food processing and petrochemicals revealed that most companies accord little importance to incentives in their foreign investment decision process (UNCTAD, 1998). In the absence of other determinants of FDI such as infrastructure, stability of policies and a distortion free environment, incentives may be of little significance for foreign investors. Developing countries may be compelled to offer such incentives only because their competitors for FDI offer them. If none of the countries offers such incentives the location decision of FDI would be based on the resource endowments of host countries and the climate they provide for efficient operations. Most such incentives are tied to performance requirements of one sort or other. Given the nature of these incentives and the fact that each of the host countries offers such incentives only because others do so, it is likely that they are yet another source of distortions in the market for FDI.

Africa's attempt at reforming FDI policies is a step in the right direction. However, given the sheer size of domestic distortions along with decades of policy failure and inefficiencies, it would take a long time for Sub-Saharan Africa to witness substantial inflows of FDI. After all, designing investment incentives is one thing and implementing the reforms is quite another. This means that incentives in themselves may constitute a necessary but not a sufficient condition; they do matter only in the presence of other ingredients of greater significance to foreign firms. In fact, empirical studies suggest that fiscal incentives offered by developing countries in general are of little significance in attracting FDI (Lim, 1983). In addition, most foreign firms regard such incentives as being much too volatile and transitory, and tax holidays to be illusory. More so, it is the stability of such incentives over time that matters not their magnitude.

In order to succeed in attracting the new wave of efficiency enhancing FDI, Sub-Saharan African countries must institute low and stable tax regimes, a non-discriminatory (transparent) regulatory environment (with an effective competition policy) and an impartial, efficient judicial system. Relevant markets (including that for labour) must be deregulated and operate efficiently with human capital enhanced appropriately to meet the needs of such investors through a suitable educational system. To this list may be added the need for support from competent technical bodies and a low-cost infrastructure. The absence of these self-evident conditions explains the disappointing performance of the region in attracting FDI. It also raises the more fundamental question of why such reforms have not been implemented.

The answer to this question is to be found largely in the political economy of African states, supported indirectly by evidence from the governance indicators compiled by the World Bank for the year 2000-2001. Of six available indicators, two are quite closely connected with economic policy (government effectiveness and regulatory quality) while the remainder include the maintenance of stability, the rule of law and the absence of corruption. On all of these criteria the SSA region fares poorly in comparison with the rest of the world, with only between 30 and 40 per cent of countries with scores as low as those typically observed in Africa (www.worldbank.org). This poor policy environment reflects a combination of weak administrative capacity (government ineffectiveness) and malfeasance. It is the combination of these elements that appears to be potentially so damaging to the attraction of FDI (as well as to overall economic performance) and proposals for policy reform must recognise the political constraints involved.

7.4 IMPACT

What has been the impact of FDI on growth and development in Africa? There are no specific statistical studies on this issue. The general impression, however, is that FDI has not had as significant an impact on employment, skill formation and growth in Africa as it has had in other areas such as the East Asian countries. The high levels of absolute poverty in most countries and the low growth rates of the region suggest as much. There are though exceptions such as Botswana and Mauritius which have benefited from FDI in terms of export growth, employment creation and wage earnings of labourers. Here, the pursuit of stable macroeconomic policies, a corruption free environment and exports of labour-intensive products such as garments, in the case of Mauritius, mostly funded and organised by foreign firms, have contributed to their success. Even so, it is arguable if FDI in these countries has resulted in technology spillovers and the establishment of viable domestic industries. Assembly operations such as manufacturing of garments are not the instruments for technology spillovers and mining of diamonds, as in Botswana, is a relatively capital intensive operation with very few backward and forward linkages. Add to this the Dutch disease phenomenon afflicting oil exporters such as Nigeria, which has rendered exports of traditional agricultural products unviable because of the appreciation of the real exchange rate.

FDI though could provide the required finances for development. It is a much cited fact that the rates of return to FDI in Africa are substantially high and compare favourably with that in other regions. Whether or not these high returns are due to the composition of FDI in Africa (oil and minerals) or they are a return to risk taking is arguable. The fact though is that the share of profits from these activities of foreign firms accruing to the host governments should ease their budgetary problems and finance development. But the sad fact is that in the case of oil rich Nigeria nearly 60 per cent of the population live below the absolute poverty line. Here again, bad governance, corruption and greed on the part of those in power are to blame.

If FDI is to have an impact on growth and poverty in Africa, it has to be channelled into those activities, apart from oil and minerals, in which African countries have a comparative advantage. These range from processed and unprocessed agricultural products to tourism. One healthy sign is that FDI from the UK and the other EU countries is increasingly directed towards these activities. But to efficiently utilise such FDI, African countries have to re-orient their trade and FDI policies and more importantly they have to improve governance, eschew corruption and bribery and streamline the bureaucracy.

7.5 FDI, CORRUPTION AND ECONOMIC GROWTH IN AFRICA: EVIDENCE FROM NIGERIA

As is well known, Nigeria is the most populous country in Africa; one in every five Sub-Saharan Africans is a Nigerian. The country is richly endowed with oil and natural gas, and it has all the necessary ingredients for development, including a sizeable labour force, natural resources and an educated elite. Nigeria is also the second largest recipient of FDI inflows in Africa, after Angola. Yet, Nigeria is an underdeveloped economy in terms of most indicators of development. With a per capita income of less than $400 Nigeria now ranks amongst the least developed countries in the world in the World Bank league tables. The Nigerian higher education system, once regarded as the best in Sub-Saharan Africa, is in deep crisis. Health services are a shamble and infrastructure (both physical and social) is grossly inadequate. Unemployment, particularly amongst graduates, is rising and so too is the crime rate.

Although all these factors are crucial determinants of FDI, it is the absence of social infrastructure, including lack of transparency, corruption and an inefficient civil service, that is of utmost concern to foreign investors. As stated earlier, one persistent and unfortunate accolade conferred on Nigeria is that it is the most corrupt country in the world. Few would dispute Nigeria's premier position in the corruption league table, as corruption is found in virtually every stratum of society. As the saying goes, "*keeping an average Nigerian from being corrupt is like keeping a goat from eating cassava*". Rarely is a distinction made between cash earned privately and cash removed from the public purse. On the one hand, this attitude could be attributed to a deep sense of obligation to one's family and ethnic group, but on the other hand it is also due to greed and avarice.

The former viewpoint is reflected in the *Financial Times* (1993) survey on Nigeria which found that a number of Nigerians see nothing wrong with "using public funds to disperse favours to a cousin or to build a well for one's village, as it is an informal means of redistributing wealth". Such an act is considered as a lubricant or a positive sum game of "give and take" which is widely practised in employment offers, award of contracts, import licences and even in obtaining admission to institutions of higher education. The visible riches of these corrupt and the greedy spur the poor to imitate their life styles and modes of acquisition of wealth. Indeed, corruption in Nigeria has become so rampant that the plastic bag which is used to carry large sums of bribe money is elevated to the status of a national symbol of corruption and it is tagged *Ghana Must Go Bag* (Jibril, 2003). Anecdotal evidence on the magnitude of corruption in Nigeria can be found in the media.[5]

Corruption is rampant in Nigeria, but it is also widespread in many other African countries. Indeed, corruption exists in every country in the world, but what is worrying is the degree to which it exists in Africa. According to the African Union (AU), corruption in Africa is "costing the continent nearly $150 billion a year, increasing the cost of goods by as much as 20 per cent, deterring investment and holding back development" (BBC World News, 18 September 2002 at http://news.bbc.co.uk/1/hi/world/africa/). It is not surprising that with such pervasive corruption, foreign investors are wary of investing in Africa, and that the impact of FDI on economic growth could be adversely affected by corruption.

A number of econometric studies, such as Asiedu (2003) and Morisset (2000), find strong evidence of a negative relationship between corruption and FDI inflows to Africa. Most empirical studies on the relationship between FDI and corruption tend to rely solely on indices of corruption published by a number of agencies. These include the corruption perception index published by Transparency International, the international country risk guide compiled by Political Risk Services, and the country risk index of the Economist Intelligence Unit. All these corruption indices are based on foreign investors' perceptions about a host country's business environment. Such corruption perception indices, however, may provide misleading information about the extent and magnitude of corruption in a host country.

In the present study, a broader concept of corruption, based on the size of the 'hidden' economy, is employed. The hidden economy is estimated on the basis of a factor analytic approach (multiple indicators, multiple independent causes – MIMIC technique). The MIMIC technique is a powerful tool because it allows for simultaneous interaction between multiple explanatory (independent) variables and multiple indicators of the hidden economy, including all directly unproductive profit-seeking economic (DUPE) activities. It is a statistical technique for estimating an equation in which the dependent variable is latent or unobservable. Since corruption is unobservable, the MIMIC methodology appears to be the most appropriate technique to estimate its extent. This technique has been pioneered by Joreskog and Van Thillo (1973) and popularised by Joreskog and Goldberger (1975), Aigner et al. (1988), Schneider (1997), and Giles (1999).

Basically, the MIMIC model can be written as follows:

$$\mathbf{y} = \boldsymbol{\lambda}\eta + \boldsymbol{\varepsilon} \qquad (7.1)$$

$$\eta = \gamma'\mathbf{x} + \zeta \qquad (7.2)$$

where **y** is a column vector of indicators of the latent (unobservable) hidden economy variable (η), and **x** is a column vector of "causes" of η. In other words, equation (7.1) denotes the measurement model for η and equation (7.2) represents the structural equation for the hidden economy variable, η. ε and ζ are the measurement and structural errors, respectively, and are assumed to be mutually uncorrelated.

The latent variable (η) is linked, on the one hand, to a number of observable indicators (reflecting changes in the size of the unreported economy); and on the other hand to a set of observed causal variables, which are considered to be important determinants of the unreported economic activity.

Figure 7.3 shows the path diagram which depicts the interrelationships between the (unobservable) hidden economy (η), its determinants (**x**) and the indicators (**y**). The theoretical literature on the hidden economy has identified four broad determinants: burden imposed by the public sector on individuals (TB), tax morality (TM), labour market conditions (L) and structural factors (SF). In this context, and for purposes of estimating the size of the hidden economy (η), equation (7.2) can be re-written as:

$$\eta = \gamma_1 TB + \gamma_2 TM + \gamma_3 L + \gamma_4 SF + \zeta \qquad (7.2a)$$

The burden on the official economy may consist of burden of taxation (measured by either the average or marginal tax rate) and the burden of regulation (measured by the number of regulators or the ratio of the number of public sector employees to total employment). The *a priori* expectation on the coefficient of the tax 'burden' is positive, implying that an increase in the burden will drive people into the hidden economy. Tax morality, however, reflects the readiness with which individuals leave the official economy. A decline in tax morality will reduce people's trust in government and will consequently increase their willingness to go underground. Frey and Pommerehne (1984) suggest that the consequences of tax morality can be checked by a growing intensity of public controls and a rise in expected punishment, which will reduce the return on hidden activities.

Figure 7.3 Path Diagram for the Hidden Economy

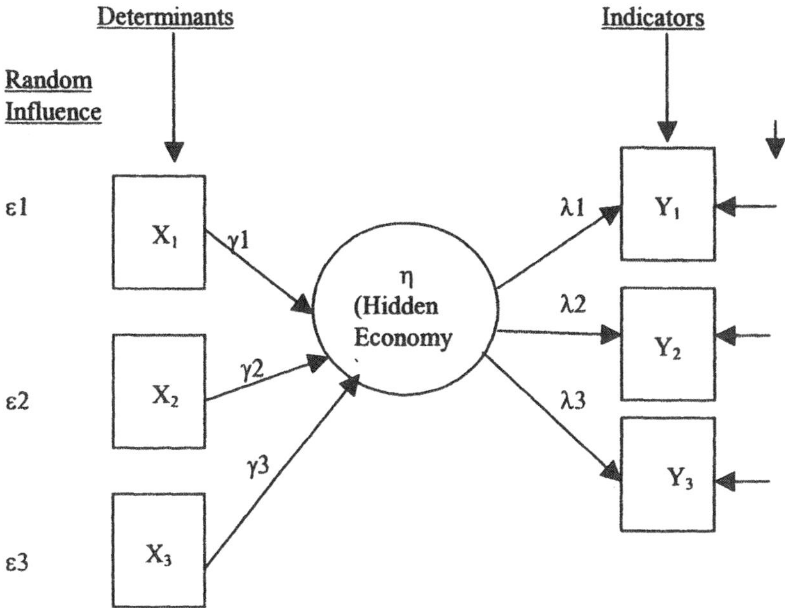

In the case of the labour market, it is hypothesised that the incentive to work in the hidden economy is high for the unemployed, since they can work in the underground economy while at the same time receiving unemployment benefits. It is noteworthy, however, that while the demand for underground activity rises with unemployment, it is also likely that the supply of job opportunities in the hidden economy will fall with rising unemployment. Overall, the effect of unemployment on the shadow economy is ambiguous, depending upon the elasticities of demand and supply with respect to the rate of unemployment.

The level of economic development can also influence the hidden economy. Individuals with low per capita real disposable income will have a strong incentive to hold multiple jobs and to pay taxes only on the first job. Empirical evidence from Italy, however, suggests that the size of underground economy in the rich North is larger than in the poor South. This positive relationship between per capita income and hidden economic activity suggests that the supply of hidden economy jobs may increase with an increase in per capita income. The expected sign of the coefficient of the level of development, however, is a priori ambiguous.

A number of studies have found that disaggregated estimates of the hidden economy are very informative in identifying the growth of corruption. For instance, evidence from India shows that the high rates of growth of the industrial sector's hidden economy during the 1980s and 1990s coincided with the timing of a large number of corruption cases uncovered by police departments in India (Bhattacharyya and Ghose, 1998).

We therefore utilise the MIMIC methodology to estimate the magnitude of hidden economy Nigeria. Three types of determinants and two types of indicators of the hidden economy are used in estimating the size of the hidden economy in Nigeria. The causal factors are: tax burden (measured by the share of taxes in GDP), inflation and real per capita income. Unemployment and sectoral variables were not included in the list of determinants due to lack of reliable data. The two indicators used in the MIMIC analysis are changes in male participation rate and changes in cash-demand deposit ratio. The growth rate of GDP is excluded from the estimation to avoid double counting.

Table 7.5 Estimates of the 'Hidden' Economy of Nigeria, 1960-2001

Year	% of GDP	Year	% of GDP	Year	% of GDP	Year	% of GDP
1960	9.64	1971	15.78	1982	36.57	1993	54.65
1961	10.02	1972	18.54	1983	45.76	1994	58.65
1962	10.42	1973	18.55	1984	31.08	1995	65.43
1963	10.72	1974	22.45	1985	35.50	1996	64.65
1964	11.20	1975	26.43	1986	36.65	1997	58.76
1965	11.54	1976	26.80	1987	37.65	1998	62.40
1966	11.54	1977	27.85	1988	39.76	1999	64.84
1967	12.10	1978	28.94	1989	42.34	2000	67.38
1968	12.36	1979	30.08	1990	40.54	2001	70.02
1969	12.66	1980	32.54	1991	42.43		
1970	12.83	1981	34.65	1992	43.54		

Source: Estimated with LISREL statistical software using the MIMIC methodology.

The estimated size of the hidden economy is then used as a proxy for corruption in the economic growth equation. Table 7.5 shows the estimates of the hidden economy in Nigeria for the period 1960-2001.[6] The size of the hidden economy increased substantially throughout the 1970s, then declined in 1984/85 before rising again. Perhaps the declining trend in the mid-1980s reflects General Muhammadu Buhari's measures to curb corruption and indiscipline.[7] With the accession of General Ibrahim Badamasi Babangida (IBB) to power, however, the level of corruption rose once again. The establishment of the Failed Bank Tribunal in 1995 by IBB's successor (late General Sani Abacha) restored some financial discipline in the banking system. This explains the decline in the hidden economy in 1996, even though Abacha himself was alleged to have massively looted the treasury.[8] With the re-introduction of democracy and the election of President Olusegun Obasanjo in 1999, many Nigerians were hopeful that the dawn of a new era in corruption control had arrived. In spite of the establishment of an Anti-Corruption Commission by President Obasanjo, the size of the hidden economy has continued to grow, reaching a peak of around 70 per cent of GDP in the year 2001 (Table 7.5).

Does corruption adversely affect the inflows of FDI in Nigeria? Contrary to the existing empirical findings on FDI determinants in Africa, the observed facts suggest that, in spite of the growth in corruption in Nigeria, FDI inflows to Nigeria have increased in recent years, apparently due to the potentially high rates of return on investment in the oil sector. It is widely believed that over 90 per cent of total FDI stock in Nigeria is in the minerals sector but disaggregated time series data on FDI do not exist to warrant a sectoral analysis of the impact of corruption on FDI. For this reason an econometric analysis of the impact of corruption on FDI in Nigeria would be futile. However, it may be worth investigating the impact of both FDI and corruption on economic growth, which has been generally overlooked by the existing econometric studies. Attracting increased FDI may be desirable but the efficacy of FDI is another issue. As stated earlier, the mere presence of FDI in a host country would not necessarily promote growth unless appropriate growth enhancing ingredients are present. This problem may be compounded by the prevalence of corruption.

Quantitative verification of the impact of corruption and FDI on economic growth can be assessed by estimating the following growth equation:

$$\text{GDPGR} = \beta_0 + \overset{-}{\beta_1}\,\text{CORR} + \overset{+}{\beta_2}\,\text{FDI} + \overset{\pm}{\beta_3}(\text{FDI} * \text{CORR}) + \sum_{i=4}^{k} \beta_i \text{Q}_i + \varepsilon \qquad (7.3)$$

where: GDPGR = growth rate of real GDP; FDI = share of foreign direct investment in gross domestic product; CORR = corruption; Q = a vector of other factors influencing economic growth, including growth in domestic capital formation, the growth rate of the labour force, and the growth rate of exports. The βs are parameters of the growth equations and ε are the error terms.

The signs of the parameters of interest (β_1, β_2, β_3) denote the *a priori* expectations based on the hypotheses that (a) corruption constrains economic growth, so its parameter in the growth equation is expected to be negative; (b) large volumes of FDI may promote growth, hence a positive sign on β_2 is expected; (c) in the presence of corruption, the growth enhancing effect of

FDI is constrained. In other words, the expected sign on β_3 (the coefficient of the interaction term between FDI and corruption in the growth equation) is ambiguous, depending on whether or not the positive impact of FDI on growth outweighs the negative impact of corruption.

Table 7.6 shows four different estimated regression equations for growth in Nigeria for the period 1965-2001. The dependent variable for the first two equations is the growth rate of recorded (official) labour productivity whilst the last two equations describe the results for growth in total (recorded plus unrecorded) labour productivity. The two sets of equations provide contrasting results. The results can be summarised as follows. First, the hypothesis that FDI promotes growth is supported by the positive and statistically significant coefficient on the FDI variable [Table 7.6, equations (a) and (b)]. Second, the hypothesis that corruption retards growth is supported by the negative and statistically significant coefficient of the hidden economy variable. Third, the growth enhancing efficiency of FDI in Nigeria is adversely affected by corruption, as the interaction term between FDI and the hidden economy is negative and statistically significant at the 1 per cent level. In the case of the growth in total labour productivity, which includes both official and unofficial (hidden) economy estimates of economic activities, the results suggest a negative but weakly significant relationship between foreign direct investment and growth in total economic activities. Another noteworthy aspect relates to the coefficients of both the hidden economy variable and its interaction with FDI. Both coefficients are positive and largely significant [Table 7.6, equations (c) and (d)]. This result suggests that the interplay between FDI and corruption results in a positive private rate of return even though the social rate of return may be negative!

The results also show that growth in real exports promotes economic growth in Nigeria. This is not surprising since oil exports account for over 90 per cent of Nigeria's foreign exchange earnings. Similarly, periods associated with the structural adjustment programme tend to experience higher rates of economic growth than pre-liberalisation periods. The Nigerian civil war has impacted negatively on the growth of the official economy, as shown by the negative and statistically significant coefficient on the war dummy.

The implications of the results of the growth equation are that Nigeria (and other corrupt African countries) should act decisively towards curbing corruption and pursue export promotion and credible liberalisation policies. Perhaps Nigeria should borrow a leaf from Botswana, which is also a natural resource based economy but has successfully overcome its problem of corruption using the Hong Kong and Singapore system of anti-corruption measures! At present, Botswana is one of the fastest growing African

Table 7.6 Estimated Growth Equations for Nigeria, 1965-2001

	Dependent Variable			
	Growth in Real Official Labour Productivity		Growth in Real Total Labour Productivity+	
	(a)	(b)	(c)	(d)
INTERCEPT	2.845***	2.505***	3.59**	3.317***
	(4.98)	(6.54)	(2.24)	(3.12)
FDI	0.054**	0.057**	-0.124*	-0.121*
	(2.19)	(2.37)	(1.80)	(1.81)
GDI	0.062***	0.069***	0.577***	0.583***
	(3.19)	(4.04)	(10.63)	(12.31)
CORR	-0.013***	-0.013***	0.021	0.021*
	(2.84)	(3.05)	(1.69)	(1.71)
FDI*CORR	-0.001***	-0.001***	0.005***	0.005***
	(3.08)	(3.25)	(3.91)	(3.98)
EXPORTS	0.281***	0.309***	0.142	0.164
	(5.21)	(7.46)	(0.93)	(1.43)
SAPDUM	0.078*	0.080**	-0.634***	-0.632***
	(1.98)	(2.05)	(5.72)	(5.81)
WARDUM	-0.176***	-0.168***	-0.001	0.005
	(4.36)	(4.31)	(0.01)	(0.05)
OILDUM	0.031		0.025	
	(0.805)		(0.23)	
$\bar{R}^2$	0.884	0.886	0.989	0.989
LM-SC	3.16	2.34	2.93	2.97
LM-FF	2.71	2.41	1.73	1.80
LM-NM	0.59	0.49	1.44	1.57

Notes: + includes both official and unofficial economic activities. FDI denotes the share of FDI in GDP; GDI is the growth rate of real gross fixed domestic capital formation per employee; CORR is measured by the share of 'hidden economy' in GDP; EXPORTS is the growth rate of real exports. SAPDUM is a dummy variable for the liberalisation period which began with the structural adjustment programme (SAP) of 1986 (1 for 1986-2001 and 0 otherwise); WARDUM is a dummy variable for the Nigerian civil war (1 for 1967-1970, 0 otherwise); OILDUM is a dummy variable for oil price increases (1 for 1973-1980, 1990-1992 and 0 otherwise). Figures in parentheses denote absolute values of t-statistics; *, **, *** denote an estimated coefficient which is significantly different from zero at the 10%, 5% and 1% levels, respectively. LM-SC, LM-FF and LM-NM denote Lagrange multiplier test statistics for residual serial correlation, functional form, and residual normality respectively. On the relevant null hypothesis the test statistics for residual serial correlation and functional form are distributed as χ^2 with 1 degree of freedom. In the case of residual normality, it is distributed with χ^2 with 2 degrees of freedom. At the 5% significance level, the critical $\chi^2_1 = 3.84$ and $\chi^2_2 = 5.99$.

countries, with a high per capita income comparable with that of a middle income economy. Botswana is also in the top 50 least corrupt countries in the world, according to the corruption perception index published by Transparency International. In contrast, Nigeria is the second most corrupt country in the world and has a per capita income that puts it in the top 20 least developed countries in the world.

Whilst Botswana provides a classic example of a country that has turned its economic fortunes around, it is worth noting three important elements in Botswana's success story. First, Botswana is a relatively small country and was therefore able to effectively implement the Hong Kong or Singapore anti-corruption model. Second, Botswana has a relatively homogeneous ethnic composition, as opposed to the 250 ethnic groups in Nigeria. This ethnic homogeneity in Botswana allows for social cohesion and stability conducive to capacity building and implementation of government policy including appropriate anti-corruption strategies. One would have expected Nigeria to use its ethnic diversity to its strength by providing a 'healthy' competition in nation building. Sadly, however, ethnic rivalry in Nigeria has been very destructive and inimical to economic growth and development. The Nigerian civil war (1967-70) was a result of bitter ethnic rivalry. Since the end of the war, ethnicity has been playing a major part in the socio-political and economic process in Nigeria! Third, Botswana, since gaining independence in 1966, has enjoyed a long period of political stability as well as stability of policy. In contrast, Nigeria, since independence in 1960, has frequent incidence of regime change and military coups *d'états*. Whilst Botswana has never experienced any military intervention, Nigeria has experienced over 15 military coups and attempted coups. In fact, African countries in general experienced a total of 327 coups and attempted coups, giving rise to a total military intervention score (TMIS) of 863 (McGowan, 2003). Nigeria ranked 7th in terms of the TMIS with a score of 40, after Sudan (70), Ghana (54), Uganda (51), Burundi (48), Sierra Leone (48) and Benin (45). In addition to such a high rate of political instability, Nigeria experienced a series of policy reversals, including a period of nationalisation and indigenisation in the 1970s, capital controls in the early 1980s, structural adjustment since the mid-1980s, and a number of policy inconsistencies in the 1990s. All these factors would make it difficult for Nigeria to make significant progress with its anti-corruption policies.

7.6 CONCLUSIONS

Decades of inappropriate trade and domestic policies have contributed to the relatively poor economic performance of Africa and the region's ability to attract and effectively utilise FDI in the growth process. Africa lags behind other comparable regions on FDI. The current stock of FDI in Sub-Saharan Africa as a whole accounts for a mere five per cent of the total FDI stock in developing countries. In spite of the unimpressive overall record of FDI in Africa, however, some countries in the region have attracted high volumes of FDI in recent years. With the exception of mineral-based economies such as Nigeria, Angola and South Africa, the success stories relating to trade and and FDI relate to Uganda, Mauritius, Mozambique and Ghana. The success of these countries in attracting FDI lies in their macroeconomic and political stability, trade reform, and the institution of a favourable climate for FDI. The FDI policy reform process is now gathering momentum in many African countries but it would serve little purpose unless it is placed within the context of a wider societal reform. More so, to effectively utilise such FDI, African countries have to re-orient their trade and FDI policies, improve governance, eschew corruption and streamline the bureaucracy.

Corruption, as the Nigerian case study illustrates, is a key factor in Africa's inability to attract FDI and to promote growth. This calls for a multi-faceted approach to deal with Africa's problems. The first step is to strengthen administrative capacity, including the bureaucracy. Politically, the leadership must promote a culture of honesty based on transparency and credibility. The legal and institutional framework for dealing with corrupt practices must be credible and independent of political control. On the economic side, African governments should scale down regulations on economic activities and other policies which contribute to the demand and supply of corrupt activities. This can be done by improving public sector wages towards market-based levels, thereby lowering the premium on errant behaviour and making dismissal from the civil service both a painful and credible threat.

Institutional reforms involving transparency and accountability, including the establishment of criminal and administrative sanctions, strengthening judicial processes, financial disclosures and open budget process, must be undertaken. All these measures are enshrined in the anti-corruption laws of most African countries but there is a lack of political will to implement them. Societal reforms and partnership with civil society must be actively promoted.

Partnerships with the international donor community are crucial. The New Partnership for Africa's Development (NEPAD), initiated by African leaders, emphasises stronger national efforts to promote FDI. The NEPAD initiative also calls for partnerships with the Triad (US, EU and Japan) on increased trade and investment initiatives to boost FDI flows to Africa. Fifth, a policy of social inclusiveness must be emphasised by all African leaders, as ethnic fragmentation in many SSA countries tends to rob Africa of much of its implementation capacity.

NOTES

1. I wish to thank Nicholas Snowden for comments on earlier version of the paper. I am also grateful to participants at the Grange-over-Sands Conference on FDI, particularly V.N. Balasubramanyam, for helpful comments. I am, however, solely responsible for any errors.
2. The top ten FDI recipients in SSA, ranked by the magnitude of FDI inflows in the year 2002, are: Angola, Nigeria, South Africa, Côte d'Ivoire, Mauritius, Uganda, Lesotho, Botswana, Swaziland and Namibia.
3. Based on information from WTO (2002).
4. These surveys include two conducted by the World Bank (World Business Environment survey in 1999/2000 and World Development Report survey, 1996/97), one by UNCTAD (World Investment Report survey) and one by the Center for Research into Economics and Finance in Southern Africa (CREFSA) survey.
5. High profile cases of grand corruption published by the media include billions of US dollars alleged to have been looted by successive Nigerian leaders, and equally huge amounts of money embezzled and mismanaged through the execution of white elephant projects such as the Ajaokuta steel plant and numerous government contracts.
6. For a detailed discussion of the estimation procedure and the choice of indicators and causes of corruption in Nigeria, see Salisu (2003).
7. General Buhari, who was Nigeria's military leader from 31 December 1983 to August 1985, is well known for his honest transparency, discipline and fight against corruption.
8. According to the Transparency International Global Corruption Report (2004), General Sani Abacha was ranked 4th in the corruption league table for global political leaders, with an estimated fortune of $2-5 billion stolen during 1993-98. The most corrupt leader was Mohamed Soharto of Indonesia ($15-35 billion stolen from 1967-98). Ferdinand Marcos of Philippines (1972-86) and Mobutu Sese Seko of Zaire (1967-97) came second and third respectively, with estimated fortunes of $5-10 billion and $5 billion each.

References

Aigner, D.J., F. Schneider and D. Ghosh (1988), 'Me and my shadow: estimating the size of the hidden economy from time series data', in Barnett, W.A. (ed.), *Dynamic Econometric Modeling: Proceedings of the Third International Symposium in Economic Theory and Econometrics*, Cambridge: Cambridge University Press.

Asiedu, E. (2003), 'Foreign Direct Investment in Africa: The Role of Government Policy, Institutions and Political Stability', Discussion Paper, Department of Economics, University of Kansas.

Balasubramanyam, V.N. and M.A. Salisu (1991), 'Export Promotion, Import Substitution and Direct Foreign Investment in Less Developed Countries', in Koekkoek, A. and L.B. M. Mennes (eds.) (1991), *International Trade and Global Development: Essays in Honour of Jagdish Bhagwati*, London: Routledge.

Balasubramanyam, V.N., M.A. Salisu and D. Sapsford (1996), 'Foreign Direct Investment and Growth in Export Promoting and Import Substituting Countries', *Economic Journal*, 106(434), 92-105.

Balasubramanyam, V.N., M.A. Salisu and D. Sapsford (1999), 'Foreign Direct Investment as an Engine of Growth', *Journal of International Trade and Development*, 8, 27-40.

Bhagwati, J. N. (1978), *Anatomy and Consequences of Exchange Control Regimes*, Balinger Publishing, New York.

Bhattacharyya, D.K. and S. Ghose (1998), 'Corruption in India and the Hidden Economy', *Economic and Political Weekly of India*, 33(44).

Bende-Nabende, A. (2002), 'Foreign Direct Investment Determinants in Sub-Saharan Africa: A Cointegration Analysis', *Economics Bulletin*, 6(4), 1-19.

Brownsberger, W.N. (1983), 'Development and government corruption: materialism and political fragmentation in Nigeria', *Journal of Modern African Studies*, 21, 215-33.

Colins, L. (1965) 'What is the Problem about Corruption?' *Journal of Modern African Studies*, 3, 215-244.

Financial Times (1993). 'Survey of Nigeria'. 20/21 October (London: FT).

Frey, Bruno S. and Hannelore Weck Hannemann (1984), 'The Hidden Economy as an "Unobserved" Variable', *European Economic Review*, 26(1), 33-53.

Giles, D.E.A. (1999), 'Measuring the Hidden Economy: Implications for Econometric Modelling', *Economic Journal*, Special Supplement, 109, 370-380.

Greenaway, D. and C. Milner (1988), 'True Protection Concepts and their Role in Evaluating Trade Policy in Developing Countries', *Journal of Development Studies*, 23, pp 200-9

Guisinger, S.E. (1986), 'Do Performance Requirements and Investment Incentives Work?' *The World Economy*, 9(1).

Jibril, M. (2003), 'Is There Not, Amongst you, a Righteous Man? The "Nigerian Factor" and the Nigerian Condition', Lecture delivered at the Fifth convocation of the Nigerian Academy of Letters, University of Lagos, Nigeria, 14 August).

Joreskog, K.G. and A.S. Goldberger (1975), 'Estimation of a Model with Multiple Indicators and Multiple Causes of a Single Latent Variable', *Journal of the American Statistical Association*, 70, 631-639.

Joreskog, K.G. and M. Van Thillo (1973), 'LISREL: A General Computer Program for Estimating a Linear Structural Equation System Involving Multiple Indicators of Unobserved Variables', Research Report 73-5, Department of Statistics, University of Uppsala.

Levine, R. and D. Renelt (1992). 'A Sensitivity Analysis of Cross-country Growth Regressions'. *American Economic Review*, 82, 942-63.

Lim, D. (1983), 'Fiscal Incentives and Direct Foreign Investment in Less Developed Countries', *Journal of Development Studies*, 19, 207-212.

Macrae, J. (1982), 'Underdevelopment and the Economics of Corruption: A Game Theory Approach', *World Development*, 10, 8, 677-687.

Mauro, P. (1995), 'Corruption and Growth', *Quarterly Journal of Economics*, 110, 681-712.

Mauro, P. (1997), 'Why Worry about Corruption?' IMF Economic Series 6 Washington DC: International Monetary Fund.

McGowan, P.J. (2003), 'African Military Coups D'etat, 1956-2001: Frequency, Trends and Distribution', *Journal of Modern African Studies*, 41(3), 339-370.

Morisset, P. (2000), 'Foreign Direct Investment to Africa: Policies also Matter', *Transnational Corporation*, 9(2), 107-125.

Mundell, R. (1957), 'International Trade and Factor Mobility', *American Economic Review*, 57.

Nye, J.S. (1961), 'Corruption and Political Development: a Cost-Benefit Analysis', *American Political Science Review*, 56, 417-35.

Sachs, J. and A. Warner (1995), 'Natural Resource Abundance and Economic Growth'. NBER Working Paper 5398, Cambridge MA: National Bureau of Economic Research.

Sala-i-Martin, X. and A. Subramanian (2003), 'Addressing the Natural Resource Curse: An Illustration from Nigeria', IMF Working Paper WP/03/139, Washington DC: IMF.

Salisu, M. (2003), 'Incentive Structure, Civil Service Efficiency and the Hidden Economy in Nigeria', in Kayizzi-Mugerwa, S. (ed.), *Reforming Africa's Institutions: Ownership, Incentives, and Capabilities*, Tokyo: UN University Press.

Schneider, F. (1997), 'Empirical Results for the Size of the Shadow Economy of Western European Countries Over Time', Working Paper 9710, Institut fur Volkswirtschaftslehre, Linz University.

South Magazine, June 1997, p. 19.

Tanzi, V. (1994), 'Corruption, Government Activities and Markets', IMF Working Papers 94/99, Washington DC.

Transparency International (2004), *Global Corruption Report* http://www.transparency.org/.

UNCTAD (1998), *World Investment Report*, New York: United Nations.

UNCTAD (2000), *World Investment Report: Cross-border Mergers and Acquisitions and Development*, New York: United Nations.

UNCTAD (2001), *World Investment Report: Promoting Linkages*, New York: United Nations.

UNCTAD (2002), *World Investment Report: Transnational Corporations and Export Competitiveness*, New York: United Nations.

UNCTAD (2003), *World Investment Report: FDI Policies for Development – National and International Perspectives*, New York: United Nations.

World Bank (2000), 'Making State Institutions More Responsive to Poor People'. *World Development Report*, 99-115.

World Bank (2002), *World Development Indicators CD-ROM Database*, Washington DC: World Bank.

World Trade Organisation (2002), *Uganda Trade Policy Review*.

Internet references:

http://news.bbc.co.uk/1/hi/world/africa/
http://www.businessage.net
http://www.worldbank.org

COMMENTS

Nicholas Snowden

An initial difficulty confronting this study is made clear at the start of section 7.2. Superficially, with the stock of FDI in Sub-Saharan Africa accounting for less than five per cent of the developing country total, there is not really much to explain (Table 7.1). Within this constrained amount, moreover, the historical pattern (especially for US and UK multinational firms) has been for most activity to be concentrated in the minerals sector.[1] Nevertheless, although flow data confirm that petroleum continues to be a key attraction for FDI in the two major cases of Angola and Nigeria, some tentative evidence of diversification has emerged in recent years.

Roughly coinciding with the post-Special Programme of Assistance era of structural reform initiatives after 1987, the absolute dollar value of FDI inflows has been rising quite strongly. During the later sub-period of 1996-2000, for instance, the ratio of net FDI inflows to GDP reached the two per cent level observed in Latin America and the Caribbean. By the 1990s, as Table 7.3 indicates, the accumulated stock of FDI was approaching the comparative importance (relative to host GDP) of some of the other non-OECD regions. While currency depreciation will certainly have flattered these trends, an important additional point made in the paper is that the ratio of total investment spending to GDP in African countries is comparatively low, implying that FDI inflows may now be around 10 per cent of the continent's annual capital formation. Expressed in these terms, FDI is clearly of economic significance for the region and deserves the further consideration supplied by the study.

These encouraging developments, however, also must be qualified. In addition to its concentration in the minerals sector, the second major fact about African FDI is correctly emphasised in the text and in Table 7.2. Other than Angola and Nigeria, South Africa has been the dominant recipient of FDI and that country accounts for the bulk of non-mineral-oriented inflows to the continent.[2] In the US case, post-apartheid re-entry appears to have been a major factor with access to the comparatively large market an important motivation. If the current state of affairs in terms of the pattern of African FDI is easily summarised, therefore, the need to spread its potential benefits beyond the mineral sector and beyond the South African sphere of economic influence is equally apparent. In this context, empirical and econometric studies of FDI determinants are reviewed usefully from an African perspective in section 7.3.

Partly based on questionnaire surveys, the role of corruption in discouraging FDI is highlighted and its prevalence is clearly a distinguishing feature of the African case. Key findings from econometric studies with an African focus are that political and macroeconomic instability both hinder inflows of FDI, with a number of other determinants (including legal system and regulatory efficiency) apparently proving significant (positive) influences. The importance of corruption in discouraging inward investment, as it emerges in the discussion of section 7.3, has both direct and indirect aspects. Costly in itself, corruption also interacts with the maintenance of distorting economic policies and the difficulty of effecting their reform. It is this pervasive quality that justifies the case study of Nigeria in section 7.5.

A novel approach is adopted here in the econometric estimation of the extent of Nigeria's 'hidden economy' over the years 1960-2001 (Table 7.5). These estimates are used subsequently as an index of corruption in a regression 'explaining' GDP growth, using FDI as a separate and interacting explanatory variable (equation 7.3). While the results of this exercise, as presented in Table 7.6, are certainly suggestive of the damaging consequences of corruption, a detailed assessment of the findings would require more information on the procedures followed than is reported in the text. The index variables for the hidden economy are summarised in equation (7.2a), although, in practice, it appears that those actually used were the ratio of tax revenues to GDP, inflation and real per capita incomes. In addition to a query over the former when most tax revenue depends on oil production (rather than on private income or expenditure), it is also noteworthy that the first and third of these variables are ratios involving measured GDP.

Attention to GDP is stimulated by a striking observation made earlier in section 7.2. It is noted there that FDI stocks in Africa represent around 30 per cent of GDP at market exchange rates, but only five per cent when GDP is measured in terms of constant international purchasing power. This implies a dramatic discrepancy between the two GDP measures, an implication readily confirmed for Nigeria (and for African countries in general). Using series from World Development Indicators for 2003, Nigeria's GDP measured (even) in current US dollars has stagnated since 1980, whereas the underlying 'growth rate' was approximately six per cent per annum using current 'international' dollars (of equivalent purchasing power across countries). The result was that by 2000-01, GDP on the less conventional measure was 2.7 times higher than that measured in dollar of the time.

Having recognised this discrepancy early in the study, it is somewhat surprising that its implications for the hidden economy index variables of tax revenue to GDP and per capita GDP are not discussed in the empirical section. Naira depreciation, for instance, would tend to raise the ratio of ($) petroleum revenue taxes to GDP and the per capita income series would also be likely to have behaved very differently on a PPP basis. While weakening of the Naira exchange rate (and declining oil prices) will have been substantially responsible for the divergence since 1980, it is noted in section 7.4 that real appreciation of the currency had earlier rendered agricultural exports uncompetitive. More explicit consideration of the exchange rate factors could probably have helped in the construction of the hidden economy variable.

These reservations should not obscure a key point from the study that the corruption (hidden economy) term does appear to capture something of actual developments in Nigerian political economy, as the discussion in section 7.5 demonstrates. Nevertheless, the new variable is used intensively in the results presented in Table 7.6 and further discussion of its properties would have been helpful. This is particularly the case in relation to the regression results (c) and (d). It appears that the dependent variable in these cases includes the growth element of the hidden economy term (CORR), which appears (in levels) as an explanatory variable.

While this procedure may need further consideration, it is certainly interesting that the structural adjustment programme dummy variable (SAPDUM) becomes strongly and negatively correlated with the measure of growth that includes unofficial activity (it is positively correlated with conventional GDP growth). This suggests, albeit tentatively, that these programmes can have their intended effects. The central requirement, as is well emphasised in the text, is the political commitment to sustaining reform. Putting the issue this way emphasises that those advocating reform must first ensure that their proposals are compatible with the interests of those who will be responsible for their execution. The weakness of 'endogenous' support for reform is well articulated here by the description provided of the Nigerian case.

DISCUSSION

John-ren Chen was of the view that corruption may be a large element of the fixed costs of investment in Africa. In addition to corruption the poor quality of labour and inefficient labour markets are major problems for most African countries. Economic incentives to boost productivity do not work in Africa due to the irrational behaviour of economic agents. Such irrational behaviour was apparent when some managers thought that raising wage rates would increase absenteeism of labour rather then result in increased productivity. Here is an example of a backward bending supply curve of labour. The question is: "Is this a general problem in Africa?" Salisu was of the view that the problem is widespread in Africa due to the poor work ethic of workers in the public sector enterprises, which for long have dominated most African economies. African public servants treat public property with disdain and their attitude to work is poor. Sadly, it is this poor work ethic that is often transferred to the private sector.

Richard Eglin argued that FDI in Africa is a mirror image of trade, which has lots to do with inappropriate policies and little to do with market access. On paper, the policies toward FDI in Africa look great. The risk is low but perceived risk is very high since very few believe in the rule of law, corruption is pervasive, and there is widespread political instability. How does one close the gap between perceived risk and actual risk? So long as the gap between perceived and actual risks remains huge, the kind of returns MNEs could be asking for must be enormous, but they simply do not exist. There is virtually nothing that MNEs could do in such an environment that would produce those kinds of return. With the exception of South Africa, there is little or no international production in most African countries.

Richard Eglin, in response to Annie Wei's question on the number of African countries in the WTO and whether or not the WTO should assist them with capacity-building, stated that there are eight African countries which are not members of the WTO but are associate members. However, he disagreed with the assertion that the problem is to do with lack of negotiating clout of the African countries. African countries get free access on most goods except bananas and sugar. African countries in general demand trade preferences. Their trade policy is inefficient, and they need to reform their trade policies. The insistence of African countries upon sticking to a host of preferences translates into saying that they do not want to reform their trade policies in the way WTO rules require them to.

Sanjaya Lall narrated his experience from a research project on FDI in Lesotho. Lesotho is a small country near South Africa with little or no corruption, has a well-managed macro economy, has no political uncertainty, and it has a competitive exchange rate and inexpensive labour. The FDI regime in Lesotho is one of the best in Africa and the country is getting relatively large amounts of FDI, basically from Taiwan. There are over 40 export-oriented Taiwanese foreign firms in Lesotho that have created over 40,000 jobs. These companies benefit from the African Growth Opportunities Act (AGOA) set up by the Clinton administration in 1999, which gives duty-free and quota free privileges and access to the US market for any manufactured product. This is a fantastic export opportunity for massive waves of FDI to Africa, particularly in clothing, footwear and other sorts of bottom-end, labour-intensive activities. At the moment, Lesotho is the biggest single African exporter of manufactured products to the USA. But the AGOA initiative is expected to run out by the end of 2008 when African manufacturing exports will be exposed to international competition. The problem, perceived by Sanjaya Lall, is that given that Southern Africa does not have the textile manufacturing capacity, is FDI in Lesotho going to stick? A major concern is that while wage rates in Lesotho and other Southern African countries compare favourably with East Asian countries, estimated labour productivity in Lesotho is 40-60% that of China or Taiwan. So, if after 15 years of operating in Lesotho and training the labour force, Lesotho cannot compete effectively with East Asian countries, then it is unlikely that Lesotho and Africa could attract substantial amounts of FDI when the AGOA initiative is phased out in 2008. The main issue highlighted by Sanjaya Lall is that Lesotho provides a classic dilemma facing Africa. Here is a country with no corruption and virtually all the ingredients for attracting FDI but it is having fundamental problems associated with competition and productivity.

Balasubramanyam wondered whether low productivity had to do with illiteracy rates, nutrition level, and other sociological factors. Sanjaya Lall was of the view that these could be factors but they might not explain all the problems. He added that maybe the MNEs operating in Lesotho import technicians and managerial staff from Taiwan/China and they do not promote the training of local African workers at the highest level. There are also problems of entrepreneurship, lack of local suppliers, lack of spillover effects, and lack of sub-contracting, all of which makes it difficult for indigenous firms and labour to benefit substantially.

Frances Ruane, drawing upon the experience of the Irish model, thought that the Lesotho experience was effectively a protectionist environment; there were exporting firms but in a highly protective environment because of privileges accorded to them. There is a lot of South African investment in Lesotho due to the sanctions and embargo imposed on the Apartheid regime in South Africa. But reported exports in Lesotho were larger than they really were. In other words, companies which had production plants both in South Africa and Lesotho were channelling their output through Lesotho because of the embargo on South African production. This therefore tends to the mask the X-inefficiency in the economy!

NOTES

1. In an earlier draft, it was noted that 75 per cent of the outstanding African stock of FDI is accounted for by nine oil exporting countries.
2. In one estimate, over half the African FDI stock is located in South Africa.

Index

Printed and bound by CPI Group (UK) Ltd, Croydon, CR0 4YY

23/04/2025

14660960-0004